MATERIALITIES OF PASSING

Passing is a common euphemism for the death of a person, as he or she is said to pass away or pass on. This open-ended saying has at its heart a notion of transformation from one state to another, which in turn grants the possibility of grasping or approximating the passage of time and the materiality of death and decay.

This book begins with the idea that since all material things – whether animals, human-beings, objects or buildings – undergo some form of passing, then the specific transformation in these passages and the materiality actively given to it can offer us a grasp of otherwise precarious temporalities. It examines how human beings strive to relate to the temporal dimension of death and decay, by giving new shape and direction to being and by examining its natural transformations. Focusing on the materiality of passing, and thereby the relationship between embodiment, temporality and death, *Materialities of Passing* offers rich case studies from Europe, Papua New Guinea, South Africa and the Russian Far East for exploring the material, spatial and directional aspects of the very interface between life and death. As such, it will appeal to scholars of anthropology, death studies, archaeology, philosophy and cultural studies.

Peter Bjerregaard is Senior Adviser of Exhibitions at Museum of Cultural History at the University of Oslo, Norway.

Anders Emil Rasmussen is Curator of Ethnographic Exhibitions at Moesgaard Museum in Denmark.

Tim Flohr Sørensen is Assistant Professor of Archaeology at the Saxo Institute at the University of Copenhagen, Denmark.

Studies in Death, Materiality and the Origin of Time

Series Editors: Rane Willerslev and Dorthe Refslund Christensen,
Aarhus University, Denmark

Eventually we all die – and we experience death head-on, when someone close to us dies. This series, *Studies in Death, Materiality and the Origin of Time*, identifies this fact as constitutive of the origin of human conceptions of time. Time permeates everything, but except for time itself all things are perishable – yet, it is only through the perishable world of things and bodies that we sense time. Bringing together scholarly work across a range of disciplines, the series explores the fact that human experiences and conceptions of time inherently hinge on the material world, and that time as a socially experienced phenomenon cannot be understood as separate from material form or expression. As such, it departs from a persistent current within Western thinking. Philosophy, biology and physics, among other disciplines, have studied time as an essential, ethereal and abstract concept. In the same way, death has often been conceived of in abstract and sometimes transcendental terms as occupying one extreme margin of human life. As an alternative, this series examines the ways in which bodily death and material decay are central points of reference in social life, which offer key insights into human perceptions of time.

Also in this series

Suicide and Agency
Anthropological Perspectives on Self-Destruction, Personhood, and Power
Edited by Ludek Broz and Daniel Münster
ISBN 978-1-4724-5791-2

Mediating and Remediating Death
Edited by Dorthe Refslund Christensen and Kjetil Sandvik
ISBN 978-1-4724-1303-1

Taming Time, Timing Death
Social Technologies and Ritual
Edited by Dorthe Refslund Christensen and Rane Willerslev
ISBN 978-1-4094-5068-9

Materialities of Passing
Explorations in Transformation, Transition and Transience

Edited by

PETER BJERREGAARD
University of Oslo, Norway

ANDERS EMIL RASMUSSEN
Moesgaard Museum, Denmark

TIM FLOHR SØRENSEN
University of Copenhagen, Denmark

Routledge
Taylor & Francis Group
LONDON AND NEW YORK

First published 2016
by Routledge
2 Park Square, Milton Park, Abingdon, Oxon OX14 4RN

and by Routledge
711 Third Avenue, New York, NY 10017

Routledge is an imprint of the Taylor & Francis Group, an informa business

© 2016 selection and editorial matter, Peter Bjerregaard, Anders Emil Rasmussen and Tim Flohr Sørensen; individual chapters, the contributors

British Library Cataloguing in Publication Data
A catalogue record for this book is available from the British Library

Library of Congress Cataloging in Publication Data
 Materialities of passing : explorations in transformation, transition and transience / [edited] by Peter Bjerregaard, Anders Emil Rasmussen and Tim Flohr Sørensen.
 pages cm. — (Studies in death, materiality and the origin of time)
 Includes bibliographical references and index.
 ISBN 978-1-4724-4197-3 (hardback) — ISBN 978-1-4724-4198-0 (ebook) — ISBN 978-1-4724-4199-7 (epub) 1. Death—Cross-cultural studies. 2. Material culture. 3. Thanatology. I. Bjerregaard, Peter, editor. II. Rasmussen, Anders Emil, editor. III. Sørensen, Tim Flohr, editor.
 GN485.5.M38 2016
 306.9—dc23
 2015028321

ISBN: 9781472441973 (hbk)
ISBN: 9781315594309 (ebk)

Typeset in Times New Roman
by Apex CoVantage, LLC

Printed in the United Kingdom
by Henry Ling Limited

Contents

List of Figures

Notes on Contributors

Jan Bill holds a PhD in archaeology from the University of Copenhagen. He is Professor in Viking Age Studies at Museum of Cultural History, University of Oslo, where he serves as Curator of the Viking Ship Collection. He works in particular with Norwegian ship graves from Oseberg, Gokstad, Tune and Borre, and is currently directing the research project *Gokstad Revitalised*. Among his other research interests are Maritime Archaeology, Medieval Ships and Seafaring, and Archaeometry.

Peter Bjerregaard is Senior Adviser of Exhibitions at Museum of Cultural History, University of Oslo. He holds a PhD in anthropology and has conducted fieldwork on exhibition processes in contemporary museums of ethnography. His current research focuses on the relation between research and exhibition practice. As part of this work he is project leader for a collaboration between the six Norwegian university museums on 'Exhibitions as research generating practice'.

Andy Clayden is a senior lecturer and landscape architect in the Department of Landscape, Sheffield University. He has published widely on cemeteries and more specifically on natural burial. His research focuses on the temporal and dynamic nature of landscape, which has had a major influence on his design teaching and how people experience and engage with the natural burial and cemetery landscape.

Martin Demant Frederiksen holds a PhD in anthropology and is Assistant Professor in the Department of Cross-Cultural and Regional Studies, University of Copenhagen, Denmark. Since 2005 he has conducted long-term fieldwork studies in the Republic of Georgia and published on issues such as urban planning, youth, crime, temporality and ethnographic writing. His current research concerns the role of meaninglessness in social life. He is author of *Young Men, Time, and Boredom in the Republic of Georgia* (2013) and co-editor of the anthologies *Ethnographies of Youth and Temporality: Time Objectified* (2014) and *Ethnographies of Grey Zones in Eastern Europe* (2015)

Per Ditlef Fredriksen is Associate Professor in archaeology at the Department of Archaeology, Conservation and History, University of Oslo, and Research Associate at the Department of Archaeology, University of Cape Town. His main research foci include critical heritage studies, archaeologies of the contemporary and studies of historical ecology in southern Africa. In addition to excavations and analysis of archaeological material in Norway, South Africa and Zimbabwe, he has also conducted anthropological field studies in Mozambique, Botswana and South Africa.

Trish Green is a Research Fellow at the Hull York Medical School, University of Hull. She has conducted research and co-authored a book and several articles on natural burial. She is currently co-investigator on a seminar series entitled 'On encountering corpses: political, socio-economic and cultural aspects of contemporary encounters with dead bodies', a three-year interdisciplinary and multi-institutional project funded by the Economic and Social Research Council (ESRC).

Jenny Hockey is trained as an anthropologist and is currently emeritus Professor of sociology at the University of Sheffield. She has published widely on death, dying and memorialisation, along with ageing and lifecourse; domestic space; gender, heterosexuality and masculinity. Much of her work is informed by a material culture studies perspective. She has been president of the Association for the Study of Death and Society (2009–2013) and is a member of the editorial board of the international death studies journal, Mortality.

Anne Kjærsgaard is a PhD Scholar in the Faculty of Philosophy, Theology and Religious Studies at Radboud University, Nijmegen, the Netherlands. She obtained her MA in Theology and BA in History and STS-Studies from Aarhus University, Denmark, where she has also lectured in Church History and acted as the secretary of the Network for the Historical Study of Religion. Furthermore, she has worked in various museums. She is one of the editors of *Kirkegårdkultur* and has published articles and chapters on funerary culture in Denmark. Currently, she is finishing her PhD thesis on the limits of secularization among Lutherans in Denmark from the angle of mortuary behaviour.

Jeanette Lykkegård is a PhD Scholar at the department of Anthropology, Aarhus University, Denmark. Since 2011 she has carried out long-term fieldwork on the Kamchatka Peninsula, Russia, mainly in and around the village Achaivayam, Koryak Okrug. Her current research concerns the Chukchi understandings of living, non-living, dying and sustaining life, including social engagement between humans and non-humans.

Susan Matland holds a post-graduate exam in archaeology from the university of Bergen, Norway, and Master of Science (MSc), in death and society, from the university in Bath, England. She is currently working on the research project 'Cremation practices in Norway; regulations, changes, challenges and innovations'. Matland was previously employed as a department head at the Museum of Cultural History, University of Oslo, Norway and is currently managing director for the university museums of Norway's collective IT-organisation.

Maja Petrović-Šteger is a Research Fellow in Anthropology at the Research Centre of the Slovenian Academy of Sciences and Arts. She also holds Research Fellowship with the Independent Social Research Foundation. Her work focuses on the ways in which past injustices may be addressed through forms of bodily accounting; the meaning and value of human remains in post-conflict, translocal, and technoscientifically oriented societies; and the military and psychological concerns with mental hygiene. Her publications are based on her fieldwork in Serbia, Tasmania and Switzerland. She is the author of *Claiming the Aboriginal Body in Tasmania: An Anthropological Study of Repatriation and Redress* (2013) and has together with Jeanette Edwards edited *Recasting Anthropological Knowledge: Inspiration and Social Science* (2011).

Mark Powell is trained in social anthropology at the Queen's University, Belfast. His research focuses on the relationship between social identity, cultural belonging and environments. Based at the School of Civil Engineering and Geosciences, Newcastle University, he works across disciplines to investigate the social and cultural dimensions of hard infrastructural environments.

Anders Emil Rasmussen is Curator of Ethnographic Exhibitions at Moesgaard Museum in Denmark. He holds a PhD in anthropology and has done extensive urban as well as village level fieldwork in Papua New Guinea and more recently in Denmark. Research interests include the anthropology of value, technology, materiality and personhood. He is the author of *Manus Canoes: Skill, Making and Personhood* (2013), and *In the Absence of the Gift: New forms of Value and Personhood in a Papua New Guinea Community* (2015).

Tim Flohr Sørensen, Assistant Professor, PhD, The University of Copenhagen, Saxo Institute. He was an Assistant Professor at Aarhus University, 2012–2014, and a Marie Curie Fellow (postdoctoral researcher) at the McDonald Institute for Archaeological Research, University of Cambridge, 2010–2012. He is an archaeologist, interested in materiality, affect, space, and movement with reference to architecture and mortuary practice in the past and present. His publications include *An Anthropology of Absence: Materializations of Transcendence and Loss* (co-edited with Mikkel Bille and Frida Hastrup, 2010) and *Staging Atmospheres: Materiality, culture, and the texture of the in-between* (forthcoming special issue of Emotion, Space and Society, co-edited with Mikkel Bille and Peter Bjerregaard).

Dylan Trigg is a Marie Curie International Outgoing Fellow at the University of Memphis/University College Dublin working on the phenomenology of anxiety. He was previously a CNRS/VolkswagenStiftung postdoctoral researcher at both the Centre de Recherche en Epistémologie Appliquée and Les Archives Husserl, École Normale Supérieure. Trigg's work has been translated into Russian, Chinese, Latvian, and French. His recent articles have appeared in Continental Philosophy Review; Chiasmi International; Emotion, Space, and Society; and Memory Studies.

Eric Venbrux is Professor of Comparative Religion at Radboud University, Nijmegen, The Netherlands. He conducted anthropological fieldwork among the Tiwi people of Australia, as well as in Switzerland and The Netherlands. His research interests are in local religion, ritual change, material culture, and the verbal and visual arts. He is author of *A Death in the Tiwi Islands: Conflict, Ritual and Social Life in an Australian Aboriginal Community* (1995), co-editor of *Ritual, Media, and Conflict* (2011) and *Changing European Death Ways* (2013), and has written numerous articles and chapters on mortuary ritual.

Rane Willerslev is Professor in Anthropology at Aarhus University and adjunct Professor at Museum of Cultural History, University of Oslo. He has his PhD from the University of Cambridge. His main field of research has been hunting and spiritual knowledge among Siberia's indigenous peoples. He is the author of the monographs *Soul Hunters: Hunting, Animism and Personhood among the Siberian Yukaghirs* (2007) and *On the Run in Siberia* (2012). From 2011 to 2013 Willerslev was director of the Museum of Cultural History, University of Oslo, Norway. He is currently the leader of an interdisciplinary research project funded by the Danish Research Council, exploring the relationship between death, materiality and time.

Preface

Eventually we all die – but more importantly, we experience death head-on, when someone close to us dies. The present book series *Studies in Death, Materiality and the Origin of Time* stipulates that this fact constitutes the origin of human conceptions of time. Time permeates everything, but except for time itself all things are perishable. Yet, it is only through the perishable world of things and bodies that we sense time. The book series explores the fact that human experiences and conceptions of time inherently hinge on the material world, and that time as a socially experienced phenomenon cannot be understood as separate from material form or expression. As such, the series departs from a persistent current within Western thinking. Philosophy, biology and physics among other disciplines have studied time as an essential, ethereal and abstract concept. In the same way, death has often been conceived of in abstract and sometimes transcendental terms as occupying one extreme margin of human life. As an alternative, this series suggests that bodily death and material decay is a central point of reference in social life, which offers key insights into human perceptions of time. The series brings together scholars from anthropology, archaeology, architecture, sociology, media studies, cultural studies, and religion, all of whom explore the topic on the basis of their particular disciplinary focus and in a range of different empirical present and historical settings.

The first volume explored the meaning, which death has for human understandings of time across cultures, stretching from the ancient Egypt and Nepal over tribal India and the Philippines to North Siberia, East and West Africa, and various parts of the Western world. The aim of this grand interdisciplinary and cross-cultural venture was to explore the various 'social technologies' used, including timework, ritual, objects and interpersonal relations, when confronted with death. The second volume examined how people, groups and institutions deal with death through processes of *mediation* (the presentation of something through media), *remediation* (the representation of one medium in another) and *mediatization*.

This volume explores materialities and practices of death, deterioration and time far beyond contexts of human death by focusing on the concept of passing. Through this concept, the contributions explore themes ranging from the decay of buildings, the manipulation and exploration of dead as well as living bodies, the architecture of graves and burial sites, and museum collections among other things. Pointing out that neither death nor time can actually be observed directly, the contributors draw attention to those specific materialities of passing that render death and time perceptibly proximate. Whether it is deteriorating buildings, the metamorphosis of the dead body, or the way people construct graves, these materialities lend themselves as concrete forms at (and with) which to approximate and conceive the otherwise ambiguous or obscure phenomena of time and death. Adopting the notion of passing allows authors from a variety of disciplines to address related issues without losing themselves in specific intra-disciplinary debates and lingo, and hence the volume ranges in empirical focus from Siberian reindeer herders, over prehistoric tombs of Southern Scandinavia and contemporary Britain, and the politics of bodily healing in post-conflict Serbia to Maurice Merleau-Ponty's philosophy of the body.

Series editors:
Rane Willerslev and Dorthe Refslund Christensen,
Aarhus University

Acknowledgements

This book is the result of the collaboration between a number of different institutions, and the academic support of several people. We are grateful for the endorsement of the series editors, Dorthe Refslund Christensen and Rane Willerslev, encouraging and stimulating our work towards this publication.

All three editors have conducted research within the research project *Death, Materiality and the Origin of Time*, which has been funded by the Independent Research Council of Denmark. Moreover, institutional support from Aarhus University and the University of Copenhagen has been necessary for the realisation of this publication. In particular we would like to thank Museum of Cultural History, University of Oslo, for allowing us to host an inspiring and thought-provoking workshop in 2013 in the preparation of this volume and for supporting the production of the volume financially.

We would like to thank Menaka Roy for her thorough copy editing of most of the chapters, and Neil Jordan, Lianne Sherlock, and Aimée Feenan at Ashgate for their kind and productive support throughout the making of the book.

Most importantly, we extend our thanks to the contributors to the volume for producing such dedicated and inspiring chapters, and for their enthusiasm in the project from its very beginning at the workshop in 2013 through the editorial stages.

Peter Bjerregaard, Anders Emil Rasmussen
and Tim Flohr Sørensen

Introducing Materialities of Passing

Peter Bjerregaard, Anders Emil Rasmussen and Tim Flohr Sørensen

Introduction

Passing is a matter of transformation, transition and transience. At the precarious and indeterminate borderlands of being and non-being, people, places and things are in motion across dubious, interstitial states of existence. Sometimes, these liminal entities are harnessed by the hope or even promise of a future, of a form of being beyond time, or they may be eclipsed by the prospects of dissolution. Even in the face of terminal existence, whoever or whatever makes the transition thus stands on the verge of emergence, either being subject to an inevitable metamorphosis or leaving behind a void filled with the potential for new beginnings. This volume argues that we may identify passing in more than the colloquial sense of the expression, which refers to human death. We hold that materialities of passing issue forth in numerous instances and forms, constituting a transport between states of being, not being and new configurations of being.

The contributions to the volume thus explore what 'passing' means through a multidisciplinary collection of studies, focusing on human death, architectural decay, soul transportation, self-diagnosis and healing, the conceptual origins of body and death, commemorative practices and exhibition practices in museums. One of the connecting themes among the diverse contributions is the contention that passing can issue forth as a movement in several directions at once, not simply back and forth between being and not being, but also into and through states of being suspended, interstitial and multiple, in essence being simultaneously in more than one state. In this book we discuss passing in relation to actual physical processes, which take many forms, *and* as an analytical term whose specific contents may be derived from those particular material processes.

Specific cases of passing provide humans with approximations for actually perceiving time and temporality: We may have seen someone pass away or observed a building fall apart over time, and we may record how the passing of time leaves marks on our body indicating the approach of our own death, but surely, as living human beings, we have never experienced death, nor seen time as such. In this volume such human approximations to the experience of death and time come together in the concept of *passing*. In developing the concept of passing we want to reflect on and explore the phenomena of death and time through the specific materialities of passing that are the closest that humans may come to perceiving the fundamental spatiotemporal confines of their being. We propose that materialities of passing are approximations to death and time that are bound to the capacities and proportions of materials that human beings are engaged with. Such material encounters are of interest to our understanding of death and time, since they add an element beyond human control. Materials strike back, so to say, and are thereby capable of generating perspectives that might not be found in textual accounts of death and the afterlife (cf. Lemonnier 2012), or in symbolic analysis of 'the materiality of death'. Indeed, practices related to materialities of passing may often counter what is given in scriptural accounts or ritual liturgy.

Even though passing may allude to an entirely cerebral imagination of a generic 'other side' or a specific otherworldly destination and destiny, the realisation of passing typically unfolds through some kind of material form or sensuous experience enabling, preventing, embodying and revealing spatiotemporal transience and transfer. By taking as its point of departure the examination of observable and material phenomena, the intention, in this volume, is to explore very specific and localised understandings of the relationship between the otherwise highly abstract phenomena of death and the passage of time through a variety of empirical registers. Forming the centre of the volume is the hypothesis that the becoming and dissolution of the material world constitutes a fundamental medium for the human recognition of time and temporality (see also Willerslev, Christensen, and Meinert 2013), and it is through the recognition and sensation of the materiality of passing that the transience and transfer of bodies and things can be shared as experience between people. The passage of time, it may be argued, emerges most dramatically and unambiguously in the encounter with the finality of bodily being – whether human or non-human – and assumes concrete form in practices connected with dying, death and decay.

The contributors to the volume explore these encounters with the temporality of the far fringes of life and material existence in a broad variety of empirical cases, such as the treatment of the dead body, perceptions of and narratives about the dead, the material forms given to that which has vanished, and the spaces that circumscribe or are subject to passing. The strength of the notion of materialities of passing is its cross-disciplinary appeal and the absence of distinct theoretical developments of the term for understanding temporal material processes and practices. Approaches in this volume emerge from a broad variety of disciplinary backgrounds and orientations. The notion of materialities of passing is addressed in a multi-vocal, multidisciplinary framework, juxtaposing different takes on and modes of analysing passing. These are not always consonant, and their (often implicit, sometimes explicit) tensions point to a number of challenges and questions for further research. The contributions offer heterogeneous approaches to social, material, affective and conceptual occurrences, providing a new vocabulary for the study of death, materiality and time.

Compasses for Passing

Myths about dying are full of metaphors of passage, movement and gateways while graves often include vehicles and equipment for travel (be they boats, horses or even suitcases) or, conversely, things that are instrumental in impeding movement, preventing the dead from travelling, or hindering the uncontrolled passage between the world of the living and the world of the dead. Such passages may cut across the mythical and material world, for instance in the landscape of the Maya of the Late Classical Period, where caves were perceived as the womb of rebirth as well as the tomb of ancestors (Bassie-Sweet 1996: 11, 160), thus marking a site of exchange between realms of what might, from a contemporary, modern perspective, be considered respectively mythical and physical, but which would be considered animate and continuous (Harrison-Buck 2012). Many other examples of archaeological, historical and ethnographic places being perceived as transitory locales of the living and the dead could be mentioned, yet the point is that we need not see the mythical or 'otherworldly' as detached from the 'real' or 'objective' world of hard facts, but instead as connected by passages that can be geographically grounded in, for example, caves, fissures, springs, rivers or lakes (see also Sørensen and Lumsden forthcoming).

In other cases it becomes evident that it is not necessarily the landscape that animates the passage, but passing can instead be instituted by vehicles or vessels. Such vehicles or containers for passing can appear to be symbolic, while at other times they are concrete. During parts of the Scandinavian prehistory, ships have thus functioned as metaphorical allusions to death and the journey beyond. Seemingly, the ship constituted a crucial symbol in parts of the prehistoric cosmology, and it figures prominently in Bronze Age iconography on rock carvings and metalwork, as well as in the form of so-called 'ship settings', which are oval settings of large stones. It has been argued that the ship was perceived as the carrier of the sun across the sky during the day and under the water at night (Kaul 1998; 2004). Archaeological evidence shows that certain individuals were in some cases also buried within the perimeter of the ship settings (Artelius 1996; Bradley, Skoglund, and Wehlin 2010; Skoglund 2008), a practice that also extends into the Iron Age (Ramskou 1976; see also Bill, this volume). Such a use of a concrete vessel or its symbolic form clearly illustrates how death can be perceived as an instance of passing from one state of being to another, aided by some form of vehicle.

Passing can thus offer a scene or medium for probing into the states of being transpiring through death or being established in processes of decay. The notion of pondering existential questions through vanishing objects or their imagery can be traced back, at the least, to classic motifs in the visual arts, such as *Memento mori*, *Dance Macabre*, *Vanitas* and *Stilleben*, or the Romantic infatuation with ruins (Ariès 1985; Ginsberg 2004; Woodward 2002; Zucker 1961). The continued fascination with ruins and dilapidated architecture, for instance in the form of so-called urban exploration (which may roughly be described as the non-destructive practice of entering industrial and institutional architecture that is condemned and off-limits), also points to the use of decay as a vehicle for reflecting on life, death and time, and for getting in touch with material instruments for perceiving passing. In an academic context, architectural dilapidation, decay, entropy and material transformation constitute media for delving into the past, creating links and presences that are otherwise obliterated by time. These spatial and temporal nexuses allow for a two-way transport in time, where traces are not simply the remains of the past, but also the compasses for navigating in the present or even probing into the future (DeSilvey 2006; Lucas 2008; Olivier 2011; Shanks, Platt and Rathje 2004). In many respects, this is precisely the *raison d'être* for archaeology, because without these traces, the past would be truly 'gone', and our sense of time would potentially lose its scale, tempo and directionality (whether linear or not). Or, in the words of Michael Shanks, David Platt and William Rathje (2004: 64):

> ... the archaeological refers to ruin and responses to it, to the mundane and quotidian articulated with grand historical scenarios, to materializations of the experience of history, material aura, senses of place and history, choices of what to keep and what to let go.

The archaeological endeavour fundamentally hinges on an attention to material phenomena and their temporal properties; their states of emergence and dissolution suspended in processes of formation, fossilisation, conservation, destruction, decay and transience (Holtorf 2014; Lucas 2012; Sørensen 2015). Thus, physical dilapidation can often act as a sensuous instrument for getting in corporeal contact with a sense of finality or even offer the potential for breaching finitude, in the process again facilitating or encumbering passage. It is precisely the quality of getting in touch with a sense of finality, and through this the sublime, often emphasised as one of the characteristics of the early modern obsession with ruins and architectonic decay. The tension between the forces of life and death can thus be said to characterise Georg Simmel's (1959) discussion of ruins, where the ruin itself assumes the role of physical entity and trope simultaneously. Simmel stipulates that ruins mark a 'cosmic tragedy' as they decentre the balance between the 'upward striving' of the soul and the 'gravity' of nature (ibid.: 259). The ruin is at the same time past and present, and it 'creates the present form of past life', and thus 'constitutes an immediately perceived presence' (ibid.: 265).

At the heart of the volume lies the idea that materialisations of the dead, the dying and the decay of bodies – human and non-human – offer ways of getting a grasp on otherwise precarious temporalities. Thus, rather than a complete annihilation, the challenge suggested by the death of people and the decay of material objects may be a 'certain uncertain', which is at once both empty and full of untamed potential. While ethnographies dealing with doubt and uncertainty tend to deal with these phenomena as relationally defined in pairs with certainty and belief (Pelkmans 2013: 3–4), several contributions to this volume deal with doubt and uncertainty as basic conditions for dealing with time and death (Petrović-

Šteger, this volume; Rasmussen, this volume). As time and the actual condition of being dead are both beyond human perception, doubt and uncertainty cannot be reduced to the temporary results of collapsed systems of belief or processes of religious conversion (Rasmussen, this volume). As several contributions to this volume demonstrate, doubt and uncertainty is experienced not as the temporary absence of belief or knowledge but as a basic condition of existence and modes of knowing, which is not confined to methodological scientific doubt (Descartes 1996).

Through 'passing' the contributors explore how humans strive to relate to the temporal dimension of death and decay, by giving new shape and direction to the potential unleashed by the dissolution of bodies. By focusing on the materiality of passing – and thereby the relationship between embodiment, temporality and the state of being or becoming dead – we believe that the volume offers readers insights into the specifically proportional, spatial and directional aspects of the interface between life and death as reflected in various materialities of passing as they are produced or experienced in a variety of socio-cultural milieus. The contributors to this volume thus deal with this interface by examining a variety of materialities of passing: the last perceptible frontier towards death and temporality. That is to say, while decay, objects of commemoration, death rituals and images of the dead are all accessible to human experience, this is not the case for either death or time.

The Unreality of Death

Death and passing are frequently explored in terms of bereavement and social institutions, such as practices through which people may reconstitute social relations or otherwise render the event of death meaningful or bearable. Yet contributors to the volume turn the focus towards the material, affective and sensuous qualities that influence or direct human understandings of the temporality of being. It may appear tempting, then, to speak of 'materiality of death' (Fahlander and Oestigaard 2008; Stefanou 2012; Sørensen 2009; Tarlow 2013; Williams 2003) as the material facticity of death. But the question is whether what people encounter in material form can ever be death *per se*, or if what humans are confronted with is, rather, decaying matter, dead bodies, cremated bodies, pyres, graves, urns, memorials, or, in other words, materialities of *passing*. Making this distinction may at first seem a cumbersome play on words, but the contributions to this volume demonstrate the need to discriminate between death and dead matter, precisely because of the concrete temporality of all things material and the conjectural nature of death.

In this way, we not only contend that death is a subjective fact, which can only be understood through the death of the other (Willerslev, Christensen and Meinert 2013: 4), but we further stipulate that death cannot be realised empirically. The death of the other is a proxy through the confrontation with dead matter, with processes of dying and decay, and the experience of loss. There can never be any materiality of death as such, only approximations, intimations and speculations concerning death. In that sense death is not an empirical fact. Therefore this volume focuses on the far fringes of life, the passing into, towards and onwards from the process of dying. The 'materiality of death' will always be metaphorical, referential or otherwise symbolic. Materialities of passing, on the other hand, refer to actual handling of decaying matter and the vanishing of life through which the passage of time may be observed; with things passed on prior to dying, with the anticipation of death, and with the material forms with which people attempt to transcend or interact with the ultimate nothingness of those who have – or that which has – passed.

There are, in other words, reasons to challenge the frequently used notion of death as the one certain thing in human life and, accordingly, as life's ultimate temporal horizon. On the basis of human experience, it would be more accurate to hold that there is no such thing as the condition of death. The concept of 'death' is, in a sense, a merely self-referential symbol pointing to no specific entity other than itself as the certain unknown of potentially nothing at all. In other words, there can be no empirical observations made of an actual materiality of death. Perceiving death as the 'only certain thing in human life' is therefore mistaken, as its only certainty is the uncertainty that defines it. Death is, at best, to be conceived of as a kind of moment or a relational disruption, rather than as a singular fact.

Framing death as a disruption places the issue of time at the foreground of the phenomenon, and we may return to the hypothesis stated at first that dead and decaying matter is the matter or medium through which humans achieve a conception of time. However, the hypothesis needs to be qualified in terms of how we understand time, because just like death as such is inaccessible to observation, time itself is beyond human perception. As noted above, time has no materiality. We do not see time itself, but arms on a clock moving, seasonal change, or the movement of the moon and the sun, and we argue that those very movements find their primordial form in the decay and transition of all bodily being, even if, in a positivist sense, it might appear to be the other way around. The empirical reality of death and of time as singular, factual phenomena thus remain entirely speculative; in their stead we place another concept: *passing*.

Passing as Interstitial Being

But before we venture on to elaborate on the wider purchase of such an understanding of passing, we will dwell a while on some of the established uses of 'passing' and unpack some of the connotations and meanings of the term. Apart from allowing us to logically contest the empirical reality of death, an important reason for employing 'passing' as the overarching term in the current cross-disciplinary framework is the fact that in contrast to similar concepts such as 'transience' or 'trans-substantiation', passing is not already inscribed within particular disciplinary discourses. Thus, the notion of 'passing' allows us to trace a theme recognised in a number of different disciplinary perspectives without hinging on established disciplinary understandings of a specific concept.

Pointing out that death and time have no materiality is perhaps stating the obvious, but it allows us to pinpoint specific cases in which people are able to conceive of time and death by intimating, interrogating, negotiating and in fact diagnosing and exploring what is at the fringes of perceived life through specific materialities of passing. But perhaps also in much more general ways, materialities of passing (whether such materialities are instituted by human agency or simply observable natural processes) can be conceived of as a *method* of exploring death and time. Therefore, we will take the notion of passing literally and explore how particular sensuous and material qualities constitute frameworks for reflecting on or understanding the temporality of death and decay. In different ways, time and temporality assume pace, scale or volume, and essentially become available to the senses and not simply to abstract reflection. The human body grows and decays, buildings deteriorate at varying paces, museum collections accumulate and demand evermore attention and care.

However, the lack of an empirical grounding of death and time does not mean that they have to be studied in exclusively speculative terms. Anthropologist Rane Willerslev (2011) has recently argued that certain essentially 'imaginative issues' (in his case the animist soul and in ours, the condition of death and the passage of time) might better be explored exactly by imaginative contemplation rather than empirical investigation (in his case 'armchair anthropology' rather than ethnographic fieldwork). A central point in our argument, however, is that even if we cannot observe death and time, people intimate and approximate that which they are well aware can only be imagined (albeit often very strongly believed in). Thus 'passing' points to the insurmountable gap between our experience of the world and our knowledge of it. In this perspective, it may be equally interesting to explore how specific materialities of passing work to close that gap or to provide a conceptual framework for achieving some form of closure. As we may only sense death and time through material passing, we may apply an experiential and explorative approach in order to deal with them.

The explorative and diagnosing practices of materialities of passing come through vividly in Loring Danforth's ethnography on burial practices in a Greek village, for example (Danforth 1982). Danforth describes how the women in a rural Greek community exhume and carefully examine the bones of the dead, thereby hoping to determine whether the dead person has reached forgiveness and access to paradise in the afterlife (1982: 48–49). But more than informing about life 'on the other side' the bones also offer the opportunity to study the moral persona of the deceased prior to passing, even after their having been dead for several years. Handling the bones of the dead person is an exploration of her moral constitution while living and thus a means of getting access to something that is otherwise concealed or made incomprehensible by the opacity of other minds. Material and social passing is thus not simply a gradual disappearance of a state of being (whether regarding personhood or objecthood), but the revelation of something concealed during life. Meanwhile, passing itself becomes a state of being as a form of interstitiality.

Passing: Approximation and Exploration

The chapters in this volume speak of different aspects of disagreement, doubt, and confusion arising from direct confrontations with and real-life speculations over death and dilapidation. As the authors show in a variety of empirical contexts and from very different disciplinary perspectives, such ambiguities seem very often to result in practices of approximation and exploration. The contributors consider the materiality of passing from the points of view of anthropology, archaeology, religious studies, landscape architecture, philosophy and sociology. The chapters deal with passing in very different ways, some strongly grounded in empirical research, while others are concerned with mediating conceptual aspects of passing in its various forms. Nevertheless, the common denominator is that passing in all of the chapters assumes *form*, or concrete material appearance, yet with different emphases. The various forms of passing may be divided into three general themes along which the volume is organised, namely, *transformation, transition* and *transience*. The individual contributions all relate in different ways to these three aspects of passing – we do not see them as different forms of passing but rather as different aspects of passing, and we believe that the respective contributions have the capacity of bringing out these particular qualities of passing in their particular case studies.

Part I: Transformation: Passing as Movement between Categories

The passing of people, things and places entails an obvious transformation of material states of being. This transformation is frequently discussed in terms of decay and dissolution of the human body or of architecture (e.g. Bloch 1995; Pétursdóttir and Olsen 2014; Tarlow 2002). In some respects this might seem to allude to a certain 'materiality of death' (as discussed above) if we accept that the corporeal decay of a body equals the corporeality of death. However, we argue that the corpse is a dead body and *not* a materiality of death itself. Metamorphosis of the body (of humans or of architecture) is a transformation as much as it is a transition, and it provides the physical and observable forms that allow for humans to perceive of different kinds of temporality, perhaps even providing clues to the 'origin' of human concepts of time as such (as suggested by Willerslev, Christensen and Meinert 2013). Hence, in the process of metamorphosis we observe the effects of time and its rhythms or speeds.

To this end, death rituals have often been conceived as 'death work' (Chapman 2003; Davies 1997; Finucane 2013; Harper 2012; Morris 1992), fixing the imbalance imposed by death in the social order and establishing a proper relation between the living and the dead. In other words, many accounts of dying and death rituals have often been described as 'rites de passage'. Famously, Arnold van Gennep (1960) developed the notion of 'rites de passage' to describe those rituals that mark social passages in the human life. Whether these are rites to transform children to grown members of the group, unmarried men and women into married persons, or living persons into (properly) dead persons, van Gennep argues that these rituals all involve three distinct phases that together finalise the passage from one structural category to another: separation, transition/limen and incorporation. For example, adolescent boys may first be taken out of their family's houses, then be isolated in a house where the secrets of the grown men's cult are revealed to them (Turner 1967: 102), and finally be reincorporated into social relations, perhaps to go and live in a men's house, reflecting their newly acquired status.

It is worth noting that in van Gennep's description, rites of passage in conjunction with death, specifically, are only rarely particularly elaborate in the phase of separation (e.g. from the living) but rather tend to dwell on rites of transition (van Gennep 1960: 146) or liminality. In other words, rites of passage in conjunction with death will most often focus on the liminal period of the ritual (according to van Gennep) in which the person is *between* categories: in a state of passing. Furthermore, death rituals present a problem to van Gennep's approach in that 'within a single people there are several contradictory or different conceptions of the afterworld, which may become intermingled with one another, so that their confusion is reflected in the rites' (ibid.: 146). While it is fairly understandable and perhaps agreed upon what the difference is between being a non-initiated adolescent and an initiated young person (you can now get married, for example), what being dead is like will remain speculative, and perhaps therefore more easily disputed, and perhaps therefore too, the liminal period is prolonged and, in some cases (see below), is never really over.

Van Gennep's notion of rites of passage has been greatly popularised by anthropologist Victor Turner, who focused precisely on the liminal period of rites of passage (Turner 1967: 93–111). Interestingly, one of the key aspects of the liminal period, according to Turner, is that the liminal 'passenger' (ibid.: 94), the person in transition during the ritual is, if not physically invisible to others (as in the case of adolescent men above), then structurally invisible, and is in fact structurally dead (ibid.: 97). This means that they are often secluded and tabooed and perceiving them is problematic since, according to Turner, people can only perceive others through their specific cultural categories, and the liminal person is neither-nor while both-and. People in limen are often therefore associated with both pollution (cf. Douglas 2002; Hertz 1960: 34–37) and with being superhuman, infinite and limitless when outside meaningful categories; they will often reside in 'another place' somewhere hidden, because their existence is a paradox, impure and scandalous (Turner 1967: 98). While in other rites of passage the liminal period unambiguously ends when the 'passenger' arrives at the destination of a new status or position in society, the same is not necessarily the case for the dead person. After all, if the destination were reached through mortuary rituals, why would the dead need the boats, horses and other means of transportation that graves are in many cases equipped with? While all other rites of passage provide transitions from one known and – in a sense materially manifest – category to another, death rites involve passage into the non-material.

Returning to Danforth (1982), who draws on van Gennep and Turner when describing 'death as passage', we find an example of this potentially infinite state of liminality. In Danforth's case the liminal period only fully ends with the second coming and 'God's Kingdom', something that his informants had little faith in. Instead they exhume the bones of the dead long after burial and '[t]he dry white bones, the product of decomposition and exhumation, are only an imperfect *approximation* of the incorruptible body promised by church teachings' (ibid.: 68, emphasis added). In other words 'the other world' of the dead remains speculative, but the materialities (such as bones) of passing, through which people may seek to perceive death, remain approximations of what is fundamentally an aporetic 'nothingness'. In line with this, the rural Greek express in songs how the dead are forced to leave the living entirely and go to 'stin xenitia', which Danforth translates as 'a foreign land' (ibid.: 59). In fact, in this case dying is not a passage into a new condition where the liminality would eventually end in the dissolution of the contradicting categories (life and death) between which the liminal (/dead) person resides. Even if the teachings promise that eventually the dead come back to life (ibid.: 68–69), Greek villagers react to such promises with disbelief. In keeping the bones of the dead after exhumation, Danforth argues, Greek villagers testify to themselves that 'the limits of the material world cannot be transcended' (ibid.: 69); exhumation is the closest they come to resurrection, and it is as such only a partial victory over death, an approximation of death through the materiality of passing.

The contributions to this part of the book relate to the liminal passages and metamorphoses in different ways, yet all clustering around distinctly architectural settings and media. First, combining landscape architecture, anthropology and sociology, Jenny Hockey, Andy Clayden, Trish Green and Mark Powell explore the construction and use of 'natural burial' in the United Kingdom. Natural burial constitutes a medium for dissolving the conventional demarcations of death, replacing them with an ecological linkage of person and nature, offering a potential for coping with the 'uncertain temporalities of death', as they describe it. They argue that passing 'assumes particular materialities or tangibilities, becoming a process of change and continuity, rather than simply a matter of dispersal or erasure'. In other words, natural burial is a mode of *making* rather than simply *marking* change, and simultaneously about not only *finding* time for commemoration, but equally about *making* time, allowing for 'far greater engagement with the uncertainties and abstractions of death'.

A similar focus, albeit in a very different empirical context, can be found in Martin Demant Frederiksen's chapter on architectural dilapidation and restoration in Tbilisi, Georgia. Frederiksen discusses the socio-political impact of the transformations of surfaces of buildings, and how the aesthetic and moral values in the exterior of architecture hinge on perceptions of the tempo of change. He argues that decaying 'old' surfaces are perceived as an anticipated state of transformation, but that the crumbling exterior of recently renovated architecture is considered untimely and hence a sign of moral dilapidation, indicating 'a frail present rather than a glorious past'. Frederiksen shows how decay and dissolution can assume very different qualities as sensory and political phenomena, as procreators rather than simply symptoms or symbols of values and morality.

Exploring a prehistoric form of architecture, Tim Flohr Sørensen discusses the interaction of burial practice and burial place in the monumental tombs of the South Scandinavian Neolithic. The tombs explored in the chapter are characterised by spacious interiors, yet with extremely confined means of access, indicating that movement in the tomb was cumbersome and highly choreographed. At the same time, burials would often revolve around the depositing or manipulation of body parts or skeletal remains. In other words, the living as well as the dead would go through a number of transformative and transient states of being, crossing several boundaries during the burial ritual. Sørensen argues that the movements across these thresholds are to be seen as instrumental in constructing new identities among the living as well as the dead.

Anne Kjærsgaard and Eric Venbrux examine a similar issue, of how people adapt to transformations occurring after the moment of dying, and the negotiation of identities. While Sørensen's prehistoric case explores the metamorphosis of the dead and their identities, Kjærsgaard and Venbrux investigate the logics of commemorative practices in contemporary Netherlands and Denmark. They show how the dead are continuously informed about the changing circumstances and events among their living relatives through photographs posted at the graves of the dead. Furthermore, the practice of posting photographs on the grave challenges the Protestant notion of the cemetery as a memorial space, turning it into a site of ongoing exchange between the living and the dead. As such, the photographs, Kjærsgaard and Venbrux argue, blur the boundaries between the living and the dead; they negotiate the finality of death.

Altogether, the chapters in this part of the book explore how passing may be extended from the perceived 'moment' of dying or vanishing to becoming an interstitial state of being, issuing forth through material transformations available for exploration through the senses. These interstices are at the same time momentary and durable, and the transformative qualities of material forms seem to offer a means of grasping the temporally grounded materiality of passing, whether as memory, architecture or corporeality.

Part II: Transition: Detachment and Continuing Bonds

The term passing obviously connotes some kind of movement. The idea of dying as movement can be traced in burial practices across the world where the dead are often equipped in the grave with means for travelling (as for instance the burial of important personages in Viking ships, cf. Bill, this volume). But we may also refer to mythical depictions of the travel from the world of the living to the world of the dead. While geographically located in landscapes of the heavens, underworlds, and so on, socially this travel may be a passage from one social category to the other, from the living to the ancestors, for example.

While the death rites pass the dead on to the unknown, the dead will often have prepared for a continuation beyond death while still alive. As anthropologist Alfred Gell (1998) has convincingly argued, material things should not always be understood in opposition to humans, but rather as extensions of human agency. Thus, through producing or attaching oneself personally to objects it is possible to create a life for oneself even after death. That way, Gell argues, people may extend themselves and cause affect long after biological death, being in that capacity what Gell refers to as 'distributed persons' (ibid.). Here Gell draws heavily on the anthropology of Melanesia in which authors such as Marilyn Strathern (1988) and Roy Wagner (1991) have argued that the person is locally conceptualised as fractal or dividual (as opposed to individual), as being 'carried' as part of another or as engendering them (Wagner 1991: 163).

In such ways, parts of the dead person live on as parts of others (e.g. Mimica 2003; see also Rasmussen this volume; Sørensen this volume). Such practices are, as one would reckon, far from unambiguous as they establish bonds that the descendants do not always approve of, sometimes causing fierce conflicts during mortuary exchange ceremonies (or during estate settlements) concerning the specific ways in which things transacted embody new locations of parts of the personhood of the person who has passed (Rasmussen 2014).

Passing can thus assume the role of a journey from life to death, severing or re-establishing the relationships between the living and the dead. Seeing love as attachment, Sigmund Freud ([1917] 1957) argued that the emotional relationship to the dead had to cease in the process of 'normal' mourning in order for the bereaved to be able to build new healthy relations and to move on in life. According to this logic, failure to abandon the dead leads to a 'pathological' state of unresolved and lasting grief, which Freud famously terms 'melancholia'. The passing of the deceased thus becomes synonymous with a severing of emotional relations, resulting in an acceptance and acknowledgement of the death of the loved one, which stands in opposition to the melancholic and reality-defying retention of the dead. The possible retention of the dead is not simply a self-induced psychological occurrence, but can be triggered by or enforced by objects that the bereaved associates with the deceased, or which somehow keep the deceased present.

This line of thinking has later led therapists to argue that objects should only be used as transitory means of adjusting to the loss of the deceased, because such 'linking objects' will otherwise blur the boundaries between the mourner and the mourned (Hallam and Hockey 2001: 19–20). Embedded in this notion of healthy grief is the temporal condition that mourning ceases at some point – that it *passes* and so does the deceased, which is also integral to Freud's initial model of healing in *Mourning and Melancholia*. However, as Tammy Clewell (2004) observes, Freud would later revise the contention that the lost object has to be repudiated in order to recover from the loss, stipulating that mourning may never cease, and that the gap left behind by the loss of the deceased may in fact never be substituted by something or someone else.

The experience of passing is thus not necessarily completed by the substitution of the lost person or object by something else, nor does the loss result in a lasting state of vacuity. Instead, as has been suggested by recent studies of grief work, the bereaved tend to establish 'continuing bonds' with the deceased (Klass, Silverman and Nickman 1996; Walter 1996; see also Field 2006; Field et al. 2013; Hockey et al., this volume; Howarth 2007; Jensen 2010; Matland, this volume; Neimeyer, Baldwin and Gillies 2006; Schut et al. 2006; Sørensen 2010; Valentine 2009). Such ties are emotional and material, and suggest that memory of that which has passed is not merely subjective or a temporal state of suspension, but can issue forth as a socially shared and durable relationship.

The proposition that the bereaved can live healthily with continuing bonds to the deceased also builds on the contention that these bonds are not static or permanent objects of memory. Rather, the passing and the temporal dimension of continuing bonds imply that relationships are prone to displacements, interruptions and transgressions (Sørensen 2012). The memory of the deceased is susceptible to change, not only in terms of the exact recollection of the deceased or of past events, but even more so with regard to the affective associations with memories. As time passes from the moment of loss, the affective texture of the memory of the deceased tends to get transformed. The memory of a person may consist of equally vivid and clear memories, but also of blurred contours of the person's moods, ways of talking and walking, of indistinct flashes of a smile, a conversation and maybe even an awareness of not being able to manifestly remember the person's face or voice.

In this sense, continuing bonds can be regarded as a medium for allowing memory to dissolve or to reconfigure into forms and contents not dictated by a fidelity to 'empirical' facts in the recollection of a person, object or event. Instead, some aspects of the memory of the deceased vanish, while other aspects may sediment into more manifest form, yet at the same time, these forms and dissolution may not necessarily be premeditated by the bereaved. As such, memory can be used as a strategy to manipulate and cope with the present, as explored by Maja Petrović-Šteger (this volume; Küchler 1999; Rowlands 1999). Here, the underlying tenet is that forgetting is the foundation for remembering, referring back to Freud's contention that humans need to filter out certain memories in order to cope with others (Freud [1923] 1961a: 50; [1924] 1961b: 199).

In her contribution, Petrović-Šteger examines the sociality of bodily health in Belgrade as a site of processing historical memory and knowability. She demonstrates that the experience of health is in many cases related to the post-conflict condition after the civil wars of the Balkans in the 1990s, meaning that healing, self-care and sometimes excessive self-monitoring becomes a means of traversing past social and political identification. Petrović-Šteger's informants often experience their bodies 'as sites bearing palpable traces of the country's conflictual past', implying a need for personal and corporeal autonomy from governmental healthcare and hence state authority. According to Petrović-Šteger, the informants' 'etiological language, compulsive checking of health indicators, naturalisation of ailments and general self-care is not only healthcare in extremis but may stand for a mode of self-discipline and of postconflict culture that aspires to record the nation's historical passage'. Memory of the conflict and the passage into a post-conflict state of being is thus implied by the body's health, because political independence becomes a property of the body.

Rasmussen's informants likewise deal with materialities of passing as methods of knowing (in Petrović-Šteger's case, diagnosing) or rather, unknowing. For many of Rasmussen's interlocutors on Mbuke Islands in Papua New Guinea, assuming one knows the destination of passing is the ultimate violation of the dead, and Rasmussen shows how a series of transactions and distributions of personhood are treated with a kind of methodological doubt. Rasmussen demonstrates how the dispersed, distributed and potentially dangerous 'soul-stuff' of the dead results in Mbuke people acting with 'precautionary approximations', granting the dead the benefit of the doubt. Discussing explorative dealings with the localities and material containers of passing, Rasmussen argues that Mbuke peoples' dealings with dying and those who have passed reflects a form of doubt that should not be understood as the temporary absence of knowledge or certainty, but as a useful knowledge proposition in its own right. For this reason, Rasmussen contends, 'the Mbuke feel they have to work to confine and contain what is potentially the stuff of the dead or those who are in the process of dying', precisely because they are painfully aware that the destination of passing cannot be known.

Exploring the tragic death of three young men at the border of Swaziland and South Africa, Per Ditlef Fredriksen demonstrates how the souls of the dead are contained in a non-human body on their way to the place of burial. This form of containment – in this case carrying the soul in a twig – illustrates how body and soul can be severed, and linger in a state of indeterminacy. Consequently, the process of transport speaks of a need to establish a contained soul, but simultaneously of the dangers of non-containment as a form of non-being. In this case, the twig carrying the soul needs to be understood in terms of its materiality, because its material decay is in essence a form of memory work. Or as Fredriksen explains, 'The slow drying, dwindling and decomposition of the twig's leaves … is a form of resistance by the life gradually deteriorating; the visual appearance of the twig becomes a way of measuring the new ancestor's distance to this world' (Fredriksen, this volume). The materiality of passing is thus the fusion of the soul and its vehicle, or the containment of the soul, pointing to past, present and future, all at once.

Susan Matland explores practices of post-mortem photography. In the chapter she goes through different types of post-mortem photography and relates them to the specific photographic techniques available. While the use of post-mortem photography has thus oscillated between the public and the private sphere, one important aspect of post-mortem photographs has been their capacity to work as a focus for continuing bonds. While the physical body of the deceased has been more or less hidden in most modern Western societies, post-mortem photography has worked as a medium for maintaining and negotiating relations to the dead. However, Matland introduces another kind of post-mortem photography that adds a highly interesting contrast to the existing literature, namely the American art photographer Sally Mann's documentation of decomposing human bodies at an American forensic anthropology research facility, 'The Body Farm'. This documentation breaks completely with the capacity of photographs to maintain identities. Instead, these photographs point to the body as a mere material container through which time passes. Thus, the dead body is introduced to the gaze, but this time in a way in which it has lost identity and makes sensible, instead, the passage of time through the human body.

In this part of the book, bodies of various kinds are shown to become places for exploration and potentiality in their capacity for being transitory. Specific materialities become temporary containers for the movement and confinement of matters associated with death, decay and temporality. We see that the human body is conceived as only one among other potential containers or access points to the 'soul-stuff' of the person. Similarly, the body itself may contain and reveal the traces of historical passages well beyond the destiny of the biological individual. Dealing in this part of the book with materialities of passing as vehicles of – or objects of – transition, these materialities are checked against perceptions of health, healing and coherence.

Part III: Transience: Passing On, Passing Through

The literature on mourning and detachment referred to above point to the need to detach oneself from the lost object; this has more recently been challenged by the concept of 'continuing bonds'. There is, however, a sense in which passing in itself reveals modes of existence that go beyond the individual person or object lost and therefore transgresses ordinary concepts of memory and mourning.

In a remarkable analysis of the clash of colonial bureaucracy and indigenous suicide in the Canadian Arctic, Lisa Stevenson (2012) observes the difference between the colonial concerns with bodily survival, and Inuit concerns with continuances that are not necessarily isolated to the human body. Thus, to state bureaucracy 'life' is an abstract and measureable unit, to be preserved at all odds. In contrast, the Inuit conception of life transgresses the individual body. Your existence is predicated on being a part of a community, most noticeable through the passing on of names. By passing on names from someone who recently died to a newborn, 'the life-of-the-name will come to reside in that newborn' (ibid.: 603).

In other words, we deal here with a concept of passing that is not predicated upon preservation or a continuation of bonds as such, but on the death – or, more generally, the destruction – of an existing form. This revelation of a larger structure or longer history within the physical body points to a supra-human perspective on time. In this sense, the dissolution of the individual reveals another temporal being which has only temporarily occupied the individual body and will later be shown to have passed over into another body.

This destruction of the known world leads us back to one of the classical texts in death studies, namely Robert Hertz's work on secondary burial (Hertz 1960; see also Venbrux 2007). Hertz argues that in cases of secondary burials, the first burial, entailing a destruction of the flesh, amounts to a destruction of the known identity, while the second burial, typically a manipulation of the bones, confers identity and marks a rebirth into the world of the dead. Thus, in order to pass into the world of the dead, the body or the object has to be destroyed. This – basically sacrificial – way of thinking marks an extreme in the way we may think of passing: in order to create a passing you have to destroy rather than preserve. Such extreme cases allow us to conceive of the ways in which passing is transformation as much as it is transience.

While the notions of passing explored so far exist in a kind of linear time, as the passage from one category to another or the extension of personhood over time, there is also a way in which passing moves through contemporary geographies. Children's literature provides us numerous examples of this kind. Just think of *Alice in Wonderland* or *The Chronicles of Narnia*. In both cases a physical passage – in the former a tree, in the latter a wardrobe – creates passages into parallel worlds that are marked by a strange relation to time. These worlds are untimely (Grosz 2004) in a double sense; they are not easily placed in a historical linearity of time, in fact they defy any ordinary experience of time (what has seemed like days on the other side of the passage has only lasted a few minutes, or even had no duration, on this side), and they seem to collapse a subjective, biographical time perspective with a non-subjective perspective of a deep time in one and the same body.

Such passages can also be found in ethnographic and historical accounts. For instance, among the Chukchi of the Siberian North, not observing the right treatment of sacrificial offerings may open a pathway for the dead to enter the realm of the living and look for relatives to take with them to the world of the dead (Willerslev 2009: 698). In medieval Norway the offering of coins in churches appears to have been practiced 'in order to assure saintly advocacy with God' (Gullbekk 2012: 7). This advocacy was particularly needed for salvation in order to avoid purgatory. Purgatory was not simply considered to be a measurable time period to follow life, but rather a parallel dimension of 'next to eternal' time expansion (ibid.). Thus, the offering of coins can in practice be considered as the opening of passages between parallel spheres activating types of agency otherwise out of reach.

In his work on Sinhalese exorcism rituals in Sri Lanka, Bruce Kapferer (1997: 176–184) argues that these rituals constitute a portal opening into a virtual world, 'which may be said to be a radical slowing down and entry within the constructional moments in which humans realize themselves and their worlds' (ibid.: 180). The virtual is non-presentable, it cannot attain any specific form, but is 'the whole' (Hallward 2006: 23), everything at once, through which the dynamics of actualised, experienced, presentable existence emerges (Hallward 2006: 31–36; Kapferer 1997: 179). In this sense the time of the ritual destroys the forces of actuality, the world as we know it, in order to activate the very dynamics of the virtual that will regenerate the sorcery victim and throw him back into actuality with new force (Kapferer 1997: 181). Thus, the passage opened by the materiality and the performance of the ritual allows not only for otherwise unattainable, mythological forces to take place within human life; it also allows for another temporal causality to operate. So, Kapferer argues, because in actuality we cannot control the unfolding of events in time, we try to control the categories of things. In the virtuality of the ritual, by contrast, categories are blurred, but the sequence of events is controlled (ibid.: 179–180).

Passages, in other words, point to material constructions through which the otherworldly may traverse to momentarily take part in the time of the living. In this way an untimeliness occurs which is of an uncertain character – potentially benign, and potentially malicious. The third part of the volume takes issue with what we frame as 'virtual' and 'transmaterial' modes of passing. This group of chapters all concern forms of passing that are characterised by cutting across established ontological boundaries of the material and the immaterial, the present and the absent. This is not simply a matter of 'mixed media' or 'multiple ontologies', but concerns passing as a concrete way of getting in touch with otherworldly entities and forms of existence, or deliberate orchestrations of materialities passing through different states. The real and the unreal are at stake at these intersections, but in ways that conflate rather than juxtapose the categories.

Jeanette Lykkegård examines passages between death and birth among the Chukchi of Siberia, and a number of cycles of traffic between the world of the living and the world of the ancestors. Key to this traffic are the material instruments and practices that make this exchange possible. The spirit of the deceased embarks on a journey towards the world of the ancestors, aided by a number of rituals, opening the precarious potential for the dead to enter the world of the living. The props involved in the ritual setting serve the purpose of creating a virtual protection of the living, and Lykkegård explains that these instruments 'are no longer just materials; they are actors, guides, enclosures, boundaries and souls'.

The traffic between the living and the dead is also a key aspect of Jan Bill's contribution, where he offers a new interpretation of the Oseberg ship burial from the Norwegian Viking Age. The Oseberg ship may at first glimpse seem to be easily interpreted as a vessel to bring the deceased from the world of the living to that of the dead. Abundant with presents of horses, dogs, sledges and other implements for travelling the deceased is apparently equipped with all necessary means to pass safely into the other side. However, the empirical findings are puzzling since the Oseberg ship seems to be anchored, and therefore not meant to travel. To understand this, Bill introduces the term 'ambiguous mobility' in order to deal with the paradoxes related to passing the dead on to another existence while keeping them within reach of the living.

Peter Bjerregaard and Rane Willerslev explore the museum as a site for engaging with death. However, in contrast to the widespread critique of the museum being a graveyard, mausoleum or even a cannibalistic process, they argue that the engagement with death provided by the museum paradoxically allows us to get a sense of the most intense life generating forces. Borrowing Deleuze's concept of 'the spark of life' they suggest that certain kinds of museum practices 'kill off' the objects' identity, returning them to a state of potentiality that allow us to imagine new futures. In this way the museum may direct our attention to objects as carriers of a non-subjectified life force that runs through all creation.

Consulting Merleau-Ponty, Dylan Trigg develops the idea of the perceiving body as an archaeological trace. While phenomenology has primarily been concerned with the perceiving body as that 'which marks the coherence of time as lived and unified by the subject', Trigg finds, particularly in the later writings of Merleau-Ponty, an attention to the trace of an anterior origin to perception, 'a structure of reality working beneath and behind the scenes of perception'. This implies that the perceiving body is structurally composed both of the subjective, experiencing body, and a trace that makes perception possible at all. This trace also means that death is not only the horizon for subjective living, but also the pre-condition of any perceiving body. In this sense, 'death registers itself not simply as something opposed to life, but instead as another life that runs parallel to our own'.

The cases presented in this part of the book thus all suggest how the death of one material state of being reveals glimpses of other temporal registers running through what is conventionally given as 'reality'. These observations may not only point to the problems involved in simply opposing death to life. They also oppose notions of death as static, suggesting, instead, that death is related to great intensity, and assumes power through its capacity to invoke a sense of transience and by being transient. This has a dual force as it concerns both the stipulation of life as transient, and the process of passing as transience.

Transformation, Transition and Transience

'He peacefully passed away'. Deceivingly innocent, the euphemism 'to pass away' covers a number of predicaments concerning death, dying and temporality. While accepting that someone or something has vanished, that it or she is 'away' or 'gone', the phrase retains a hope or belief that something has passed *on* at the same time as passing *away*. We know 'it' is not 'here' anymore, but cannot reconcile ourselves with the idea that nothing is left. The very need to say *peacefully* passed, at least among certain Western people, might provide an indication of what we argue in this introduction: By reassuring ourselves that those who die depart in peace, we reassure ourselves too that the transition was not associated with unbearable horrors. Similarly, the expression to 'rest in peace' alludes to the hope that a tranquil existence awaits the dead on the other side. In fact, in some sense the materialities given or ascribed to passing provide ways of approximating the nature of what is passed in or on to.

Materialities of passing likewise lend themselves as perceptible processes, containments and contours with which to think about time and death. But more than that, they provide a temporary body that falls prey to the transformations of time and decay. Materialities of passing constitute the actual traces and leftovers of time, death and dissolution through which these may be conceived, explored and intimated. Rather than materialities of passing constituting a set of processes and things that happen to be at hand for the Levi-Straussian *bricoleur* to think with, they are in fact all that there is. This volume presents a series of examples of how people across time and space engage these last traces and far fringes of what can be encountered or perceived: materialities situated between the near and the far, between the sensory present and the absent. Materialities of passing are the lasting remains, the cursory presence of time. In this, we identify transformation of matter, transition between ontological states and transient existence at this margin. On the verge of being and not being, new forms of existence emerge in a constant process of becoming. It is simultaneously a crossing-over of states of existence and a mode of existence in itself, and we believe that the contributions to this volume unravel how passing issues forth in a multitude of complex ways: as transformation (when an object or a person emerges in new form), as transition (when an object or person emerges in a new position, locale or realm) and as transience (when an object or person emerges as temporary and temporally grounded, leaving a fleeting or lasting trace in their void).

In all three aspects of passing, emergence is crucial, underscoring how passing is not simply about disappearance, at least not if understood as being turned into an existential nil. Rather, passing is the multi-temporal, multi-directional potentiality of becoming with the simultaneity of continuity and discontinuity.

References

Ariès, P., 1985. *Images of Man and Death*. London: Harvard University Press.

Artelius, T., 1996. *Långfärd och återkomst: skeppet i bronsålderns gravar*. Stockholm: Riksantikvarieämbetet, Arkeologiska Undersökningar.

Bassie-Sweet, K., 1996. *At the Edge of the World: Caves and Late Classic Maya World View*. Norman: University of Oklahoma Press.

Bloch, M., 1995. The resurrection of the house amongst the Zafimaniry of Madagascar. In: J. Carsten and S. Hugh-Jones, eds, *About the house: Levi-Strauss and beyond*. Cambridge: Cambridge University Press, pp. 69–83.

Bradley, R., Skoglund, P. and Wehlin, J., 2010. Imaginary vessels in the Late Bronze Age of Gotland and South Scandinavia. *Current Swedish Archaeology*, 18: 79–103.

Chapman, R., 2003. Death, society and archaeology: The social dimensions of mortuary practices. *Mortality*, 8(3): 305–312.

Clewell, T., 2004. Mourning Beyond Melancholia: Freud's Psychoanalysis of Loss. *Journal of the American Psychoanalytic Association*, 52(1): 43–67.

Danforth, L. M., 1982. *The Death Rituals of Rural Greece*. Princeton: Princeton University Press.

Davies, D. J., 1997. *Death, Ritual and Belief: The Rhetoric of Funerary Rites*. London: Cassell.

Descartes, R., 1996. *Meditations on the First Philosophy: With Selections from the Objections and Replies*. Cambridge: Cambridge University Press.

DeSilvey, C., 2006. Observed Decay: Telling Stories with Mutable Things. *Journal of Material Culture*, 11(3): 318–338.

Douglas, M. [1966] 2002. *Purity and Danger: An Analysis of Concepts of Pollution and Taboo*. London: Routledge.

Fahlander, F. and Oestigaard, T., eds, 2008. *The Materiality of Death: Bodies, Burials, Beliefs*. Oxford: Archaeopress.

Field, N. P., 2006. Unresolved Grief and Continuing Bonds: An Attachment Perspective. *Death Studies*, 30(8): 739–756.

Field, N. P., Packman, W., Ronen, R., et al., 2013. Type of Continuing Bonds Expression and Its Comforting Versus Distressing Nature: Implications for Adjustment among Bereaved Mothers. *Death Studies*, 37(10): 889–912.

Finucane, R. C., 1981/2013. Sacred Corpse, Profane Carrion: Social Ideals and Death Rituals in the later Middle Ages. In: J. Whaley, ed., *Mirrors of Mortality: Social Studies in the History of Death*. London: Routledge, pp. 40–60.

Freud, S. [1917] 1957. Mourning and Melancholia. In: *The Standard Edition of the Complete Psychological Works of Sigmund Freud, Volume XIV*. London: The Hogarth Press and the Institute of Psychoanalysis, pp. 243–258.

Freud, S. [1923] 1961a. The Ego and the Id. In: *The Standard Edition of the Complete Psychological Works of Sigmund Freud, Volume XIX*. London: The Hogarth Press and the Institute of Psychoanalysis, pp. 12–66.

Freud, S. [1924] 1961b. A Short Account of Psycho-analysis. In: *The Standard Edition of the Complete Psychological Works of Sigmund Freud, Volume XIX*. London: The Hogarth Press and the Institute of Psychoanalysis, pp. 191–209.

Gell, A., 1998. *Art and Agency: An Anthropological Theory*. Oxford: Oxford University Press.

Ginsberg, R., 2004. *The Aesthetics of Ruins*. Amsterdam: Rodipi B.V.

Grosz, E., 2004. *The Nick of Time: Politics, Evolution, and the Untimely*. Durham and London: Duke University Press.

Gullbekk, S. H., 2012. Salvation and small change: Medieval coins in Scandinavian churches. In: G. Dethlefs, A. Pol and S. Wittenbrink, eds, *NUMMI DOCENT! Münzen – Schätze – Funde. Festschrift für Peter Ilisch zum 65. Geburtstag am 28. April 2012*. Osnabrück, Numismatischer Verlag Fritz-Rudolf Künker, pp. 227–233.

Hallam, E. and Hockey, J., 2001. *Death, Memory and Material Culture*. Oxford: Berg.

Hallward, P., 2006. *Out of This World: Deleuze and the Philosophy of Creation.* London: Verso.

Harper, S., 2012. 'I'm glad she has her glasses on. That really makes the difference': Grave goods in English and American death rituals. *Journal of Material Culture*, 17(1): 43–59.

Harrison-Buck, E., 2012. Architecture as Animate Landscape: Circular Shrines in the Ancient Maya Lowlands. *American Anthropologist*, 114(1): 64–80.

Hertz, R. [1907] 1960. *Death and the Right Hand.* London: Cohen & West.

Holtorf, C., 2015. Averting loss aversion in cultural heritage. *International Journal of Heritage Studies*, 21(4): 405–421.

Howarth, G., 2007. The Rebirth of Death: Continuing Relationships with the Dead. In: M. Mitchell, ed., *Remember Me: Constructing Immortality – Beliefs on Immortality, Life, and Death.* London: Routledge, pp. 19–34.

Jensen, A. M. B., 2010. A Sense of Absence: The Staging of Heroic Deaths and Ongoing Lives among American Organ Donor Families. In: M. Bille, F. Hastrup and T. F. Sørensen, eds, *An Anthropology of Absence: Materializations of Transcendence and Loss.* New York: Springer, pp. 63–80.

Kapferer, B., 1997. *The Feast of the Sorcerer: Practices of Consciousness and Power.* Chicago: University of Chicago Press.

Kaul, F., 1998. *Ships on Bronzes: A Study in Bronze Age Religion and Iconography. Text.* Copenhagen: The National Museum.

Kaul, F., 2004. *Bronzealderens religion – studier af den nordiske bronzealders ikonografi.* Copenhagen: Det Kongelige Nordiske Oldskriftsselskab.

Klass, D., Silverman, P. R. and Nickman, S. L., eds, 1996. *Continuing Bonds: New Understandings of Grief.* London: Taylor and Francis.

Küchler, S., 1999. The Place of Memory. In: A. Forty and S. Küchler, eds, *The Art of Forgetting.* Oxford: Berg, pp. 53–72.

Lemonnier, P., 2012. *Mundane Objects: Materiality and Non-Verbal Communication.* Walnut Creek, CA: Left Coast Press.

Lucas, G., 2008. Time and the Archaeological Event. *Cambridge Archaeological Journal*, 18(1): 59–65.

Lucas, G., 2012. *Understanding the Archaeological Record.* Cambridge: Cambridge University Press.

Mimica, J., 2003. The Death of a Strong, Great, Bad Man: An Ethnography of Soul Incorporation. *Oceania*, 73(4): 260–286.

Morris, I., 1992. *Death-Ritual and Social Structure in Classical Antiquity.* Cambridge: University of Cambridge Press.

Neimeyer, R. A., Baldwin, S. A. and Gillies, J., 2006. Continuing Bonds and Reconstructing Meaning: Mitigating Complications in Bereavement. *Death Studies*, 30(8): 715–738.

Olivier, L., 2011. *The Dark Abyss of Time: Archaeology and Memory.* Lanham, MD: Altamira Press.

Pelkmans, M., 2013. Outline for an Ethnography of Doubt. In: M. Pelkmans, ed., *Ethnographies of Doubt: Faith and Uncertainty in Contemporary Societies.* London: I.B.Tauris, pp. 1–42.

Pétursdóttir, Þ. and Olsen, B., 2014. An archaeology of ruins. In: B. Olsen and T. Pétursdóttir, eds, *Ruin Memories: Materialities, Aesthetics and the Archaeology of the Recent Past.* London: Routledge, pp. 1–30.

Ramskou, T., 1976. *Lindholm Høje gravpladsen.* Copenhagen: Herm. H.J. Lynge og Søn.

Rasmussen, A. E., 2014. Infinity in a Spear: Things as Mediations among the Mbuke (Papua New Guinea). In: D. R. Christensen and K. Sandvik, eds, *Mediating and Remediating Death.* Farnham: Ashgate, pp. 63–74.

Rowlands, M., 1999. Remembering to Forget: Sublimation as Sacrifice to War Memorials. In: A. Forty and S. Küchler, eds, *The Art of Forgetting.* Oxford: Berg, pp. 129–145.

Schut, H. A. W., Stroebe, M. S., Boelen, P. A. and Zijerveld, A. M., 2006. Continuing Relationships with the Deceased: Disentangling Bonds and Grief. *Death Studies,* 30(8): 757–766.

Shanks, M., Platt, D. and Rathje, W. L., 2004. The Perfume of Garbage: Modernity and the Archaeological. *Modernism / Modernity,* 11(1): 61–83.

Simmel, G., 1959. The Ruin. In: K. Wolff, ed., *Georg Simmel, 1858–1918. A Collection of Essays, with Translations and a Bibliography.* Columbus, OH: Ohio State University Press, pp. 259–265.

Skoglund, P., 2008. Stone ships: Continuity and change in Scandinavian prehistory. *World Archaeology,* 40(3): 390–406.

Stefanou, E., 2012. The materiality of death: Human relics and the 'resurrection' of the Greek maritime past in museum spaces. *International Journal of Heritage Studies,* 18(4): 385–399.

Stevenson, L., 2012. The psychic life of biopolitics: Survival, cooperation and Inuit community. *American Ethnologist,* 39(3): 592–613.

Strathern, M., 1988. *The Gender of the Gift.* Berkeley: University of California Press.

Sørensen, T. F., 2009. The Presence of the Dead: Cemeteries, cremation and the staging of non-place. *Journal of Social Archaeology,* 9(1): 110–135.

Sørensen, T. F., 2010. A Saturated Void: Anticipating and Preparing Presence in Contemporary Danish Cemetery Culture. In: M. Bille, F. Hastrup and T. F. Sørensen, eds, *An Anthropology of Absence: Materializations of Transcendence and Loss.* New York: Springer, pp. 115–130.

Sørensen, T. F., 2012. Delusion and disclosure: Human disposal and the aesthetics of vagueness. In: M. L. S. Sørensen and K. Rebay-Salisbury, eds, *Embodied Knowledge: Historical Perspectives on Technology and Belief.* Oxford: Oxbow Books, pp. 27–39.

Sørensen, T. F., 2015. Transience and the objects of heritage: A matter of time. *Danish Journal of Archaeology,* 3(1): 86–90.

Sørensen, T. F. and Lumsden, S. (forthcoming). Hid in Death's Dateless Night: The Lure of an Uncanny Landscape in Hittite Anatolia. In: J. Fleisher and N. Norman, eds, *The Archaeology of Fear and Anxiety: Emotive States Materialized*. New York: Springer.

Tarlow, S., 2002. The aesthetic corpse in nineteenth-century Britain. In: Y. Hamilakis, M. Pluciennik and S. Tarlow, eds, *Thinking through the Body: Archaeologies of Corporeality*. London: Kluwer Academic, pp. 85–97.

Tarlow, S., 2013. *Ritual, Belief and the Dead in Early Modern Britain and Ireland*. Cambridge: Cambridge University Press.

Turner, V., 1967. *The Forest of Symbols: Aspects of the Ndembu Ritual*. New York: Cornell University Press.

Valentine, C., 2009. Continuing bonds after bereavement: A cross-cultural perspective. *Bereavement Care*, 28(2): 6–11.

van Gennep, A. [1909] 1960. *The Rites of Passage*. London: Routledge & Kegan Paul.

Venbrux, E., 2007. Robert Hertz's seminal essay and mortuary rites in the Pacific region. *Journal de la Société des Océanistes*, 124(Année 2007–1).

Wagner, R., 1991. The fractal person. In: M. Godelier and M. Strathern, eds, *Big Men and Great Men: Personifications of Power in Melanesia*. Cambridge: Cambridge University Press, pp. 159–173.

Walter, T., 1996. A new model of grief: Bereavement and biography. *Mortality*, 1(1): 7–25.

Willerslev, R., 2009. The optimal sacrifice: A study of voluntary death among the Siberian Chukchi. *American Ethnologist*, 36(4): 693–704.

Willerslev, R., 2011. Frazer strikes back from the armchair: A new search for the animist soul. *Journal of the Royal Anthropological Institute*, 17(3): 504–526.

Willerslev, R., Christensen, D. R. and Meinert, L., 2013. Introduction. In: D. R. Christensen and R. Willerslev, eds, *Taming Time, Timing Death: Social Technologies and Ritual*. Farnham: Ashgate, pp. 1–16.

Williams, H. ed., 2003. *Archaeologies of Remembrance: Death and Memory in Past Societies*. London: Plenum.

Woodward, C., 2002. *In Ruins: A Journey Through History, Art, and Literature*. London: Vintage.

Zucker, P., 1961. Ruins – An Aesthetic Hybrid. *The Journal of Aesthetics and Art Criticism*, 20(2): 119–130.

PART I:
Transformation: Passing as Movement between Categories

Chapter 1

Temporalities of Transience and the Mortuary Landscape: The Example of Natural Burial

Jenny Hockey, Andy Clayden, Trish Green and Mark Powell

Since 1993 interring the dead in a natural burial ground has been a disposal option in the UK. Drawing on a study conducted in Great Britain between 2007 and 2010,[1] this chapter asks how natural burial might inform experiences of passage or transience at the time of death. Natural burial grounds typically contain few traditional symbols of death: there are no broken columns or draped urns to signify a boundary between life and death, no references to a Christian afterlife in inscriptions, marble crosses, bibles, angels or cherubs. Instead, the dead 'disappear', often into woodland or fields where only ephemeral markers stand for their passage (Hockey et al. 2012). How, then, can such sites generate experiential knowledge of death?

As we show, such 'knowledge' might be less a matter of cognitions or well-articulated beliefs, and more a case of emotionally generated understandings particular to individuals or families. Taking the form of approximations, intimations and negotiations, such understandings may reflect differing values and priorities, as well as diverse relationships with the dead. With the senses as their source, they may become evident in memories and imaginings that enable continuities to be created and the temporalities of passage between being alive and being dead to be accessed. Time, we therefore argue, can be both 'found' and 'made' in such settings. Transitions between seasons, for example, and associated changes in vegetation and weather, provide evidence of temporal change; once 'found' in this way, time can also be 'made' through practices that allow the absence of the dead to be engaged with. For example, as a new and less common disposal option, natural burial affords mourners more extended 'ritual' time than cremation. This feature, plus the personal support owners and managers often provide, enables mourners to 'make' more time for the funeral and indeed to involve themselves with the deceased in the days prior to their burial.

Where these conditions are in place, 'passing' may assume a particular material or tangible form, becoming a process of change *and* continuity. In this respect,

1   We are grateful to the Economic and Social Research Council for funding the project 'Back to Nature? The Cultural, Social and Emotional Implications of Natural Burial'.

as our data evidence, natural burial can enable the kind of liminal period (Van Gennep [1909] 1960) that *makes* rather than simply marks changes.

'Passing on', 'Passing away', 'Passed'

Practices such as dressing the body and actively participating in the funeral are not, however, unique to natural burial. Instead, like natural burial itself, they contribute to a strand of cultural change that has been occurring in the UK since the late twentieth century. In part, it is a form of resistance to traditional deathways that not only involve removing or sequestering the dead, but are also often at odds with ambivalent belief systems. Open to alternatives that promise more direct or personal engagement between the living and the dead, between bereaved people and society, members of many Western societies now disparage *euphemistic* phrases for announcing a death – 'laid to rest', 'gone to meet his Maker', 'departed'. Yet there is no unified cultural consensus; 'passed on', 'passed away' and 'passed' remain in routine use to soften the news. Within this mix of new and more traditional mortuary cultures, then, what the concept or metaphor of 'passage' might actually refer to is uncertain, particularly in the absence of a consensus of belief as to what happens to someone when they die. While passing 'on' or 'away' hint at a location that is not 'here', 'passing' simply suggests movement.

Meanwhile the process of *dying* has become well defined and extended – partly through medical debates that pursue precise definitions of death in order to support organ harvesting (Lock 2002). Yet journeys once mapped through limbo or purgatory towards a permanent afterlife have become less persuasive. Bereavement, similarly, has been re-configured, now no longer an extended, structured pathway once evidenced in the sequencing of nineteenth-century women's mourning dress (Taylor 1983). Even mid-twentieth-century staged models of a grief 'process' (Kübler-Ross 1969) have been supplanted by the more fluid notion of 'continuing' bonds (Klass, Silverman and Nickman 1996) between the living and the dead.

To borrow irreverently from the UK comedy *Blackadder*, when the downtrodden servant, Baldrick, wants to know what caused the First World War, he can only frame his question as, 'How did the one state of affairs become the other?' His struggle for words resonates with the similar challenge of understanding how the state of 'being alive' becomes the state of 'being dead'. Bille, Hastrup and Sørensen call for attention to 'the mutual inter-dependence in people's lives of the materially present and the materially absent' (2010: 4). In their view, absences make themselves *felt* – sensuously, emotionally and ideationally (ibid.: 3) – acquiring a potentially challenging presence within the here and now.

In relation to the dead, however, it is not simply their static immanence within the everyday, or at key calendrical moments. The challenge or uncertainty associated with their simultaneous absence and presence pertains to the dynamic nature of what has happened, the process whereby someone who has irrefutably *been* is now no longer. Materially, this transition is evidenced in the transformation of vital embodiment into decaying corpse. Both the living and the dead body are, at particular points, present. Yet, while one embodies the presence of the individual, the presence of the other confirms their absence. This chapter therefore addresses the interplay of absence and presence, so exploring the scope and limitations of mortuary culture as a set of materially grounded practices and entities, to enable human beings to understand how 'the one state of affairs becomes the other'.

Ambivalence and Sequestration

Not a self-evident pair, these terms nonetheless intersect within many Western social environments where death neither elicits a consensus as to its nature or aftermath, nor occurs within everyday settings. This is not to impute a false collectivity to members of traditional societies among whom much anthropological work is rooted, to stake some exclusive Western claim to experiences of difference and doubt. It is, however, to highlight 'a shift into a this-worldliness in Europe through the second half of the 20th century' (Davies 2005: 57), one within which the idea of a heavenly afterlife is 'more therapeutic than theological' (ibid.: 58).

It is in relation to such settings that the 'sequestration thesis' was developed. Its critical focus included the containment of the dying within medicalised hospital space where their families and friends became similarly marginalised; once dead, their corpse was likely to 'de-materialise' at least temporarily, under the custodianship of the funeral director, or, in the case of an unexplained death, become a possession of the coroner. Sociologists such as Elias (1985), Giddens (1991), Bauman (1992), Mellor and Shilling (1993) and Seale (1998), as well as anthropologists such as Gorer (1965), cited urbanisation, industrialisation, professionalisation and secularisation as core to the sequestration of death-related practices and environments. Earlier in the twentieth century, individuals familiar to the dying person and their family, the priest, the layer-out, the carpenter and the sexton, were likely to accompany their passage. By the second half of that century, however, the doctor, the funeral director and Bereavement Services were occupying the bedside and the graveside (Illich 1975; Parsons 1999). As Jupp and Walter wrote in 1999, '[m]ost English people die in old age, out of sight, in hospital or nursing and residential homes. These are the all-too-frequent unseen deaths of the confused elderly, victims of strokes, or in coronary care or suffering Alzheimer's' (278).

As a result, the 'passing' of someone known, respected and perhaps loved, became a less 'knowable' process of change, if indeed it was experienced as a process at all, or simply remained a medically defined *event*, the cessation of brain-stem activity. After death, until the legitimation of 'continuing bonds' (Klass, Silverman and Nickman 1996) in the late twentieth century, even retaining the belongings of the dead was likely to be a covert, even furtive, pursuit. However, while Davies identifies a place for 'default religion' where the Christian church offers 'the easier option for people, even those with little or no active religious belief or commitment (Davies 2005: 58), he views its current mix of 'personal readings or personal music as markers of individuality set within the traditional framework' (ibid.: 59), as a response now vulnerable to alternative ritual options.

Evidence of ambivalent beliefs and sequestered practices might therefore seem to undermine any 'mutual inter-dependence in people's lives of the materially present and the materially absent' (Bille, Hastrup and Sørensen 2010: 4), at least in ways that allow death and its temporalities to be 'known' and understood. As the Introduction to this collection explains, its aim is to 'explore how particular sensuous and material qualities constitute frameworks for reflecting on or understanding the temporality of death and decay'. Yet according to the sequestration thesis, members of Western societies became all but starved of such qualities – in the name of professionalism, hygiene, convenience and 'care' of bereaved people's sensibilities and a deteriorating body. These conditions were, moreover, likely to be experienced without resort to a socially authenticated belief system that might render 'death' accessible or meaningful.

The sequestration thesis has, however, been challenged as an all-encompassing account of Western deathways (Hockey 2011). Empirical evidence of other sites and practices complicates the idea that Europe is an 'exceptional case' when compared with parts of the world where religious beliefs and practices proliferate (Davies 2005: 56). While natural burial has no affiliation with ideas about a heavenly afterlife, it does stand for an explicit set of belief and values, ones that our data suggest can support engaged participation in the passage of someone who has died. It is this orientation that many of those who choose alternatives to traditional deathways have espoused. Davies describes natural burial emerging 'from an interplay between science of an intuitively acceptable kind and a sense of self that is not dependent upon either belief in an otherworldly afterlife or the fragility of the enduring memories of one's descendants', something he encapsulates in the concept of 'ecological immortality' (ibid.: 87).

Into the Field

The study drawn on here combines perspectives from landscape architecture, social anthropology and sociology. It has generated a geographic information system (GIS) database of all the natural burial grounds in the UK, a survey of 20 such sites that included interviews with owners/managers plus a photographic and textual record of the site, ethnographic work at four natural burial grounds that represented a diversity of providers – a farmer, a charitable trust, a local authority and a funeral director – and an ongoing observational study at one site with data recorded photographically and textually. This extensive material relating to one among a number of new or alternative deathways in the UK allows us a particular perspective on the concept or metaphor of passage.

Natural burial originated at Carlisle municipal cemetery in the UK in 1993. Here the manager, Ken West, established a new area of the cemetery where only a tree would mark a grave, a response born of his own disillusionment with chemically resourced maintenance practices that undermined the cemetery's ecological stability, as well as a conversation with two single women who wished to somehow avoid being buried in an unvisited grave with decaying headstone and curtilage (see West 2010).

Ken West's approach to natural burial reflects Davies's (2005) notion of 'ecological immortality', a morally esteemed bodily merger with a sustainable environment. It gives form to the metaphors of 'passing away' or 'passing on' since an explicit emphasis on 'passing away' into a wider organic milieu also means 'passing on' one's habitat to future generations, for example by being buried into a habitat that is thereby protected. This orientation is enhanced by site owners/managers who ban or discourage embalming and hardwood coffins, the corpse thereby disintegrating readily into the landscape. Indeed, at Green Lane Burial Field in Powys, Wales, bodies are interred relatively close to the surface of the burial field; their decomposition is thus accelerated through readier access to air and water. Above the surface of the grave, as noted, little of an immutable nature marks the deceased's passage. Headstones, grave curtilage, informal memorials and, in some cases, site boundaries and signage that help define UK burial grounds (Rugg 2000) may well be missing. In many ways, then, the deceased simply disappears into an anonymous landscape, the materiality of this process potentially making 'passing' more imaginable. Amy Salter,[2] whose father was buried in woodland at the East Meon site, said:

> Yeah, down there and the same with the flowers on top of him are turning over and the colours going out of them, and all, I feel, I don't think it's horrible personally, I just think all the water and the rain is washing through him and then he'll become part of the trees, it's not a horror image at all but I think he's not in his body so it doesn't really matter.

East Meon was among many diverse landscapes that we encountered during our study. The desire to preserve and to create particular environments that motivates many site owners/managers, means that they may be located in existing woodland, orchards or fields – or, conversely, occupy areas that will *become* woodland as a result of grave-related planting, or fields that will be enhanced by a reduction of grazing or chemical fertilisers. In this way, then, the dead help 'pass on' a valued landscape.

To what extent, though, can a natural burial ground afford experiences that might generate knowledge of death? People seeking to pre-purchase their grave or bury a friend or relative are more likely to experience the deep time of Great Britain's rural heritage, something one of our participants described as

---

2   All personal names used are pseudonyms, to ensure confidentiality.

**Figure 1.1   No other form of memorialisation is permitted other than a
native oak tree planted on each grave (September 2012)**

both 'a timeless experience' and one that 'built bridges'. Their words suggest
that, in transcending the unstable here and now of loss, timelessness can enable
connection, an apparent paradox explored below.

Bringing it All Back Home

To show how natural burial has acquired its status as a more materially grounded
and participative experience of death, we present ethnographic data gathered
during fieldwork at the East Meon site in the south of England. Rather than a set of
routinised procedures, we observed how people's contribution to a funeral resulted
from negotiations that are key to manager Al's relationship with his clients. This
was also described by bereaved people when interviewed. Unlike most cemetery
managers, Al accompanied people around the site and helped them choose a grave
location. This helped him assess their emotional state and available networks of
support. It also allowed him to discover whether they understood what it meant
to bury naturally, what a funeral in this setting might involve and whether they
might wish to consider managing it themselves. Those clearly traumatised by the

death, he advised to contact a funeral director. Yet he made this suggestion gently because, as he explained:

> The difficulty is … if I say … do this and do that … get rid of the men in black at the gate [funeral directors], I don't want them to feel they're having an inferior do … doing anything lesser because they have chosen to have the funeral director there … or the minister.

Al thus practised his established style of negotiation, ensuring that people did not envisage natural burial occupying some higher moral ground where duties of care could not be delegated to professionals. Indeed, if people were keen to participate in ways that might result in their going to pieces on the day, he would advise against this option. His was therefore a very personal relationship with bereaved people. Compared with staff at a municipal cemetery whom mourners are unlikely to meet, he felt a personal responsibility to look out for his clients and ensure everything went well on the day.

If his clients appeared emotionally resilient and had sufficient informal support, Al would encourage them to consider an active role in arranging the burial, something he saw as a cathartic involvement that could help them work through their grief. If they were fit, he might suggest that they used the hand bier[3] to transport the coffin, and then help lower it into the grave. Perhaps they might consider speaking at the burial service. Through these mechanisms, people could engage directly with the materialities of the corpse and the practicalities of disposing of it.

As a site and a practice natural burial is therefore at odds with the idea that Western death is sequestered, that dying people, their families and indeed the corpse are routinely rendered passive. The question remains, however, as to whether – and if so, how – a more embodied, indeed vibrant engagement between dying, dead and bereaved people informs understandings of death and its associated temporalities. Without shared religious, spiritual or in some cases ecological beliefs, how were the materialities of natural burial experienced?

No Direction Home?

Our data show that site owners/managers do see themselves undertaking something that differs from traditional mortuary culture. While templates and indeed texts are available to them (for example, West 2010), establishing a site is by no means a 'one-size-fits-all' endeavour. For a start, the landscapes adopted are hugely varied. When Ken West, a cemetery manager, undertook his makeover of adjacent land, he adapted the cemetery's linear layout of graves and retained the practice of grave-based memorialisation. The resulting site is laid out on a grid system with rows of

---

3   A slatted stretcher that rests on two wheels with handles at either end.

trees planted above the bodies, one per person. By contrast, when Andrew Gifford, a farmer, turned one of his fields into a burial ground, he drew on the model of rigg-and-furrow[4] ploughing, creating low embankments into which bodies could be buried (Clayden et al. 2010).

These are design issues, but as people began burying their dead in such diverse settings, the idea of natural burial as a *practice* also came under scrutiny. The assumption that it involved a minimal footprint with only the simplest, most bio-degradable marker proved counter to some bereaved people's felt needs. While present at the grave, many had difficulty passively contemplating an anonymous patch of grass. Instead, like the owners/managers who designed the site, they drew on what they knew, importing contemporary memorialising practices such as weeding and planting the soil, and creating personal shrines with rocks, benches, crosses, toys, ornaments, cards, photographs and letters.

In this way the fabric of the natural burial ground took shape; enormously diverse in geography, design, values and management style, many sites had to subsume inherent contradictions and indeed tensions. These might be between bereaved people and the site owner/manager and their guidelines or rules; or between different family members who lacked a shared vision of natural burial and what the nature of the grave should be; or indeed between different bereaved people, some of whom saw 'nature' as an absence of traditional grave goods and memorials, others for whom the desire to create and elaborate a focus for their grief was only 'human nature' (Clayden, Hockey and Powell 2010: 157.

The result of this lack of fixed templates or established mores is a fluid mortuary landscape in which the materialities of burying, planting and maintenance may be subject to ongoing negotiation. Our data therefore show that a resource through which individuals may seek to overcome the non-empirical nature of death – where passing can somehow be fleshed out – involves approximations and intimations, while speculations predominate. Instead of some direct correspondence between material and inchoate entities – as when the cross where Jesus died becomes an item worn round the neck that meshes with the *idea* of sacrifice –, the ambiguities and contradictions that constitute natural burial can become a resource for creative contemplation and engagement. In addition, as we demonstrate, the decay of the body and its inevitable disappearance into an ever-changing landscape provide an absence or nothingness of the kind referred to in the Introduction to this collection – something at once empty and full of untamed potential. In the sections to follow, we describe experiences of and orientations towards time, arguing that these can enable site visitors to discover what death might mean for them.

---

4   'Rig and furrow' is a medieval system of working the land that was common in upland areas and is closely related to its lowland equivalent of ridge and furrow.

Figure 1.2   The rapid and unrestricted growth of herbaceous plants in spring and summer make it increasingly challenging to find and access a grave

Finding Time

We begin with the notion of time 'found' and focus on the natural burial ground landscape and its implications for interring the corpse in a place where grass and brambles supplant manicured lawns, where shoulder-high summer growth may make access to a grave challenging as trees gain both width and height. While the appearance of any burial ground will undergo seasonal change, in the natural burial ground the diversity of plants and trees and their freedom from pruning provide powerful evidence of cycles of growth, decay and re-growth. Unpaved, a site's terrain generates experiences of walking towards or sitting by a grave that contrast radically with the cemetery landscape; rain, ice, snow and indeed sustained sunshine shape the nature of both the soil and what grows upon it. Passage through such a landscape may therefore evoke particular kinds of temporal experience: the first year after the death can acquire an extended linearity, for example, as one season slowly cedes to another; subsequent years potentially generate a more cyclical temporal experience as the grave returns to some version of its original appearance, perhaps lit by spring sunshine or snow- and ice bound in February.

As Bille, Hastrup and Sørensen (2010) argue, things 'present' themselves to us, and at the time of death this may occur in striking ways. Their presence can evoke absences which make material items 'truly noticed', as Gibson (2008) explains in relation to domestic objects such as a sewing box that survived her mother. Time and the temporalities of passing may thus be 'found' rather than actively created. They are a kind of *objet trouvé* that may be pressed into service in a variety of creative ways.

To engage with the dynamic nature of this mortuary landscape, our study included a longitudinal project that produces a monthly visual and textual record of one of our four ethnographic sites. By taking photographs from the same six vantage points, a wealth of comparative data has been generated, so demonstrating the temporalities of this setting. Below we present observations drawn from this record.

The South Yorkshire Woodland Burial Ground opened in 1995, the first burial being marked with the planting of a rowan tree. Choice characterises the owner's motivation for this project and its parallel activity of a funeral-directing business. Bereaved people and those wishing to pre-purchase a grave can choose its location

Figure 1.3   Taken from the same place in the burial ground, these images reveal how the landscape has changed over a period of 10 years (2002, 2006, 2009, 2012, Ulley South Yorkshire)

without conforming to a grid layout. Similarly, the owner has exercised less control over informal memorialisation than at many other natural burial grounds. Such items remain evident, although their earlier proliferation drew criticism from some bereaved people and resulted in the owner's attempts to curb their scale and nature. Data from the site's burial register reveal how each burial has contributed, incrementally, to its contemporary landscape. Our photographic record also shows how the emergent woodland changes with each season as new trees are included. Moreover, the absent presence of the dead, materialised through their gravesite and the tree likely to be planted upon it, fosters this new woodland's identity as a sacred landscape, a quality that comes into and out of focus through the seasonal cycle of growth and decay.

Early burials at this site clustered along the field's perimeter hedge and stream, its banks now colonised by alder and willow, an immediate connection with an established nature and an anchor for anyone wishing to locate a particular grave. By 2006, however, the burial 'field' had changed significantly, the experience of walking there and contemplating the surrounding landscape now framed by the diversity of trees chosen by bereaved people. As a result the initial landmarks of hedge, stream and pathway had been supplemented by a network of semi-mature and mature trees stretching across the site, which transformed the previously open field into a more intimate and private landscape.

In winter the site's appearance is stark, untidy and uninviting, particularly in cold grey light. Short wet grass, leafless trees, the bare earth of new graves, memorial plaques and cut flowers are especially visible – and the presence of the dead more prominent. If snow comes, the site is again transformed, not slowly as one year follows the next, but overnight, each grave now hidden under a thick blanket that briefly captures the passage of visitors and wildlife. It leaves the site looking clean and uncluttered, the trees' dark silhouettes newly prominent against a white backcloth. Towards winter's end, delicate patches of snowdrops surface, planted by bereaved people on some of the graves in previous years – evidence of the season's turning.

Change then becomes more dramatic with a flourish of colour as daffodils emerge from many of the graves. When March gives way to early summer more and more bulbs and annuals appear, evocations of seasonal gardening in more domestic settings. By the end of spring these changes have accelerated. In warm, wet weather, the grasses and herbaceous vegetation may have grown by over a meter between our monthly visits. Like the snow, this herbaceous layer conceals the graves, only their memorial trees and occasional clusters of floral plantings betraying their presence.

At this time of year the contrast between the municipal cemetery and the natural burial ground is greatest. In the former, the grass is kept short and the individual graves remain prominent; in the latter, dense vegetation creates a private, sheltered landscape. Away from the main pathway the passage of visitors is identifiable in trails of broken and folded grass, like winter footprints in the snow. Their presence in the burial ground is also evidenced in cleared patches of unwanted 'weeds'

**Figure 1.4   These images reveal how the passing seasons dramatically
change the appearance of the burial ground as individual
graves come in and out of focus**

Note: Clockwise from top left: Winter, Spring, Summer and Autumn.

and the planting of summer bedding. A number of graves display some bereaved
people's resistance to the advances of nature: tall grass is cut back and removed,
a practice Nassauer (1995) would locate among shared visual language 'cues to
care'. Such 'cues', she argues, refer to landscape interventions that signal human
care for that environment. At this point in the annual cycle, the natural world is
also present in what can be touched, smelled and heard, the whole site alive with
insects and birdsong.

By late June or early July, another kind of seasonal intervention is visible
as the seeded grass is cut to the ground, something that occurs annually
and radically alters the appearance and feel of the burial ground. Individual
memorials and the bare earth of new graves return to view and a more managed
landscape briefly usurps wild messy nature, creating the appearance of a
suburban park. However, by early September the environment has changed yet
again, as the new flush of growth materialises. Along with green shoots there is
the red autumn colour of cherry trees and bright orange and red rowan berries.
Pumpkins and offerings of fruit supplement these during Halloween (All Souls'
Day) celebrations – until November brings the frost that quickly returns the

burial ground to its winter state, strong winds stripping the oak trees of their remaining leaves.

As the Introduction to this collection reminds us, the becoming and dissolution of the material world – here evidenced in seasonal cycles of growth and decay – constitutes a fundamental medium for the human recognition of time and temporality. Thus Mary Stanton, who had buried her father at Green Lane Burial Field in Powys, said:

> I think returning to the earth, at nature's pace, is the best solution really. I mean, it gives everybody around long enough to come to terms with it … I think long enough for a burial site to start to heal over and plants to start to re-grow and things. It sort of … and to return one's sort of vehicle to the earth, just on a physical level … just seems to be the right thing to do really. And I think to actually, to actually be around an object like that and actually see it returning to the earth, I think it's very, well, it's sort of obvious, but I think sometimes a body in grief needs obvious things to kind of make it plain …

Within this dynamic landscape, we now consider not just the 'finding' or 'truly noticing' of temporalities, but also the 'making' of time, an active process that, we argue, enables the twin abstractions of time and death to be grasped and understandings to be shared among those who visit the site.

Making Time

Out of the materialities of weather, vegetation, earth and water, the individuals we spoke to wove a set of temporalities that located the event of a death, both spatially and temporally, creating a presence for the deceased and materialising their ongoing contribution to familial and calendrical rituals: Christmas, Valentine's Day, Mother's Day, Halloween, along with existing birthdays, new births, new deaths. As the South Yorkshire Woodland Burial Ground's owner had gradually discouraged extensive use of artificial decorations, one family had hung pine cone Christmas 'decorations' unobtrusively in the sweet chestnut they had planted on the deceased's grave. Leaving carved pumpkins and fruit on the grave was another 'legitimate' way of incorporating the deceased into calendrically organised family practices. Plantings too were more than mere ornament: forget-me-not clusters grew in the footprints of mourners who had encircled a burial, re-appearing annually and now intersected by plantings from a newer adjacent grave. Spatio-temporal connections were also made by blanketing a grave with rose petals gathered in the deceased's former garden, a gesture repeated annually at the time of their death and their birth, a conjoining of life-course transitions, or forms of passing.

Exposure to seasonal time, the discovery of sudden changes and cyclical repetitions, can thus resource an active making of time, a marked characteristic of natural burial more generally. When Al weighs people up and encourages participation where appropriate, East Meon's landscape itself comes into play: access to the burial area involves walking down through uneven, wooded terrain, something that affords scope for a drawn-out, measured processional dimension to the funeral, the coffin slowly borne down to the grave on either the hand bier or a horse-drawn cart.

Within our data, many people thus 'made' time for death – creating the temporalities that constituted passage, passing, passing away or passing on. Since the forms of participation they chose 'took' time, they thereby shaped new death-related temporalities. Planting a tree directly above a burial is a common way of extending the social life-time of the deceased. If it flourishes, it will, over time, come to stand in for the previous vitality of their embodied life. Indeed, its trunks, limbs, foliage and fruit can be seen to occupy a metonymic relationship with the person themselves in that its roots are often imagined to be drawing sustenance from their body. As sites that have buried using a grid system with one tree per grave have found, however, this kind of design can become problematic. As trees mature they not only compete with one another but may also curtail access to the grave. At the Green Lane Burial Field in Powys, by contrast, trees were planted at the field edges, so providing future screening for the site. Bearing small wooden plaques with details of the deceased, they nonetheless bore no direct relationship with their grave itself. At sites such as this, however, bereaved people may find the presence of their relative or friend somehow more accessible in that evidence of other burials is absent, and again, a visit may be a way of making temporal continuities of a very personal nature.

Through such practices, passing away and passing on take tangible form: the landscape that encompasses the deceased constitutes a vibrant site for continuing visits, for the re-animation of the deceased's social life. At the South Yorkshire Woodland Burial Ground we met a couple tending their son-in-law's grave. They recalled a previous visit and a picnic taking place at a grave across from his. Partly obscured by trees, they could nonetheless hear laughter and singing as a group spanning three generations gathered around a grave. Balloons were finally released to cheers and whoops, as young children played nearby. Not only did the couple see this as very 'natural' in that people were expressing themselves uninhibitedly, in their view, but it was something they felt could not happen in a cemetery.

The natural burial ground was therefore seen to permit 'natural' behaviour and this perception underpinned many of the ways in which individuals 'made' time, not just after but also before a death. During another visit to South Yorkshire Woodland Burial Ground, while chatting with one of the grave diggers, we observed a middle-aged couple approach him with questions about the burial ground, what was permitted, whether grave locations could be chosen freely and if gardening was allowed after burial. The husband had a life-limiting illness and when they heard about the site on a radio programme they decided to visit together – after looking at images of the burial ground on its website. Already they were aware of the dynamic quality of this landscape, noting the large size of the trees compared

Figure 1.5 **Bereaved people deploy a range of purchased and often homemade grave markers to mark calendrical rituals of Christmas, Valentine's Day and Halloween**

with how they appeared in the photos; it was more enclosed, felt more private than they had expected. They liked what they had seen. The grave digger was relaxed and informative with them, 'passing on' his knowledge and understanding of the site while preparing the grave for another person's passing, something that could not have escaped the couple. When illness brings the husband's life to an end, the grave digger they spoke to will probably prepare the man's grave and back fill it after his funeral. When the grave digger next meets the wife, she will already be a widow.

This example contrasts markedly with the deathways described in the sequestration thesis. As a picturesque location, away from the institutions of the hospital and the cemetery, the natural burial ground enabled this couple to engage with future time via the materialities of becoming dead, of a body lowered into the ground and covered over with soil – of the wife's post-mortem visits as a widow. At the point when a death has occurred, however, there remains further scope for expanding and elaborating the 'moment'. Thus, what happens at death can be the outcome of *anticipatory* participation, which not only extends the time surrounding the death but also the personhood of the deceased.

For example, when Arthur Westthorpe described the route the funeral director took when transporting his wife's body to the natural burial ground, he felt it was likely to have been arranged previously by his wife, who had contributed significantly to planning her funeral. In shaping the temporality of her final journey, then, Arthur's wife extended her personhood, her agency and her scope for affective action (Gell 1998). Arthur said:

> On the funeral day ... the journey to the woodland site went past all the places again where I'd been involved, they went on a road past Arthur Lees on, where, on, through Sheffield, that is where I started work, they passed Tinsley where I lived, they went back that way and they passed the woods where I used to play as a kid and then down the road I used to ride ... so it followed a route of my life going backwards.

> ... I couldn't believe it because I didn't know which way they were going to go. I thought they were going to go through Sheffield, all way, but they turned off, went over Ecclesfield and then back on the road, Tinsley, over the Tinsley bridge where I lived, up through Brinsworth where I, past the ... woods where I'd played as a young child, so it was a journey back in time.

This practice is not unusual. Another widowed man created a similar journey, re-animating the past he shared with his wife. Other members of his family had been engaged with her body and their example appears to have prompted his actions:

> I went down, saw the funeral directors and all sorts of things and then I saw my daughter and my daughter-in-law fussing round, they dressed my wife and everything ... it [transporting her body] was something I could do, a little bit extra and, and someone said, oh it costs you so much for a hearse and all, this, that and the other. I said, well I've got a big estate car, why don't I take her to her resting place in my car, our car? So I rang up the funeral people and they said course you can, so I took all the back seats out and ... my wife came up here with me.

As in Arthur Westthorpe's case, Harold Riggthwaite's spatio-temporal experience resonated with time past, the married life he shared with his wife. He said:

> Well I just didn't drive straight here, we went for miles round the country lanes. We went to Winchester Hill, sat up there. Chatting to her all along, all the stuff

we liked doing when we were, when she was alive was driving the country lanes, we loved it, one of our favourite pastimes.

The journey had taken him about an hour and a half and when he described it he said:

> I did that for her and I was talking to her all the time and was lovely ... beautiful day, it was November. Crisp and cold, beautiful sunrise and I drove all the way up here and Winchester Hill and we sat there for about twenty minutes, chatting away ... and then we drove back and, and ... there was two buzzards flying round on the road and I just said to her, we're a couple of buzzards up there, look. Hope she heard me.

When Harold undertook to insert a 90-minute journey into the day of his wife's funeral he created a form of passing that reversed the day's temporality, steering him – and his wife – back into 'one of our favourite pastimes'. Moreover, the material presence of her corpse afforded him the opportunity to re-animate their relationship within a shared landscape, in a car where she had often sat beside him. Throughout his description, he refers to 'we' and includes the reciprocal activity of 'chatting away'. Heading for the natural burial ground, he keenly notes the seasonal temporalities of crisp cold November weather, of the sunrise. And in the flight of buzzards he finds their coupledom materialised, the birds' passage through the sky standing in for the major transition he and his wife were undergoing.

As noted, at the burial ground itself, mourners commonly experienced a freedom from constraint as the space and time afforded by the site enabled participation in the shared materialities of the funeral and the burial. Rather than the rapid journey up the aisle of the church or into the crematorium – on the shoulders of funeral directors and mourners or wheeled on a trolley – at both Powys and East Meon the terrain was difficult, requiring bodily control and exertion. In bad weather mourners got cold and wet while processing. Yet as Carolyn Salter described, this physical journey could evoke emotional transitions. While her mother-in-law had been against natural burial, in her view an undignified, cheapskate option, once she joined in the procession down to the grave, things changed, as Carolyn explained:

> Because everything changes you, doesn't it? And she's gone from all this, "Oh, what's it going to be like and blah, blah, blah?", to, "That was a beautiful hearse, that horse and cart". And it was a timeless experience and it built bridges, it was, it was a healing experience.

Diversity, Agency and Choice

When discussing East Meon natural burial ground, Carolyn Salter said she appreciated manager Al's open-minded approach to whatever arrangements people wanted, his resistance to imposing an imagined set of values upon them: 'he didn't come across pompous or arrogant or like, oh, we've got all the answers because we're the green people'.

Al's concern not to make bereaved people feel that a conventionally distant approach to the funeral was less valid raises the question of how varying deathways intersect in the UK. Certainly natural burial could be chosen as an antidote to the depersonalising sequestration of hospital. Carolyn Salter embraced East Meon natural burial ground enthusiastically and would hear nothing against it. When interviewed she explained this in relation to the hospital treatment her father received at the end:

> I really have tried to think hard of something bad to say about this place, but …
> if you want me to say something bad I'd say about dying in a conventional
> hospital situation, which is like being kept alive and poked, it's horrible, but
> here was brilliant.

In sites such as this, and at Green Lane Burial Field in Powys, the funeral may be felt as an unbounded period of time. Indeed some owners/managers recognise the need to signal to bereaved people when they may leave the site, thereby creating a temporal boundary without which the party may feel disoriented.

This sense of uncertainty could, however, animate mourners, inspiring an agency unnecessary in traditional death rites where familiarity may produce a blandness that fails to stimulate the senses, the memory or the imagination – where death remains an abstraction. Phyllis Cowell, whose mother was buried at the South Yorkshire Woodland Burial Ground, described her distress when the funeral director left many of her mother's floral tributes in the hearse instead of transferring them to the grave:

> I said, you can't leave those flowers in car, they're my mum's. And he's trying
> to calm me down, somebody from the funeral directors, he says, Phyllis it's all
> right, we'll take them up after, I says, no they're my mum's flowers you've got
> to take them now.

This hiatus about etiquette at an unfamiliar burial ground, the practicalities of a complicated transition from hearse to grave, inspired a set of innovations, which Phyllis went on to detail:

> Jessie [her grand-daughter] says, "Granny can I carry some?" And somebody
> just gave her a bunch of flowers and after that all the other kids came forward
> and you know when you wish you'd got a camera but you don't really take your
> camera to your mum's funeral do you? And we walked up this field, my mum
> was in front, the kids didn't follow because they don't know what you do at a
> funeral, so everybody knows that this is what you're supposed to do, get in an
> orderly line don't they? But kids don't know the format and there was Jessie,

there was our Joanne who's a bit older and then our Harry ... so there was all age ranges from little tots, they, and they'd all got a bouquet of flowers and they were just running up here and the sun was shining and I just said my mother would love this, she would absolutely love these kids running and laughing because they didn't know they shouldn't and, and then we just all gathered round at the top and it was absolutely beautiful.

As Phyllis suggests, it was the departures from existing practice and the inventiveness of the children that provided a memorable occasion leading her to vividly imagine her mother's response to it. Amy Salter, Carolyn's sister, described a similar experience at East Meon site:

what was funny was we started traipsing off down there and a big trail of people and then we got down towards the bend and I suddenly realised I'd forgotten the tape machine, so my pal Simon that had come up with us, sort of, yelled to him so he ran back up and I was thinking it's fine, running is fine at funerals, you know ... because it's a break with convention isn't it? You know, you know, you don't run at funerals, it's like running in school corridors and so, and then he came back down with the tape machine and I'd sort of fallen back so I wanted to catch up with Dad, so I thought, well, I'm going to have to run now because otherwise I'm not going to catch up, so I said I'm sorry everybody I'm going to catch up with my dad, you know, and I sort of ran up to the front but again I thought, well I don't care actually, because I want to catch up with my dad.

Time Re-Configured

In conclusion, this chapter has explored one example of cultural and social practice around the time of a death. While the participation and engagement fostered by natural burial is shared by DIY funerals and informal graveside practices found in other mortuary environments, we have focussed on the way in which temporalities are 'found', discovered or 'truly noticed' in a setting where the seasonal cycles of the natural environment are accessible to people contemplating their own deaths or managing that of someone close.

In that people 'find time' in these settings, many of them then 'make time' in ways that allow for engagement with the uncertainties and abstractions of death. Re-configuring the temporal processes of dying, disposal and mourning, social life is engendered while building more nuanced understandings of death becomes a collective endeavour, thereby acquiring a local, cultural dimension. As the conventional linearity of time is ruptured, so new continuities are established through the ongoing social presence of the dead: for example, the scope for re-generating the pastimes of a marriage now ended.

As we argue, in disturbing or discarding the clock time of a conventional funeral, new kinds of familial or marital time may be established. In this way, the dead remain as agents within their own families, their passage structuring the temporalities of everyday life and the seasonal cycle of calendrical rituals. Thus death, as an abstract or speculative entity, becomes less of a rupture or departure from a deathless life and instead contributes – often via the dead themselves – to the patterning and animation of the lives of those left behind.

References

Bauman, Z., 1992. *Mortality, Immortality and Other Life Strategies*. Cambridge: Cambridge University Press.

Bille, M., Hastrup, F. and Sørensen, T. F., 2010. Introduction: An Anthropology of Absence. In: M. Bille, F. Hastrup and T. F. Sørensen, eds, *An Anthropology of Absence: Materialisations of Transcendence and Loss*. New York: Springer, pp. 3–22.

Clayden, A., Green, T., Hockey, J. and Powell, M., 2010. From Cabbages to Cadavers: Natural Burial Down on the Farm. In: A. Maddrell and J. D. Sidaway, eds, *Deathscapes: Spaces for Death, Dying, Mourning and Remembrance*. Farnham: Ashgate, pp. 119–139.

Clayden, A., Hockey, J. and Powell, M., 2010. Natural Burial: The De-materialising of Death? In: J. Hockey, C. Komaromy and K. Woodthorpe, eds, *The Matter of Death: Space, Place and Materiality*. Basingstoke: Palgrave Macmillan, pp. 148–164.

Davies, D.J., 2005. *A Brief History of Death*. Oxford: Blackwell Publishing.

Elias, N., 1985. *The Loneliness of the Dying*. New York: Continuum.

Gell, A., 1998. *Art and Agency: An Anthropological Theory*. Oxford: Clarendon Press.

Gibson, M., 2008. *Objects of the Dead: Mourning and Memory in Everyday Life*. Melbourne: Melbourne University Press.

Giddens, A., 1991. *Modernity and Self-identity: Self and Society in the Late Modern Age*. Cambridge: Polity Press.

Gorer, G., 1965. *Death, Grief and Mourning in Contemporary Britain*. London: Cresset.

Hockey, J., 2011. Contemporary Cultures of Memorialisation: Blending Social Inventiveness and Conformity? In: S. Conway, ed., *Governing Death and Loss: Empowerment, Involvement and Participation*. Oxford: Oxford University Press, pp. 27–36.

Hockey, J., Green, T., Clayden, A. and Powell, M., 2012. Landscapes of the Dead? Natural Burial and the Materialization of Absence. *Journal of Material Culture*, 17(2): 115–132.

Illich, I. 1975. *Medical Nemesis: The Expropriation of Health*. London: Caldor and Boyars Ltd.

Jupp, P. C. and Walter, T., 1999. The Health Society: 1918–98. In: P. C. Jupp and C. Gittings, eds, *Death in England: An Illustrated History*. Manchester: Manchester University Press, pp. 256–82.

Klass, D., Silverman, P. R. and Nickman, S.L., eds, 1996. *Continuing Bonds: New Understandings of Grief*. Washington DC: Taylor & Francis.

Kübler-Ross, E., 1969. *On Death and Dying*. New York: Macmillan.

Lock, M., 2002. *Twice Dead: Organ Transplants and the Reinvention of Death*. Berkeley: University of California Press.

Mellor, P. and Shilling, C., 1993. Modernity, Self-identity and the Sequestration of Death. *Sociology*, 27(3): 411–431.

Nassauer, J. I., 1995. Messy Ecosystems, Orderly Frames. *Landscape Journal*, 15(9): 161–170.

Parsons, B., 1999. Yesterday, Today and Tomorrow: The Lifecycle of the UK Funeral Industry. *Mortality*, 4(2): 127–146.

Rugg, J., 2000. Defining the Place of Burial: What Makes a Cemetery a Cemetery? *Mortality*, 5(3): 259–75.

Seale, C., 1998. *Constructing Death: The Sociology of Dying and Bereavement*. Cambridge: Cambridge University Press.

Taylor, L., 1983. *Mourning Dress: A Costume and Social History*. London: George Allen & Unwin.

Van Gennep, A. [1909] 1960. *The Rites of Passage*. Chicago: University of Chicago Press.

West, K., 2010. *A Guide to Natural Burial*. London: Sweet & Maxwell.

Chapter 2

Material Dys-appearance: Decaying Futures and Contested Temporal Passage

Martin Demant Frederiksen

Introduction: Political Landscapes and Material Dys-appearance

On 23 November 2011 a statue of the former US President, Ronald Reagan, was unveiled in central Tbilisi. The bronze statue figures Reagan sitting on a bench looking towards the newly finished residence of the then Georgian president Mikheil Saakashvili. An inscription on the bench reads, 'Freedom is never more than a generation away from extinction' – a Reagan quote referring to the end of the Cold War. 'Europe Park', in which the statue is located, also features tiles decorated with images of roses – the symbol of the revolution in Georgia in 2003, after which Saakashvili had originally come to power. The political symbolism underpinning the reconstructed park was unmistakable: after 70 years of Soviet rule and a further 20 years of post-Soviet political turmoil, Georgia had finally found its proper place as a distinctly European nation with strong political ties to the US. Of course, not everyone in Tbilisi (or in Georgia at large) subscribed to the political opinion expressed in these material forms, but the message was clear.

The statue of Reagan in Europe Park was but one in a long series of new constructions undertaken by Saakashvili during his final years in power. Many of these constructions sparked protest and criticism among the population. However, as I will argue in this paper, it was not necessarily the political *content* symbolised in these materialities that people protested against. Rather, it was the absence of content in the supposed political form and, more importantly, the *tempo* in which the buildings were constructed or reconstructed that was contested. The central issue was that many of the newly built structures began to decay shortly after having been built, turning immediately into ruins despite being envisaged as political visions of the future. It was this ambiguous form of material passing taking place in the new 'political landscapes' – and perceptions that time was not passing in a proper way – that came to animate protest.

Ruins are often depicted as having an aura of eternity even though they are in a state of decay (cf. Manning 2008), and since the Renaissance, ruins, particularly in terms of architectural remnants, have often been invested with historical and aesthetic qualities (Edensor 2005; Trigg 2006; Buchli 2007; Hell and Schönle 2010: 5; DeSilvey and Edensor 2012). Despite in one sense being tragic as signs or symbols of death, as Georg Simmel observed in his short essay 'The Ruin',

Materialities of Passing

Figure 2.1   Statue of Reagan in Europe Park
Source: Photo by the author.

there can be a certain calmness surrounding ruins as present forms of a past life (Simmel 1958: 383). Ruins have even been taken as a political aesthetic, as infamously promoted in Albert Speer's 'Theory of Ruin Value' (Stead 2003). But what is at stake when cracks and crumbling surfaces begin to look wrong, when the passing of time that ruins signify can no longer glide into the background as a form of calmness? How can we approach the ambiguities surrounding decay when the decay at stake is not nested in historical or aesthetic qualities and a perceived orderly passing of time because the process of decay happens too quickly – decay that occurs in an incorrect manner? Probing these questions I will make use of Drew Leder's notion of 'dys-appearance'. In his book, *The Absent Body* (1990), Leder argues that certain forms of disappearance are essential to the body's functioning. That is, on an everyday basis we rarely take notice of our body's surface; 'the body simply "moves off to the side"; at any time, parts of the surface of the body are left unused or rendered subsidiary, placed in a background disappearance' (ibid.: 69). Yet, in moments of disease or pain, the body suddenly emerges to our consciousness as an alien presence, the body no longer disappears but 'dys-appears' as in a *dys* state (ibid.: 84). When this happens the surface of the body becomes an affective disturbance and an explicit awareness. In relation to the body, Leder writes, 'dys-appearance tends to arise when we are away, apart, from our ordinary mastery and health. There is the sense of privation, a reversal of a normal or desired state, which can then provoke a bodily thematisation' (ibid.: 87). In what follows I will apply this perspective on dys-appearance and thematisation to the empirical situation from Georgia outlined above. More specifically, I will explore the surfaces of emergent materialities in Tbilisi and the ways in which this 'urban body' came to *dys*-appear in the eyes of many local residents. On an empirical level, my aim is to show that the protests emerging against these constructions should not necessarily be seen as politically motivated. I do so by focusing on various forms of material dys-appearances in Tbilisi and the ways in which decaying surfaces, historical residues and even political visions of houses yet-to-be-built came to animate both social and political life. I will present a series of short empirical cases that depict particular buildings or neighbourhoods in Tbilisi and use these to approach the temporal tropes of material dys-appearance. On a broader level, my aim is to outline a possible approach or vocabulary for the study of the material and temporal qualities of surfaces and their decay. The notion of passing is instructive in this regard. As the editors suggest in their introduction to this volume, the encounter with the finality of the body may result in the most direct realisation of the otherwise abstract phenomenon of temporal passage. The 'normal' body may not reveal time in the same manner as an unhealthy or dying body does. Likewise, the decay of a ruin in itself may not draw attention to temporal passage – under normal circumstances it simply transcends time with its aura of eternity. This changes, however, if the ruin begins to dys-appear, leading its temporal passage to become an object of attention and contention. Drawing on the empirical examples from Georgia, I suggest that conflicts about appropriate forms of temporal passage provide an arena for disputing and discussing specific temporal connections to past, present and future (cf. DeSilvey 2006). As will become clear, the problem in Tbilisi was not that the materialities described in these cases were decaying, but that they were decaying *in the wrong way*, for instance by decaying too quickly, and that this incorrect form of material-temporal passage from life to death came to serve as an anchor of critique towards the politicians who built them – a critique directed not against the ideological content of their politics, but rather against a form of politics lacking content.

Immediate Ruins

Originally constructed in the 1880s by the German contractor Friedrich Vezel, Aghmashenebelis Avenue is the main street on the left embankment of the Mtkvari River cutting through central Tbilisi. The stylistic inspirations of the buildings that were constructed on the street during this period were mainly the neo-byzantine architecture of the Russian empire and, more often, the then-new wave of *Stil Modern* or Art Nouveau that had made its way to the country from Europe through the Black Sea. Many houses on Aghmashenebelis Avenue thus came to feature fences and balconies in wrought iron, intricate plaster-decorations on facades, and paintings and carvings decorating both interiors and exteriors.

In 1921, not long after many of these houses were constructed, Georgia became part of the Soviet Union, and the architectural styles of Aghmashenebelis Avenue came to be seen by the new political leadership as bourgeois art forms. Moreover, as with houses elsewhere in Georgia, the buildings went from being privately owned to state-owned and, due to the official indifference towards the architectural style dominating the street, little if anything was done to preserve or repair these buildings during the following decades. During the Soviet period, not least in the Khrushchev era from 1953 to 1964, material constructions in larger cities throughout the Union involved both the modernising and the standardising of urban landscapes (Luehrman 2011: 100; see also Buchli 1999, Gozak 2005, Lahusen 2006 and Fehervary 2013). In Tbilisi this mainly took place through the building of new suburbs constructed as residential areas. Many older houses, such as those on Aghmashenebeli Avenue, would become offices of the state administration.

When once again privatised, as Georgia gained independence from the Soviet Union in 1991, the socioeconomic detour faced by the vast majority of the population in the country rendered most of the buildings too expensive to renovate (Walker 2012). However, a few years after Mikheil Saakashvili came to power and under the heading 'Old Tbilisi New Life', the municipality of Tbilisi initiated a rehabilitation project of Aghmashenebelis Avenue in 2010. This was done with the support of the government of Saakashvili, which aimed at reconstructing the country itself. Initially this had been done with little guidance other than the personal preferences of politicians themselves, but increasingly art critics, architects and geologists were involved in the processes. A total of 70 houses on Aghmashenebeli Avenue were included in the first stage of the rehabilitation project. A year later, after the project was completed, the street was 'reopened' by President Saakashvili at an official ceremony in November 2011 (Edilashvili 2011). Yet, curiously, despite the previous poor condition of the buildings, the rehabilitation project was met with both scepticism and despair by many residents in Tbilisi.

Having conducted fieldwork five years earlier in Tbilisi in the office of an NGO located in the neighbourhood, I was struck by the extent of the alterations that had been made on Aghmashenebeli Avenue as I visited the NGO's office in early 2012. The staff members in the office, however, were not in any way impressed, not least due to their knowledge of the way in which these reconstructions had been carried out. Although they appreciated the fact that experts had actually been consulted in the process (something which had been missing in a series of previous reconstructions), they believed that the *speed* of the process had been problematic. In an interview, one of my interlocutors in the NGO explained that the president's push to complete renovations as soon as possible had resulted in a series of haphazard acts. For instance, she recounted, since much of the paint job had been done in mid-winter it was, due to the weather, difficult to ensure that the paint dried. But because the president insisted on the schedule being kept so that he could 'reopen' the Avenue as planned, everything had to be

Figure 2.2   New decay on Aghmashenebeli Avenue
Source: Photo by the author.

ready no matter the cost, speed or time of year. Consequently, workers had, for instance, been forced to use ordinary house-fans to dry the walls immediately after they had been painted. This procedure had meant that the paint did indeed dry in time for the official presentation of the finished renovation, but it had also meant that the newly applied layer of paint was extremely fragile. By the time of the interview in January 2012, only one and a half months after the project was completed and the street re-opened, the paint had begun to peel off. The speed of the renovation had thus resulted in an almost instant process of decay taking place. Indeed, if one took a closer look at the facades on the street, it was clear that cracks were to be found everywhere. Residents of Aghmashenebeli Avenue further recounted how entire plaster ornamentations had fallen to the streets, not only endangering passage on sidewalks but also leaving the 'new' buildings scarred.

A local acquaintance, Beka, noted how this was typical of the government. He agreed with the NGO worker that it was indeed positive that experts such as historians and art critics had been consulted to ensure that 'things looked right' but the manner of construction was still hasty and reckless. 'In the end', Beka noted, 'they are only interested in the outside, and not the inside, like their politics it's only superficial'. In this sense, there was only form but no content and everything thus depended on the surface. And the problem was that even the surface had come to look wrong.

Lost Minutes and EUtopia

On Aghmashenebeli Avenue the process of reconstruction was obvious. In other parts of central Tbilisi, however, reconstructions took place behind tall wooden fences. In others still, there were fences with images of what would-be reconstruction would look like, but with no particular signs of anything actually going on. One such place was the site of the former Institute of Marxism and Leninism located by Rustaveli Avenue, another main street in centre of the city. The 'Imeli' building (as it is known in short) was originally constructed by the architect Alexey Shchusev in 1938 and it achieved the status of national heritage in 1986. Yet, after a meeting in the municipality in 2010 this status was suddenly removed from official records. The minutes of this meeting magically disappeared, which made it impossible for anyone outside the municipality (and the Ministry of Culture) to determine why it had been done and by whom. Not long after the status was changed the premises of the building were sold to a Dutch construction company. The company's plan was to demolish 'Imeli' and build an entirely new luxury hotel in its place. The historical interiors of the building were removed and one wing was completely demolished, as were parts of the roof. But public protests against the demolition slowly started to emerge and a series of petitions arguing for the preservation of the original structure were circulated. One such public petition was named 'Stop IMELI Demolition' and addressed to the President, the Parliament, Tbilisi City Hall, Tbilisi City Council and the Ministry of Culture. It read:

> We are appealing to those who understand that cultural heritage is not a matter of taste, but a fact, in other words, a value that should be protected; to those who know that Stalinist architecture (especially as because [*sic*] this architectural monument belongs to A. Shchusev), is equally valuable for our culture as other civic or religious facilities built in various periods of our history; to those who think that "new" should not be built at the expense of "old". (Gogishvili 2010)

Due to such protests and petitions, the Dutch company eventually backed out, leaving behind a gutted and ruined shell that was no longer salvageable in its original form, and a fence surrounding the premise featuring deteriorating posters with images of the hotel-never-built.

Burgeoning civil dissatisfaction and protest also surrounded another site in the heart of Tbilisi's Old Town: Gudiashvili Square. Known for its aesthetic and historical qualities, the square was one of the oldest surviving residential areas in the city. When rumours spread that an Austrian firm, Zechner & Zechner ZTGmbH, had won a competition for rehabilitating Gudiashvili Square, it caused immediate protest among locals (Lekishvili 2012). On 16 December 2011 the Austrian architectural firm posted images on its website showing their proposed redesigning of the square. Aiming at developing an area with restaurants, offices and shops, this design involved substantial changes in the appearance of the square. A note on the website made it clear, however, that the intention was not to completely alter

Figure 2.3   The newly ruined Imeli building
Source: Photo by the author.

the square, but rather to incorporate classic Georgian architecture in the façade-design: 'The choice of keeping the structure divided into individual buildings, carries on the old town's habitual growth pattern, interweaving the new parts with the existing fabric of the city … Similarly the architectural design follows the urban integration concept in attempting to respond to the scale and character of the location. The result of the study will be the basis of an intense discussion and process together with interested participants and the urban government' (Zechner and Zechner 2012). Sensitivities, in relation to both existing architecture and local interest groups, seemed to have been taken into account. This, however, was not how it was perceived. In the period following the publication of the proposed plans, local and international newspapers began to flourish with articles on the rehabilitation of Gudiashvili Square and the perceived likelihood of its negative consequences (e.g. Jashi 2012; Lekishvili 2012; Lobzhanidze 2012; Nikuradze 2012; Saralidze 2012). Through rallies and petitions, local protesters argued that the political ideal of bringing Georgia closer to Europe had begun to damage the surface of the Old Town – it was beginning to look wrong. Although many still welcomed the political goal of strengthening ties to Europe and of Georgia entering the European Union at some point, they still held that this should be done through actual reform processes that would improve living standards rather than merely serving as showcases of intentions (Frederiksen 2014); in other words, it should not be done through a material 'EUropeanization' (e.g. Harboe 2012) of urban space. Further, due to the fact that the buildings that had already been reconstructed had started decaying once again, and in an improper manner (such as those on Aghmashenebil Avenue), critics argued that the decaying facades were an expression of 'EUtopia' – an idealised future that would never come into being and would leave non-historical ruins in its wake.

Heritage and Untimely Decay

> More damage has been done to our city in the last two years than in the entire Soviet period ... "new life" should be renamed "new death". (Elderly resident from central Tbilisi commenting on the *Old Tbilisi, New Life* reconstruction programme, quoted from Nonidze 2010)

Protests steadily grew, with increasing concern about the general governmental reconstruction and rehabilitation of Tbilisi's Old Town (Nasmyth 2011). Among the most prominent opponents to the projects was the group 'Tiflis Hamqari'. It was founded in 2005 in response to the dissatisfaction with the physical appearance of the reconstructed buildings. 'Tiflis' refers to the former name of the city (which was officially altered to 'Tbilisi' in 1936), 'hamqari' to the historical craftsmen's guilds in the city (originally meaning 'joint actions'). Its mission was to protect cultural heritage in Tbilisi and to ensure that development and modernisation projects were undertaken in accordance with both legislation and respect to historical values. Furthermore, it was an initiative seeking to actively engage the citizens of Tbilisi in protecting and preserving the city's urban environment and cultural heritage. Its aim was thus not to ensure that nothing was done to the historical buildings in Tbilisi, but rather that something was done *in the right way*.

In the summer of 2012 I met with Nona, a staff member in Tiflis Hamqari, in her office in central Tbilisi. Our conversation consisted mainly of shouting to each other, not out of disagreement but in order to drown out the noise made by the bulldozers, hammers, drills and concrete mixers at work in the streets surrounding the office. She said that not only was the quality of the reconstructions poor, so was the methodology. For instance, on Aghmashenebeli Avenue, where the new facades on the old Art Nouveau buildings had already started to crumble, there were suddenly many more Art Nouveau buildings than there had been before. This was, she explained, because there had also been a few Soviet buildings on the street that had suddenly, under the guise of renovation, re-emerged in Art Nouveau style. Despite it being a dark chapter of the country's history, she continued, the Soviet period was still part of their national history. But with the 'new life' project the architectural remnants had now disappeared from Aghmashenebeli Avenue and, due to the hasty and bad quality of work, many buildings on the street now also had a wrong appearance as the new facades of the buildings were decaying. In Nona's opinion, the very soul of the city was slowly dying. Bringing it back to life – the goal of the 'Old Tbilisi-New Life' project – was thus paradoxically now putting to death some of its trademarks. In the words of Nona, 'it's no longer old Tbilisi, it's something absolutely new, the materials are very different, and it looks kitchy too, it loses [sic] its spirit'. What was more, that which was being done in order to ensure that the city did not decay resulted in the city merely decaying in another way: urban surfaces were passing from one state of ruin into another.

Again, it is important to note that neither Nona nor the majority of those protesting against the restorations were against the idea that such work should be done. There was no question that Aghmashenebeli Avenue, The Institute of Marxism and Leninism, Gudiashvili Square, and many other places like them, were in dire need of restoration. The problem was that the municipality (and the government) was in such a hurry. 'They want', said Nona, 'to develop tourism, to show how effectively they work, to show the image of the work they have done, that they are rebuilding the country and that this is the physical manifestation. And they want to do it before an election. But none of it anticipates what will follow, what kinds of problems we will face afterwards. The speed is so rapid, they are fixing only facades and not what is in the building – it is only for tourists. Indeed, parliamentary elections were only months away and the President was under serious pressure due to a new opposition leader who was ahead in most polls. In order to materialise their promises of a new Georgia, time itself had had to be sped up. This meant, according to Nona, that they had not taken the time to find the correct materials and this had resulted in facades decaying almost instantly. Furthermore, it meant that they had not taken the time to ensure the rights of the local residents who had been forced to leave their houses, resulting in gentrification in some neighbourhoods. And, finally, it meant that they had not taken the time to find out whether the constructions would in fact improve tourism – which had been one of the main arguments for initiating them.

In his book, *Untimely Ruins*, Nick Yablon (2010) depicts modern American ruins and the ways in which they, in contrast to 'ancient ruins', are seen as being too banal or cheap to be considered as 'proper' ruins. They do not have the temporal distance to the past that would allow them to be looked upon with nostalgia (see also Pálsson 2012). Instead, these 'day-old' ruins spawned by rapid urbanisation interrupted ideas of linear progress, becoming instead symbols of impermanence. There are obvious parallels between this situation and the one found in contemporary Georgia; as with the American ruins described by Yablon, the decay appearing on renovated buildings in Tbilisi bespoke a frail present rather than a glorious past. In Tbilisi, images of the past (in terms of national heritage) were turned into kitschy replicas whose decay was untimely rather than eternal. We can find another parallel example in the political and public debates about what was to be done with Lenin's body after his death – debates that have taken place both during and after the Soviet period (e.g. Tumarkin 1981 and Gill 2008, respectively). One aspect of these debates was the question of whether Lenin would not in fact 'live on' in a better, or more proper, way if he was given an actual burial instead of remaining on display in the Mausoleum in Moscow. Here, as with the buildings in Tbilisi, permanence and eternity becomes a question of 'natural' decay taking precedence over a constructed and frozen form of ancientness that forces time to stand still rather than pass (for similar examples of temporality and dead bodies see Verdery 1999 and Bernstein 2011).

Contested Temporal Passage

Visually presenting the passage from one period to another via material constructions and deconstruction has almost become a political tradition in independent Georgia, starting with the removal of Soviet symbols after 1991. Since then, statues have been removed or resurrected, bodies been dug up and reburied, buildings been demolished, abandoned, rebuilt or reconstructed, depending on the signal attempted to be sent (e.g. Manning 2009; Vann Assche, Vershragen and Salukvadze 2010; Vann Assche and Salukvadze 2011; Frederiksen 2013; Gotfredsen 2013; Dunn and Frederiksen 2014). When the businessman Bidzina Ivanishvili entered the political stage in Georgia in 2012 as a challenger to Mikheil Saakashvili he remarked that if he was elected he would immediately tear down the newly erected 'Bridge of Peace' connecting Old Tbilisi to Europe Park – a bridge that had been built by Saakashvili.

Attempts to inscribe political visions and ideologies in material structure have been seen both during and after the Soviet Union (e.g. Humphrey 2005; Darieva, Kaschuba and Krebs 2011; and Fehérváry 2013) – and also in other political contexts (e.g. Weszkalnys 2007; van der Hoorn 2009; Bennett 2010; and Abram and Weszkalnys 2011). Particularly in the 1920s and 1930s, Soviet architecture was aimed at creating a new way of life. By constructing certain kinds of living quarters for its citizens it was believed that individualistic conditions could be eliminated – the private would give way to the collective. But rather than this occurring, writes Caroline Humphrey, architecture in the early days of the Soviet Union came to act like a prism from which alternative ideas were deflected. Hence, despite attempting to channel diverse meanings into a single one through material objects, new meanings in fact emerged. These meanings were not random; they were directed as subtle critiques visible, for instance, in imaginative literature and satire (Humphrey 2005). This chapter has equally focused on what happens when there is a political meddling with material surroundings and the critiques it animates. In the empirical context depicted here it may be argued that there is also an ideological aspect at play. Considering the construction of 'Europe Park' and the statue of Ronald Reagan mentioned in the introduction, and the political symbolism inherent to it, this certainly seems to be the case. However, the local protests and criticisms aimed at politically motivated constructions and reconstructions were not necessarily directed towards the political *content*. Rather, it was a question of dissatisfaction with the *lack* of content, the superficiality, of politics and the manner in which something was made to pass into another (and perceived wrong) state of being, for instance the ways in which buildings decayed.

In the introduction I stated my intention to examine the processes of reconstruction taking place in Tbilisi, and criticism against them, through Drew Leder's notion of dys-appearance, considering it not in relation to the surface of the biological body but in relation to the surface of materialities, thus turning Leder's concept into a spatial rather than a merely bodily optic. Seeing the city as a body is not a novel approach within the social sciences. In fact, writes Andrew Irving, anthropological and sociological studies have often seen 'the city as modelled on the corporeal body – with the various constituent parts corresponding to different body parts and performing corresponding functions' (Irving 2011: 19). Urban residents themselves also often describe places in their cities in bodily terms, talking about the city centre as the 'heart' of the city (Weszkalnys 2007), old neighbourhoods as the 'soul' of the city (Eckstein 1990) and the walls and surfaces of buildings as the 'skin' or 'complexion' of the city (Irving 2011). Keith Basso has argued that our relation to places may be taken for granted until we are somehow robbed of our customary relation to them. This may be because we find ourselves in new surroundings that we either do not understand or which have no meaning for us (Basso 1996). However, just as with an unanticipated bodily change – *pace* Leder – a change may take place *within* a certain space itself which entails or provokes a new awareness or thematisation, such as when a crack appears in a place where it ought not to be. Unlike Leder's analysis of bodily dys-appearance, which is an individual experience, the material dys-appearance depicted here in terms of surfaces and decay comes to include a distinctly social aspect; it is something which is discussed in private homes, in work-places, and in parks and streets; it sparks criticism towards political practices and results in protests, and it becomes a focal point for local NGOs. It is not merely a question of whether reconstructions or decay are being seen as negative per se in such discussions or protests, but rather a question of concerns about whether or not materialities decay in the proper manner and, more importantly, at the proper tempo. At the root of such discussions, criticisms and actions we thus find concerns about the passage of time rather than concerns about political, ideological content.

Conclusion

However heterogenous their colors may have been when new, the long common destinies, dryness and moisture, heat and cold, outer wear and inner disintegration, which they have encountered through the centuries produce a unity of tint, a reduction to the same common denominator of color which no color can imitate. In a similar way, the influences of rain and sunshine, the incursion of vegetation, heat, and cold must have assimilated the building

abandoned to them to the color tone of the ground which has been abandoned
to the same destines. They have sunk its once conspicuous contrast into the
peaceful unity of belonging. (Simmel 1958: 383)

Ruins can be seen as a reminder that everything will at some point perish. But they
can also be seen as humanity's defiance against nature (Manning 2008: 4). For many
locals in Tbilisi the old houses, squares and streets in the city had the latter quality.
Indeed, many of them were in a state of decay but exactly because of this they
had the appearance of something having survived; something uniquely Georgian
that had transcended time and remained unique despite dramatic sociopolitical
changes throughout history. To be sure, it is likely that when the neo-byzantine
architecture of the Russian empire and European Art Nouveau were introduced
in Tbilisi in the late nineteenth century these material forms also sparked local
concern by not being traditionally Georgian. But after well over a century's wear
and tear these buildings, paraphrasing Simmel's observation quoted above, have
gained 'a unity of tint, a reduction to the same common denominator', which
has merged them with other buildings in the city into 'a unity of belonging'. It
was this national heritage that the 'Old Tbilisi – New Life' programme sought to
reinvigorate, but relations between the old and the new became difficult to handle.
In an article on the building of new churches in Georgia, Paul Manning has argued
that the material quality of oldness represents a problem for newly built orthodox
churches. Whereas old churches (qua their age and state of decay) can be seen as
symbols of the survival of ancient Georgian traditions and the orthodox belief,
'many Georgians see these new churches as not reflecting a miraculous spiritual
renewal, but rather a materialistic degradation of Georgia' (ibid.: 2008: 18).
Similarly, renovated buildings, streets and squares in Tbilisi have come to look
'too new' (thus losing both their aura of ancientness and their aura of eternity) –
they have become, as Yablon puts it, untimely. However, the criticism and protests
that arose among parts of the local population at the time of these renovations
and reconstructions was not only related to the newness, it was also related to the
fact that the new had started to decay due to being badly and hastily constructed,
and that this form of decay looked wrong. Hence, while the renovations made
the former decay disappear, it made new decay *dys-appear*, and rather than being
reminders of a continuity of Georgian history and national heritage (as decaying
pasts), the surfaces of old Tbilisi became reminders of decaying futures and
collapsed political visions.

In 'Europe Square', during the final phase of its construction in 2012, a section
of marble boxes that were meant as decorations were placed in one of the corners
of the square. They featured images of roses – the symbol of the revolution. Unlike
similar looking boxes these ones were unlikely to ever be put in place in the park,
as they had all cracked. Although supposed to be reminders for future generations
of the accomplishments of Saakashvili, these symbols fell apart even before
Saakashvili was forced to leave office a year later.

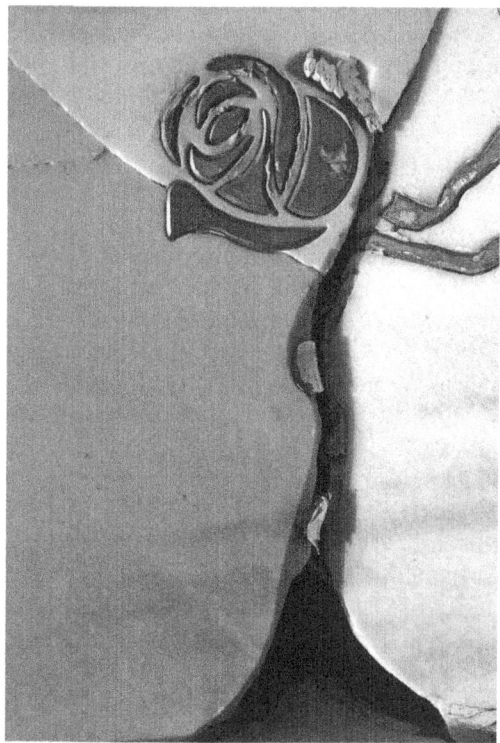

Figure 2.4   Cracked rose in Europe Park
Source: Photo by the author.

Acknowledgements

Research for this chapter was made possible through a travel grant from the Ethnographic Collections at Moesgaard Museum, Denmark. For their valuable input I owe my thanks to Paul Manning and Manouchehr Shiva for their comments on an earlier draft of this chapter, to the participants at the 'Materialities of Passing' workshop held in Oslo in 2012, and to my colleagues at University of Copenhagen, Andreas Bandak, Regnar Kristensen, Birgitte Møller Kristensen, Michael Ulfstjerne and Marie Ørum Wikman.

References

Abram, S. and Weszkalnys, G., 2011. Introduction: Anthropologies of planning – temporality, imagination, and ethnography. *Focaal*, 61: 3–18.

Basso, K., 1996. *Wisdom Sits in Places: Landscape and Language Among the Apache*. Albuquerque, New Mexico: University of New Mexico Press.

Bennett, J., 2010. *Vibrant Matter: A Political Ecology of Things*. Durham and London: Duke University Press.

Bernstein, A., 2011. The post-Soviet treasure hunt: Time, space, and necropolitics in Siberian Buddhism. *Comparative Studies in Society and History*, 53(3): 623–653.

Buchli, V., 1999. *An Archaeology of Socialism*. Oxford & New York: Berg.

Buchli, V., 2007. Astana – materiality and the city. In: C. Alexander, V. Buchli and C. Humphrey, eds, *Urban Life in Post-Soviet Asia*. London: Routledge, pp. 40–70.

Darieva, T., Kaschuba, W. and Krebs, M., 2011. *Urban Spaces after Socialism – Ethnographies of Public Places in Eurasia*. Chicago: University of Chicago Press.

DeSilvey, C., 2006. Observed decay: Telling stories with mutable things. *Journal of Material Culture*, 11(3): 318–338.

DeSilvey, C. and Edensor, T., 2012. Reckoning with ruins. *Progress in Human Geography*, 37(4): 465–485.

Dunn, E. and Frederiksen, M. D., 2014. Introduction: Ethnographies of absence in contemporary Georgia. *Slavic Review*, 73(2): 241–246.

Eckstein, S., 1990. Poor people versus the state and capital: Anatomy of a successful community mobilization for housing in Mexico City. *International Journal of Urban and Regional Research*, 14(2): 274–296.

Edensor, T., 2005. *Industrial Ruins: Space, Aesthetics and Materiality*. Oxford: Berg.

Edilashvili, N., 2011. Reconstructed Aghmashenebeli Avenue gets new image and appeal. *Georgia Today*, No. 589.

Fehervary, K., 2013. *Politics in Color and Concrete: Socialist Materialities and the Middle Class in Hungary*. Bloomington and Indianapolis: Indiana University Press.

Frederiksen, M. D., 2013. *Young Men, Time, and Boredom in the Republic of Georgia*. Philadelphia: Temple University Press.

Frederiksen, M. D., 2014. The would-be state – reforms, NGOs and absent present in post-revolutionary Georgia. *Slavic Review*, 73(2): 307–322.

Gill, G., 2008, 'Lenin lives': Or does he? symbols and the transition from socialism. *Europe-Asia Studies*, 60(2): 173–196.

Gogishvili, D., 2010. 'Stop IMELI Demolition', www.gopetition.com.

Gotfredsen, K., 2013. *Evasive Politics: Paradoxes of History, Nation and Everyday Communication in the Republic of Georgia*. PhD. University of Copenhagen.

Gozak, A., 2005. Attitudes towards modern architecture in the USSR and Russia. In: Jean-Yves Andrieux and Fabienne Chevallier, eds, *The Reception of Architecture of the Modern Movement: Image, Usage, Heritage*. Saint-Etienne: Publications de l'Université de Saint-Etienne, pp. 433–437.

Harboe, I., 2012. *New Lithuania in Old Hands – Effects and Outcomes of EUropeanization in Rural Lithuania*. London: Anthem Press.

Hell, J. and Schönle, A., 2010. Introduction. In: Hell and Schönle, eds, *Ruins of Modernity*. Durham and London: Duke University Press, pp. 1–14.

Humphrey, C., 2005. Ideology in infrastructure: Architecture and the Soviet imagination. *JRAI*, 11: 39–58.

Irving, A., 2011. Foreword. Fading Ads: An Urban Archaeology of Life and Photography. In: Frank Jump, ed., *Fading Ads of New York City*. Charleston and London: History Press. pp. 11–25.

Jashi, S., 2012. Tbilisi – Where 'Restoration' Means Redevelopment. *OpenDemocracy Russia*, 4 July 2012.

Lahusen, T., 2006. Decay or endurance? The ruins of socialism. *Slavic Review*, 65(4): 736–746.

Leder, D., 1990. *The Absent Body*. Chicago: University of Chicago Press.

Lekishvili, K., 2012. Gudiashvili Square – protest and protect. *Georgia Today*, No. 596.

Lobzhanidze, D., 2012. Showing civil solidarity in Tbilisi streets. *Georgia Today*, No. 607.

Luehrman, S., 2011. *Secularism Soviet Style: Teaching Atheism and Religion in a Volga Republic*. Bloomington: Indiana University Press.

Manning, P., 2009. The Hotel/Refugee Cqamp Iveria: Symptom, Monster, Fetish, Home. In: Kristof Van Assche, Joeseph Salukvadze and Nick Shavishvili, eds, *City Culture and City Planning in Tbilisi: Where Europe Meets Asia*. Lewiston: Mellen Press, pp. 319–334.

Manning, P., 2008. Materiality and cosmology: Old Georgian churches as sacred, sublime, and secular objects. *Ethnos*, 73(3): 327–360.

Nasmyth, P., 2011. The dilemma over Georgian architecture. *The Art Desk*, 20 August 2011.

Nikuradze, M., 2012. Protesting the destruction of an old square in Tbilisi. *Democracy and Freedom Watch*, 21 May 2012.

Nonidze, G., 2010. 'Tbilisi: Tearing Down the Past'. *OpenDemocracy*, 23 November 2010.

Pálsson, G., 2012. These are not old ruins: A heritage of the Hrun. *International Journal of Historical Archeology*, 6: 559–576.

Saralidze, A., 2012. Gudiashvili Square, Tbilisi. *Europa Nostra*, 1 January 2012.

Simmel G., 1958. Two essays. *The Hudson Review*, 11(3): 371–385.

Stead, N., 2003. The value of ruins: Allegories of destruction in Benjamin and Speer. *Form/Work: An Interdisciplinary Journal of the Built Environment*, 6: 51–64.

Trigg, D., 2006. *The Aesthetics of Decay: Nothingness, Nostalgia and the Absence of Reason*. New York: Peter Lang.

Tumarkin, N., 1981. Religion, Bolshevism, and the origins of the Lenin cult. *Russian Review*, 40(1): 35–46.

Van der Hoorn, M., 2009. *Indispensable Eyesores: An Anthropology of Undesired Buildings*. London: Berghahn Books.

Vann Assche, K. and Salukvadze, J., 2011. Tbilisi reinvented: Planning, development and the unfinished project of democracy in Georgia. *Planning Perspectives*, 27(1): 1–24.

Vann Assche, K., Vershragen, G. and Salukvadze, J., 2010. Changing frames: Citizen and expert participation in Georgian planning. *Planning, Practice & Research*, 25(3): 377–395.

Verdery, K., 1999. *The Political Lives of Dead Bodies: Reburial and Postsocialist Change*. New York: Columbia University Press.

Walker, J., 2012. On the brink of extinction: Tbilisi's hidden art nouveau. *Kunstpedia*, 25 August 2012.

Weszkalnys, G., 2007. The disintigration of a socialist exemplar: Discourses on urban disorder in Alexanderplatz, Berlin. *Space and Culture*, 0(2): 207–230.

Yablon, N., 2010. *Untimely Ruins: An Archeology of American Urban Modernity, 1819–1919*. Chicago: University of Chicago Press.

Chapter 3

Passage and Passing: Movement, Boundary and Presence in Neolithic Mortuary Architecture

Tim Flohr Sørensen

Introduction

Across the world, death seems almost always to result in some form of formal disposal of the dead body. The handling of the dead body is in its own right a cultural site for marking or exploring the ethics, politics and aesthetics of death. As such, mortuary practices often seem to be just as much about the living as they are about the dead (e.g. Hertz 1960; Bloch and Parry 1982; Metcalf and Huntingdon 1991; Hallam and Hockey 2001). In this light, the English colloquialism and euphemism 'passing' may appear to broadly describe the journey that the living *and* the dead will have to go through in order to arrive at some 'other side' beyond burial or in death.

In a number of cases, instruments or vehicles facilitate that actual passing, either in symbolic or practical form, and some of these allude concretely to the perception of death as a passage or transition that the dead have to go through (for examples, see Bjerregaard, Rasmussen and Sørensen, this volume). The vehicle can thus be in the form of a coffin within which the deceased is subject to a transportation or movement. In other cases, we may suggest, the transfer takes place as a movement of the body in the sense of metamorphosis, that is, a corporeal transformation in the form of putrefaction or cremation (Tarlow 2002; Rebay-Salisbury, Sørensen, and Hughes 2010; Kuijt, Quinn and Cooney 2014). In this sense, passing is at the same time movement and conversion, because the dead individual is being transported and transformed. Passing thus becomes synonymous with 'crossing', 'going over' or 'transgressing' a perceived boundary, and breaching the boundary can simultaneously be physical and conceptual, turning out to be a division and a passage at the same time.

This notion of the boundary is in line with philosopher Martin Heidegger's contention that the boundary is not so much an instrument of separation, but rather a beginning or a moment of transformation. Or, as he explains, the 'boundary is not that at which something stops ..., the boundary is that from which something *begins its presencing*' (Heidegger 1971: 154, emphasis in original). In this chapter I adopt this contention as the starting point for exploring death as passage and passing. In doing so, I seek to unpack and elaborate on the philosophical notion of the boundary, and contextualise its relevance in a concrete empirical case study. I scrutinise the kinds of presencing that are at stake when crossing a boundary at the confrontation with death and burial. Certainly, the dead are located at a margin and, depending on cosmology, they may be at the boundary of an ultimate nothingness or on the verge of a new beginning (whether in the form of rebirth or some form of metaphysical existence).

So while death may in one sense be seen as the moment when a person passes away (as in disappearing or vanishing), it may also be defined as the passage across a boundary revolving around identity or ontology, where a person passes into a new state of being (Fowler 2004: ch. 4; Willerslev 2007; 2009; also Marcussen and Venbrux, this volume; Nielsen, this volume; Rasmussen, this volume). The biological changes taking place in the dead body suggest that this passing is autonomous and determined by the agency of the dead body (agency sensu Gell 1998; e.g. Williams 2004; Sørensen 2009; Harper 2010; Bille 2013). At the same time, the handling of the body by the mourning community also suggests that a certain degree of assistance, direction or control over the passage has to be exercised by the society of the living. This passage, as anthropologist Robert Hertz (1960: 81) would have it, does not simply occur as an instantaneous event at or after the moment of dying, but is most often 'a transitory state of a certain duration' (see also Nielsen, this volume).

The quality of this 'certain duration' is particularly pronounced in so-called 'secondary' mortuary practices. This category of mortuary practices challenges us to understand the connection between passing, temporality and the boundaries between life and death, as the passage is not straightforward and unidirectional. Secondary burials or mortuary practices cover a range of variations, but with the common theme of being circumscribed by a ceremonial return to the dead body after an initial – primary – burial. As such it may be defined as a reburial, for example after exhumation, defleshing, excarnation or cremation, or in the context of an initial yet not necessarily complete process of putrefaction, upon which bones or corporeal remains are cleansed, sorted, organised, reburied and/or distributed. The order of activities and their timing can vary greatly, and may extend from days to decades. Archaeology and ethnography offer numerous examples of secondary mortuary practices, (e.g. Hertz 1960; Bloch 1982; Metcalf and Huntingdon 1991; Chesson 2001; Å. M. Larsson 2003; Kuijt 2008; Poyil 2009; Quinn and Kuijt 2013), and while anthropological analyses often explore the conceptual and social dynamics of these forms of burial, archaeological studies tend to emphasise their spatial and material dimensions (as suggested by the reference above, several exceptions to this gross generalisation can, of course, be found).

In this chapter I seek to bridge such social and spatial perspectives through an examination of the architectonic and conceptual materialisations of passing in megalithic tombs from the South Scandinavian Middle Neolithic. It is, thus, a particular form of passing that is explored in this chapter, where the double connotation of passing – as movement and transformation, or as passage and conversion – is at stake. I will try to make a connection between conceptual passing and spatial passage, departing from the rather obvious linguistic (and coincidental) connection between *passing* and so-called *passage graves* from a part of the South Scandinavian Middle Neolithic (built ca. 3300–3100 BC). I am going to argue that (spatial) passage and (ontological) passing may actually be seen as mutually engendering forces in the understanding of death and temporality in these Stone Age communities.

Passage graves are particularly interesting as a source material for the exploration of passing due to their architectonic structure and the multiple ways in which dead people were buried within them. Both architecture and burial practices highlight the qualities of transition and transformation, and they do so with regard to the living as well as the dead. This opens up the question of what the passage transpiring at a burial and within the space of burial actually achieves. What is the reason for the elaborate architectural setting and the cumbersome endeavour of handling human remains instead of a simple earthen grave? I will use the passage graves as a starting point for considering how architecture, body and movement constitute connections and disconnections between the living and the dead, exploring boundary and body in philosophical and ethnographic perspectives in order to complement the archaeological evidence. Boundaries and passing are thus examined as spatial *and* bodily phenomena, with the aim of understanding the synchronicity of these factors and the qualitative constituents of passing.

Passage Graves in Southern Scandinavia

Passage graves are burial monuments that are distributed across the landscapes of Southern Scandinavia and were built during a part of the Middle Neolithic (3300–3100 BC). During this time, communities were practicing a low-intensity form of farming based on relatively small-scale production of crops and more intense animal husbandry. These activities took place in a landscape composed of woodland and pasture, dotted with dispersed, temporary settlements, probably constituted by extended family groups, judging from the archaeological evidence (Tilley 1996; Nielsen 1999: 163; Richards, Price and Koch 2003: 289; L. Larsson and Brink 2013). Carbon 14 dating of organic material from the passage graves indicates that they were built in the time span between 3300 and 3100 BC (Dehn and Hansen 2002: 47), yet earlier dates are sometimes suggested (Clausen, Einicke and Kjærgaard 2008: 216). In the Danish area alone, on which this chapter primarily focuses, around 500 passage graves are preserved, out of an estimated original number of up to 5,000 (Dehn, Hansen and Westphal 2004: 153).

Despite being more than 5,000 years old, many of these graves persist in almost pristine conditions to this day due to their sturdy architecture and the exceptional engineering skills behind their construction. Basically, passage graves are composed of an internal chamber and a corridor – or a passage, which gives them their name – and an intricate construction of several layers of smaller rocks,

Figure 3.1   Exterior view of Birkehøj passage grave, North West Zealand, showing the entrance to the corridor

Source: Photo by the author.

pebbles, soil and organic materials, circumscribed by a line of kerb stones and turf coating. The chambers are constructed with a ceiling of enormous capstones of up to 25 tons on which further layers of rocks and soil were placed. The chambers can be up to 16 metres in length, and up to 2.5 metres in width and height, and thus offered room enough for numerous burials (Dehn and Hansen 2002, 2007). This makes for a domed, grass-covered mound of 10 to 30 metres in diameter on the exterior, accessible from an opening in the façade.

The corridor – or the passage – is set perpendicularly to the chamber, and ordinarily runs from the middle of the long side of the chamber to the edge of the mound encapsulating the entire construction. The length of the corridor can vary from 3 to 10 m, and is normally approximately 0.5 m wide and about 1 m high, enclosed by granite boulders. While the chamber is high enough for an adult to stand up, and may reach 2.40 m (Dehn and Hansen 2006: 26), the corridors are usually are significantly lower (60 to 120 cm; see Skaarup 1985 for examples), which means that a person moving through the corridor has to bend down and crawl or squat to get through to or from the chamber.

Passage graves were used for the collective internment of people, in some cases more than 100 individuals (Nordman 1918: 80ff; Persson and Sjögren 2001: 227), including both sexes, and children and adults alike. The nature of internment in the passage graves has been debated by archaeologists for around a century, and

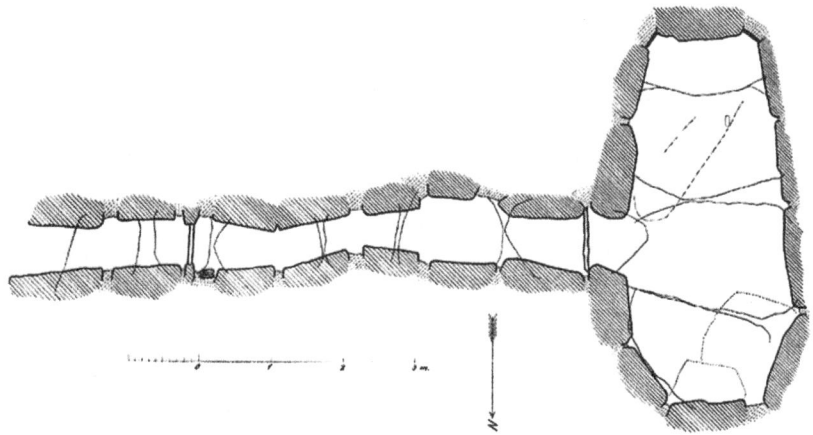

Figure 3.2   Plan of Mogenstrup passage grave, East Jutland
Source: Nordman 1918, Figure 67.

a number of interpretations of the skeletal remains have been proposed (Shanks and Tilley 1982; Kaul 1992; Tilley 1996; Bradley 1998; Ahlström 2001, 2003; Å. M. Larsson 2003, 2009a, 2009b; Sjögren 2010; Sørensen, 2015b). The main confusion stems from the fact that the passage graves were in most cases in use for decades, sometimes for centuries, and in a few cases for millennia. The use of the burial chambers was not necessarily continuous, and often there are signs that later burials interfered with older ones, resulting in what has been termed a 'chaotic' assemblage of more or less disarticulated skeletal distributions in the chambers and corridors (Nordman 1917: 241; Rosenberg 1929: 214; Schuldt 1972; Kaul 1992; Midgley 1992: 450ff; Holten 2000: 289; Å. M. Larsson 2009b). The main dispute in the archaeological debate is whether the passage graves were: 1) used for the internment of complete and coherent dead bodies with the purpose of remaining in the chamber for posterity; 2) used for the deposition of dead bodies whose putrefied or skeletonised remains were subsequently removed and circulated or deposited elsewhere; or 3) used for the deposition of body parts or skeletal remains after temporary burial or excarnation elsewhere.

The aim of this chapter is not to review the debate on this matter, so I will bypass a lengthy recapitulation of the arguments in the debate (see instead Shanks and Tilley 1982; Damm 1991; Ahlström 2003; Sjögren 2010, 2015; Sørensen 2015a, b). In the context of this chapter it is enough to establish that we can say with confidence that dead bodies did not remain in an intact and complete form in all passage graves throughout Southern Scandinavia. Body parts were from time to time moved around in the chambers, and also taken out of the tombs, and the bottom line is that the passage graves were the sites of processes of bodily transformation – either in the form of a gradual organic decomposition or the assisted fragmentation of the integrity of the dead body. In many cases is seems that the disarticulation of human remains was intentional, and that the breaking up of the body was associated with a particular form of burial, which we may recognise as so-called secondary burial or secondary mortuary practice (as described above). The fragmentation of individual bodies would thus either mean that the dead body was deposited temporarily in the chamber and then subsequently partially removed, or that the dead body had been buried temporarily elsewhere and that fragments of the body were deposited in the chamber at a later time or event.

The disarticulation and, in a number of instances, rather creative re-articulation of dead bodies in passage graves are of course important for our hopes of understanding boundaries and passing in the South Scandinavian Neolithic. In the context of this chapter, the treatment of dead bodies influences the potential for establishing a connection between passing and passage in relation to death, bereavement and identity. But more importantly, the fragmentation of bodies also relates directly to passing and passage as the simultaneous movement of the body and affective movement. The fragmentation and transport of the dead body involve the movement of a living body, being subject to simultaneous bodily and affective movement (following James 1884; Spinoza 1996; Massumi 2002; Sheets-Johnstone 2011). It is difficult to speak of one specific interpretation of the burials in the passage graves, despite the fact that their architecture and spatial organisation conform to a relatively standardised framework. It may thus tentatively be argued that it is precisely the durability of the architecture that offers itself to a multitude of forms of burial. Or, in other words, the durable architecture can be seen as constituting a spatial stability against the ephemerality of performance. As such, the temporal qualities of architecture and the particular form of burial are conceptually juxtaposed in the passage graves, and in the remainder of the chapter I will focus on the contrast between the breakable corpse, the transience of the moving body of the bereaved and the solid architecture, exploring how these temporal and material regimes coexist.

Bodies in Passing and Bodily Passage

In the following I want to explore a few selected cases of burials in passage graves in Denmark for furthering reflections on boundaries and passing in this form of burial space. It can be debated whether these cases are representative of burial customs more widely in the South Scandinavian Middle Neolithic, yet the aim of the chapter is to focus on these particular cases and explore their character and potential motives, regardless of whether they are the expression of unique events or a more widespread mortuary tradition. One potential reason for the peculiarity of some finds may be that mortuary practices were highly explorative fora, leading to very diverse and even unique burial practices. So, regardless if the cases I draw upon are unique, we are still compelled to try to understand them.

One specific find is particularly curious and does not seem to be the expression of a common practice, but it nevertheless calls for a consideration of its possible

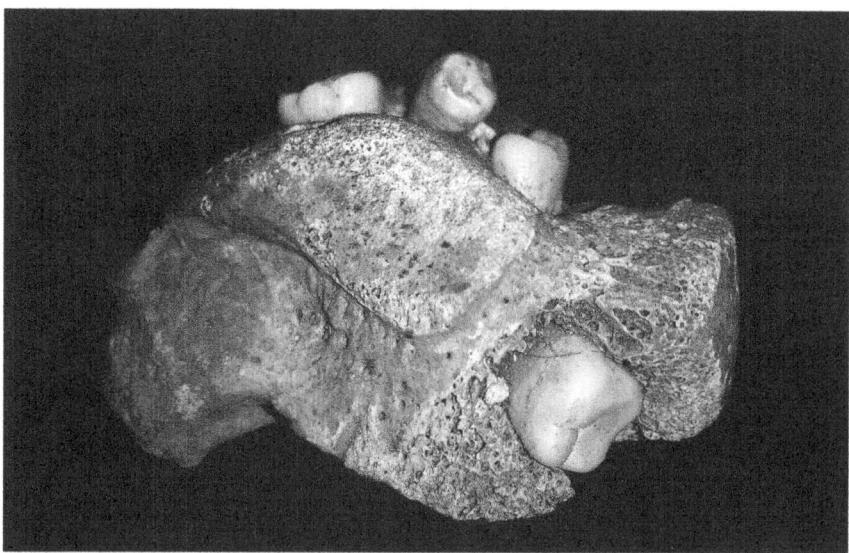

**Figure 3.3   Human ankle bone mounted with human teeth;
Birkehøj passage grave, North West Zealand**

Source: Photo by Severin Tobias Mortensen, reproduced with permission.

logics. This find derives from the Birkehøj passage grave (Dehn, Hansen, and Westphal 2004) in north-western Zealand and emphasises just how malleable the body seems to have been perceived in death: the ankle bone (*talus*) from a human foot was found with four human teeth inserted into it. The teeth were placed in sockets drilled into the bone, evidenced by a fifth socket, where the tooth is absent. It is unclear whether the teeth belonged to the same person as the ankle bone, but in other passage graves it is clear that remains from different individuals were combined.

Also, in passage graves at Rævehøj and Kyndeløse on Zealand, respectively 9 and 20 crania and other bones were piled in corners of the chambers. Likewise, three piles of long bones from several individuals were each topped by a cranium in a passage grave at Uggerslev on Funen. It has been argued that these piles were assembled in the context of tidying up the chambers, rather than being the expression of mortuary practices as such (Kaul 1992: 22), even though it is not entirely clear how it is possible to tell the difference archaeologically, or whether such activities would be distinguished in the Middle Neolithic. At any rate, it appears that individually bounded bodiness was transgressed in death, and the collection of bones from different individuals might instead have been perceived as a potential for creating or confirming notions of personhood exceeding the modern concept of the individual. Some archaeologists have suggested that the deconstruction of human bodies was carried out at ceremonial structures known as causewayed enclosures, such as a particularly well-documented structure at Sarup on south-western Funen, and argue that bones or body parts were circulated between passage graves and open-air ceremonial sites in the landscape (Andersen 1997: 309; see also Andersen 2009; Madsen 2009). The collections of crania or other skeletal remains should thus not be seen as a carefully curated and lasting form of memorialisation. On the contrary, body parts or bones could be piled, sometimes as collections of long bones, an assemblage of ribs, and what have you, and be complemented by remains of the more recently deceased. And just as bones and other forms of human remains could be compiled, so could they be reconfigured, moved about or taken out of the chamber. As such, the passage grave largely defies the notion of the cemetery as a final resting place.

The composition of body fragments implies that the dead body was seen as a source of assemblage or collage, which could be built across individual or personal identities to form a montage of dead people. This form of assemblage may concur with the 'collective assemblage of enunciation' that philosophers Gilles Deleuze and Félix Guattari (1987: 98) describe as an assemblage of 'acts and statements, of incorporeal transformations attributed to bodies' (1987: 98). Building a heap of bones deriving from different individuals thus implies engaging in a playful substitution of body-related identity formation in favour of a spatially situated enunciation of fluid and continuous identity processes that extend beyond the physical assemblage itself in the form of the collection of skeletal remains. Moving skeletal remains about may accordingly be seen as an aspect of dead bodies as 'unfinished objects' (Julier 2009: 96–98), that is, as things in transformation, circulation, movement; ensembles of things that are actively orchestrated in ongoing states of being un-fixed and unsettled. This suggests that bodily unity was an element of the identification of the individual as a member of a social community, whereas the breakable and divisible corpse may offer a source for articulating – enunciating – the relationship between the living community and the realm of the dead.

In the passage graves, these organisations of skeletonised bodies, whole bodies and partially coherent bodies in creative assemblages were intimate and immediate to the senses. This suggests that the tactile and sensuous interaction with the dead was a means of learning and knowing what to do with them; touching, smelling and seeing the dead matter would thus be a way of establishing the state of the deceased. The larger cycle of movements that dead bodies went through at this time might therefore be connected with this intimate and sensuous engagement. The tactile sensation encountered while assembling dead bodies would thus offer the experience of *feeling* the slippage of the individuals into a more vaguely defined form (Sørensen 2015a, b). The dead person being deposited in the passage grave remains identified in the act of burial, while the bones that are moved around, reconfigured, placed in the chamber or removed from the chamber, are being reworked along the lines of an active reconfiguration of the personhood of the deceased. The purpose of this process is to move the dead from a state of individual 'deadness' towards a larger assemblage of dead people or a more abstract sense of community in death (cf. Shanks and Tilley 1982).

Touching bones and rearranging them in an order that defies the anatomical structure of the integrated living body is a process of dis-identification; a way of distancing the bones from the person that was once part of those very bones. Thus, touching and feeling the body parts or bones becomes an integral part of creating attention towards the aspects of the dead person that are considered important to explore. It does not just involve a translocation of body parts or skeletal remains, but is rather a medium through which the experiences of the deceased are negotiated and learned. This also transgresses the mere forgetting or elimination of individual identities and may have more to do with transgressing the boundedness of the individual body form in death and allowing it to enter into an assemblage of identities akin to those suggested in Marilyn Strathern's (1988) notion of 'dividuality' or Roy Wagner's (1991) 'fractal personhood' (contra Ahlström 2003; Sjögren 2010; see also Sørensen 2015b).

Architecture, Passage and Passing

For the person who enters the passage grave for the first time, the architecture choreographs certain vistas while playing down others, and channels perception of the cemetery and the dead matter in a way that emphasises proximity and attention to one's presence in a very special place. The disappearance of visual identification of details in the tomb – the concealment of some perceptual stimuli – highlights other sensations and, as demonstrated, touch, sound and smell take centre stage at the expense of sight. Orientation in the chamber and the recognition of putrefying bodies thus need to issue forth through sensory engagements that require greater proximity and intimacy, in comparison with sight. The architectonic framework of the passage grave is an important factor in the creation of vague notions of identity and experience. Movement into the chamber – whether accompanied by a dead body or not – is part of a sensory choreography that simultaneously emphasises an intimacy with matter and a lack of optical clarity.

As illustrated above, passage graves are characterised by an inherent darkness. The use of artificial lighting has not left unequivocal archaeological traces, but even if fires or torches had been use to light up the chamber, it would only have created a dim and smoky interior with a vibrancy of constantly moving shadows. Vision, thus, does not offer the most pronounced or primary mode of engaging with the passage grave and seeing does not facilitate the identification of its interior environment. Philosopher Maurice Merleau-Ponty argues that sight is a distancing faculty, or in his words, 'to see is *to have at a distance*' (Merleau-Ponty 1964: 166, emphasis in original). Rather, touch, smell and sound are more readily available sensory regimes within passage graves, and if sight is – as Merleau-Ponty contends – a distancing faculty, then we may propose that these other senses serve to draw things closer, making them immediate and pressing.

Figure 3.4   Person moving through the corridor of Birkehøj passage grave
Source: Photo by the author.

The notion of presencing again turns out to be crucial, as the body or body parts of the dead cannot simply be seen and reflected upon at a distance. Rather, they must be integrated as an extension of the body of the living through touch. In this way, touch goes both ways: what we touch, touches us, and object and body thus mutually transgress any well-defined boundary of self and other. To illustrate this, Merleau-Ponty uses the example of pressing his two hands together:

> ... the two hands are never touched and touching at the same time with respect to each other. When I press my two hands together, it is not a matter of two sensations felt together as one perceives two objects placed side by side, but of an ambiguous arrangement in which the two hands can alternate in the role of "touching" and "touched". (Merleau-Ponty 2002: 93)

The architecture of the passage grave contributes actively in the staging of this exchange between object and body, and it assumes an important role in the choreography of the senses. Most significantly, it directs movement through the corridor in a particularly confined way, forcing the body into close contact with the architecture of and with the objects transported in and out of the passage grave. It is not possible to pass through the corridor without bumping into its granite walls and ceiling as one's body needs to assume an awkward squatting or crawling posture with a strong capacity for directing movement. Adding to this choreography the fact that people would be entering the monument with the purpose of depositing or removing a dead body, body parts or skeletal remains, it is clear that multisensory experience and exchange with the elements would be immediate. Moreover, the architecture choreographs the sequencing of persons going into the chamber, restricting movement in the passage towards the chamber.

After crawling through the passage, one can stand up comfortably and go either left or right. As such, passing from the corridor to the chamber can be seen as crossing another threshold, where the body is once again free to stand up and extend spatially. It is tempting to see the distal ends of the chambers as 'dead ends', yet they should rather be perceived as turning points, where the person or persons in the chamber need to turn around and return towards the world outside. The precise activities that took place in the chamber in the Middle Neolithic are not entirely clear from the archaeological material. It is evident, however, that people did leave behind manipulated human remains and seem to have removed parts of dead people, while also depositing flint objects, pottery and amber ornaments. Some of the archaeological evidence suggests that the passage graves were used as mortuary repositories, where bodies were placed in order to decompose and then subsequently be removed and relocated elsewhere. In this perspective, the dead, too, would return from the tomb, and the passage grave turns out to be a host of thresholds or boundaries to be transgressed in several stages and in multiple dimensions.

If we return to Heidegger's contention that the boundary is not where something ends, but where it begins its presencing, we may suggest that the crossing of the boundary requires some form of friction in order for a *feeling* of presence to occur. In the case of Middle Neolithic passage graves this feeling of presence, moreover, appears to hinge on a simultaneous oscillation with experiences of absence. This absence emerges in the megalithic tombs in the form of disappearing senses, dissolving bodies and a moving and removal of distinct, bounded identities. Heidegger's 'presencing' resonates well with historian Eelco Runia's notion of 'presence' in the context of commemoration, which he describes as '"being in touch" – either literally or figuratively – with people, things, events, and feelings' (2006: 5). Importantly, Runia underlines that presence is not 'the fulfillment of a wish to stop time, and preserve, respect, and honour what you happen to possess' (ibid.). Instead, Runia understands presence in the commemorative act as a quality that opens up future contingency, consonant with Heidegger's understanding of the boundary as a point of departure, or the beginning of a presencing.

The material infrastructure of these scenes of presence and presencing thus needs to be given its due. Presence is not divorced from a material and spatial grounding, and in the spatial and material practices circumscribing the passage graves it can be argued that the juxtaposition of architecture and corporeality points precisely to the temporal character of presence. Movement through the passage grave and the corporeal metamorphosis of the dead body are crucial to the quality of this form of burial structure, emphasising the temporality of passing and passage. The architecture of the passage graves offers a sensuous scene for experiencing the material and conceptual reconfiguration of the dead. The spatial and material cultural framework reveals and conceals experiences through movement, creating perceptual foregrounds and backgrounds and a certain aesthetic experience of the mortuary sphere and the practices carried out there: some things are seen, others are not; some things are sensed through other media, while others are not. Bodies, body parts and identities are coming and going in and out of sensuous immediacy, and they eventually disappear without necessarily losing their affective presence. In this sense, the friction that occurs in the passage revolves around not only the ways in which the body touches the architecture of the tomb, but also around the friction between the living body and the dead body as the interaction with dead bodies in the passage graves were characterised by a high degree of intimacy with the dead matter.

Betweenness and the Power of Interstice

The empirical evidence from the passage graves suggests that the cultural attitude to phenomena like transition, passing, passage, borderline occurrences and boundaries are at stake in the mortuary practices of the Middle Neolithic. A key aspect and unifying feature of burials in the passage graves is the act of *returning*, in bodily and spatial as well as in emotional and mnemonic terms (see also Sørensen 2014). While it has been suggested that burials and architecture in and of the passage graves can be understood through the conceptual frameworks of Victor Turner's transitional notion of the 'liminal' (Tilley 1991) or Julia Kristeva's boundary concept of 'abjection' (Sørensen 2010), I want to explore in greater detail how the thresholds that are embedded in these frameworks may offer a particular purchase for the understanding of the passage graves. As outlined above, passage graves are instruments of bodily conversion and at the same time spaces of movement. This compels us to explore the temporality of passing and passage, but also how the architectural environment works on the senses, taking seriously the particular affective agency of the passage graves.

As demonstrated earlier, the passage graves challenge a visually dominated, detached and reflected mode of interacting with or comprehending space, and instead exploit a 'feel' of space and a temporal emphasis on space as unfolding and ongoing, mutable, and morphing through movement. Such a perception of space challenges a conventional modern, Western notion of space as something seen and static (Thomas 1993; Bender 1999; Casey 2001; Lefebvre 2004). Exploring spatial perception among autistics, Erin Manning and Brian Massumi (2014) argue that the perception of space experienced by some autistics is not simply a pathological condition, but is frequently classified as such due to a 'neurotypical' normativity, foreclosing an experientially flat ontology. This normativity considers it unsustainable – and pathological – to experience space as engagements with a multitude of continuously emergent relations; that is, to experience the world 'without discrimination' (2014: 4) between heterogeneous relations that mutually texture one another simultaneously, where everything is 'somewhat alive' through the 'immediacy of the environment' (2014: 4). The immediacy and simultaneity of experience implies that everything is perceived as an immersion in space, rather than by singling out individual elements in the spatial experience. As such, space and experience is emergent (see also Sørensen 2015a; Bille and Sørensen in press) as a 'co-motion' and qualitative texturing of bodies and elements (Manning and Massumi 2014: 4).

As Manning and Massumi contend, this mode of perception need not be pathologised or seen as an anomaly, but may rather be appreciated as an ability not to discriminate or give a priori priority to certain sense modalities. Space recognition should instead be seen as issuing forth as an 'intermodal' way of thinking *in* movement and of perceiving things in co-motion (2014: 8). Manning and Massumi argue that the normative attitude to experience is the product, on the one hand, of a 'neuroreductionism', hinging on embodied cognition and enactive perception, and, on the other, of phenomenological concerns first and foremost, with subjectivity (2014: 19), both of which are firmly grounded in a modern, Western – and hence Cartesian – preconception that humans separate themselves from their surroundings in their perception of the world.

In addition to Manning and Massumi's examples, alternative modes of perception may be found in numerous ethnographic accounts that prescribe a continuity of body, landscape, movement, time and modes of perception. Thus, according to Eric Hirsch, we cannot speak of an 'absolute' body, because 'the body is a locality, a form of ambience and a perceptual surround' (Hirsch 1995: 23), while Maurice Leenhardt observed that among the Kanaks of New Caledonia, prior to the introduction of Christianity, personhood was diffused into a world of person and thing with no particular locus or concept of body (Leenhardt 1979: 164). Similarly, the Ambonwari people of Papua New Guinea do not have a term for the bounded physical body, but only of a bodily relation to the totality of human existence; the body as a physical phenomenon may only be referred to with respect to the individual body parts, such as organs, bones and bodily fluids. The term that comes closest to a Western notion of body is a reference to the way that the body acts in terms of body functions, movement and motility (Telban 1998: 62; see also the notion of body in Amerindian ontologies according to Viveiros de Castro 2004: 474–475). André Grau found that the Tiwi of Arnhem Land in north Australia do not have a word for the living body as a self-contained entity. The only word the Tiwi have for the body is that of the dead body, because death imposes boundaries on the body: 'Life, on the other hand, expands the body into the world, both natural and social' (Grau 2005: 153). This also means that the body may serve as a reference beyond itself and constitute a totality with the landscape of the Tiwi land. Since their land – like their bodies – does not have a single unifying name, each place and part of the landscape is identified in the course of dances, where the dancer 'emplaces' the land in his or her own flesh (Grau 2005: 158).

I take these ethnographic examples and Manning and Massumi's exploration of autism as clues in the pursuit of the notion of the bodied space, and evidence supporting a need to transgress the notion of the boundary as a barrier. Rather, it may be helpful to understand the spatial or bodily boundary as a moment of passing between states or modes of being. In this sense spatial, social and perceptual passage as immersed in one another. Spatial and ontological movements are thus connected in this way and – more importantly – their separation is unthinkable. Or, as Brian Massumi argues, '... boundaries are not barriers; they are not impermeable. They are more like filters than walls' and 'are set and specified in the act of passage. The crossing actualizes the boundary – rather than the boundary defining something inside by its inability to cross' (1993: 21).

Returning to the fragments and assemblages of dead bodies in the Middle Neolithic passage graves, it may thus be suggested that the formation of experience and identities resides in the interstices that emerge in the transgression of boundaries, both spatial and corporeal. The disintegration of the individually bounded body in death appears to have produced not so much a crisis in the ontology of the person, but rather an open-ended potential for entering and constituting new relations. As stated previously, the burial chamber inside the passage grave is not to be considered a resting place, but probably more a transformative interstice. The potentiality of such an opening is described by Elizabeth Grosz in this way:

> The space of the in-between is the locus for social, cultural, and natural transformations: it is not simply a convenient space for movements and realignments but in fact is the only place – the place around identities, between identities – where becoming, openness to futurity, outstrips the conservational impetus to retain cohesion and unity. (Grosz 2001: 92)

Conclusion

The strict opposition between life and death that is widespread in contemporary Western society does not appear to be a useful model for understanding burial practices in Middle Neolithic Southern Scandinavia. People were entering and re-entering tombs on several occasions, seemingly to manipulate dead bodies in the tombs or to collect or deposit parts of dead bodies or skeletal remains. A number of boundaries are crossed in this context. First, the dead seem not to have been separated from the world of the living, and relegated to a segregated mode of existence, but were recirculated in a new state of being. Second, movement in the passage grave appears to be characterised by a number of boundaries and perceptual restrictions, which in fact seem to act as incitements to transgress limitations, and to make conceptual and experiential connections across the boundaries rather than serving as impenetrable or categorical divisions.

The philosophical discussion of boundaries above suggests that it is possible to approach mortuary spaces in ways that are not confined to the logics of modernity's concern with categorisation and separation in the sense of organising the dead and the living into fixed, binary positions. In the Middle Neolithic passage graves the materiality through which passing issues forth implies a concern with exploration. First and foremost, this seems to have revolved not so much around the dead *or* the living, but around the transition of their relations. In the spatial passage and the ontological passing, the mourners' knowledge and memory of the dead would be challenged, creating potentially new or altered identities of the dead, and new modes of identifying, through the dead, for the living.

As the archaeological evidence is not uniform, not only across regions but also within local areas, mortuary practices seem to have been malleable and marked by contingency, and by the lack of a predefined course in terms of the directionality and speed of passing. So, rather than seeing the burial practices in the passage graves as representing a concrete mortuary tradition or some clichéd form of 'ancestor belief', as is often suggested, the movement through the visually opaque interior of the passage graves and the confrontation with various states of decomposed human remains would be a means of exploring passing as a conceptual and material quality of life and death.

Ultimately, I argue that bodily movement or the movement of bodies – in the sense of transformation – is central to seeing the threshold or boundary as a place or moment of 'presencing' in the context of the mortuary practice. For the living, such movements are about changing postures and modes of movement, and about transforming means of perception during the passage through the monument, including the experience of presence (see also Runia 2006; Bille, Hastrup, and Sørensen 2010: 9–11). For the dead, they are about changing states of integration and fragmentation, and about becoming, through passing, members of new social assemblages.

Acknowledgements

I am grateful for comments on an earlier version of this chapter provided by Anders Emil Rasmussen, and to the other contributors to this volume for their comments on a very early draft of the ideas presented here.

References

Ahlström, T., 2001. Det döda kollektivet. Bioantropologisk analys av skelett-materialet från Rössbergagånggriften. In: P. Persson and K.-G. Sjögren, eds, *Falbygdens gånggrifter. Undersökningar 1985–1998*. Göteborgs: Göteborgs Universitet: 301–362.

Ahlström, T., 2003. Grave or ossuary? Osteological finds from a recently excavated passage tomb in Falbygden, Sweden. In: G. Burenhult and S. Westergaard, eds, *Stones and Bones: Formal Disposal of the Dead in Atlantic Europe*

During the Mesolithic-Neolithic Interface 6000–3000 BC. Archaeological Conference in Honour of the Late Professor Michael J. O'Kelly. Proceedings of the Stones and Bones Conference in Sligo, Ireland, May 1–5, 2002. Oxford, Archaeopress: 253–269.

Andersen, N. H., 1997. *The Sarup Enclosures: The Funnel Beaker Culture of the Sarup Site Including Two Causewayed Camps Compared to the Contemporary Settlements in the Area and Other European Enclosures, Sarup.* Aarhus: Jutland Archaeological Society.

Andersen, N. H., 2009. Sarupområdet på Sydvestfyn i slutningen af 4. årtusinde f. Kr. In: A. Schülke, ed., *Plads og rum i tragtbægerkulturen. Bidrag fra Arbejdsmødet på Nationalmuseet, 22 September 2005.* Copenhagen: Det Kongelige Nordiske Oldskriftselskab: 25–44.

Bender, B., 1999. Subverting the Western Gaze: Mapping Alternative Worlds. In: P. J. Ucko and R. Layton, eds, *The Archaeology and Anthropology of Landscape.* New York: Routledge: 31–45.

Bille, M., 2013. Dealing with dead saints. In: D. R. Christensen and R. Willerslev, eds, *Taming Time, Timing Death: Social Technologies and Ritual.* Farnham: Ashgate: 137–155.

Bille, M., Hastrup, F. and Sørensen, T. F., 2010. Introduction: An Anthropology of Absence. In: M. Bille, F. Hastrup and T. F. Sørensen, eds, *An Anthropology of Absence: Materializations of Transcendence and Loss.* New York: Springer: 3–22.

Bille, M. and Sørensen, T. F. (forthcoming). Into the Fog of Architecture. In: M. Bille and T. F. Sørensen, eds, *Elements of Architecture: Assembling Archaeology, Atmosphere and the Performance of Building Space.* London: Routledge.

Bloch, M., 1982. Death, Women and Power. In: M. Bloch and J. Parry, eds, *Death and the Regeneration of Life.* Cambridge: Cambridge University Press: 211–230.

Bloch, M. and Parry, J. eds, 1982. *Death and the Regeneration of Life.* Cambridge: Cambridge University Press.

Bradley, R., 1998. *The Significance of Monuments: On the Shaping of Human Experience in Neolithic and Bronze Age Europe.* London: Routledge.

Casey, E. S., 2001. Between Geography and Philosophy: What Does It Mean to Be in the Place-World? *Annals of the Association of American Geographers,* 91(4): 683–693.

Chesson, M. S., 2001. Social Memory, Identity and Death: Ethnographic and Archaeological Perspectives on Mortuary Rituals. In: M. S. Chesson, ed., *Archaeological Publications of the American Anthropological Association.* Arlington, VA: American Anthropological Association: 12–26.

Clausen, C., Einicke, O. and Kjærgaard, P., 2008. The Orientation of Danish Passage Graves. *Acta Archaeologica,* 79(1): 216–229.

Damm, C. B., 1991. Burying the Past: An Example of Social Transformation in the Danish Neolithic. In: P. Garwood, D. Jennings, R. Skeates and J. Toms, eds,

Sacred and Profane: Proceedings of a Conference on Archaeology, Ritual and Religion. Oxford: Oxford University Committee: 43–49.

Dehn, T. and Hansen, S. I., 2002. Megalithic Architecture in Scandinavia. In: R. Joussaume, L. Laporte and C. Scarre, eds, *Origine et Développement du Mégalithisme de L'ouest de L'Europe. Actes du Colloque International, 26–30 Octobre 2002, Bougon, France.* Bougon, Musée des Tumulus de Bougon (Deus-Sèvres): 39–61.

Dehn, T. and Hansen, S. I., 2006. Birch bark in Danish Passage Graves. *Journal of Danish Archaeology*, 14: 23–44.

Dehn, T. and Hansen, S. I., 2007. Examples of megalithic technology and architecture in Denmark. In: J. H. F. Bloemers, ed., *Tussen D26 en P14: Jan Albert Bakker 65 jaar.* Amsterdam, Amsterdam Archeologische Centrum: 17–32.

Dehn, T., Hansen, S. I. and Westphal, J., 2004. Jættestuen Birkehøj. Restaurering af en 5.000 år gammel storstensgrav. *Nationalmuseets Arbejdsmark*, 2004: 153–174.

Deleuze, G. and Guattari, P. F., 1987. *A Thousand Plateaus: Capitalism and Schizophrenia.* London: Continuum Books.

Fowler, C., 2004. *The Archaeology of Personhood: An Anthropological Approach.* London: Routledge.

Gell, A., 1998. *Art and Agency: An Anthropological Theory.* Oxford: Oxford University Press.

Grau, A., 2005. When the Landscape becomes Flesh: An Investigation into Body Boundaries with Special Reference to Tiwi Dance and Western Classical Ballet. *Body & Society*, 11(4): 141–163.

Grosz, E., 2001. *Architecture from the Outside: Essays on Virtual and Real Space.* Cambridge, MA: MIT Press.

Hallam, E. and Hockey, J., 2001. *Death, Memory and Material Culture.* Oxford: Berg.

Harper, S., 2010. The social agency of dead bodies. *Mortality*, 15(4): 308–322.

Heidegger, M., 1971. Building dwelling thinking. In: A. Hofstadter, ed., *Poetry, Language, Thought.* New York: Harper & Row: 145–161.

Hertz, R. [1907] 1960. *Death and the Right Hand.* London: Cohen & West.

Hirsch, E., 1995. Landscape: Between Place and Space. In: E. Hirsch and M. E. O'Hanlon, eds, *The Anthropology of Landscape: Perspectives on Place And Space.* Oxford: Clarendon Press: 1–30.

Holten, L., 2000. Death, Danger, Destruction and Unintended Megaliths: An Essay on Human Classification and its Material and Social Consequences in the Neolithic of South Scandinavia. In: A. Ritchie, ed., *Neolithic Orkney in its European Context.* Cambridge: McDonald Institute Monographs: 287–297.

James, W., 1884. What is an Emotion? *Mind*, 9(34): 188–205.

Julier, G., 2009. Value, Relationality and Unfinished Objects: Guy Julier Interview with Scott Lash and Celia Lury. *Design and Culture*, 1(1): 93–104.

Kaul, F., 1992. Ritualer med menneskeknogler i yngre stenalder. *Kuml*, 1991/92: 7–53.

Kuijt, I., 2008. The Regeneration of Life: Neolithic Structures of Symbolic Remembering and Forgetting. *Current Anthropology*, 49(2): 171–197.

Kuijt, I., Quinn, C. and Cooney, G. eds, 2014. *Transformation by Fire: The Archaeology of Cremation in Cultural Context*. Tucson: University of Arizona Press.

Larsson, L. and Brink, K., 2013. Lost and Found: Houses in the Neolithic of Southern Scandinavia. In: D. Hofmann and J. Smyth, eds, *Tracking the Neolithic House in Europe*. New York: Springer: 329–348.

Larsson, Å. M., 2003. Secondary Burial Practices in the Middle Neolithic: Causes and Consequences. *Current Swedish Archaeology*, 11: 153–170.

Larsson, Å. M., 2009a. *Breaking and Making Bodies and Pots: Material and Ritual Practices in Sweden in the Third Millennium BC*. Uppsala: Uppsala University.

Larsson, Å. M., 2009b. Organized Chaos. Defleshing, Cremation and Dispersal of the Dead in Pitted Ware Culture. In: I.-M. Back Danielsson, I. Gustin, A. Larsson, N. Myrberg and S. Thedéen, eds, *Döda personers sällskap: gravmaterialens identiteter och kulturella uttryck*. Stockholm: Stockholm University: 109–130.

Leenhardt, M. [1948] 1979. *Do Kamo: Person and Myth in a Melanesian World*. Chicago: Chicago University Press.

Lefebvre, H. [1992] 2004. *Rhythmanalysis: Space, Time, and Everyday Life*. London: Continuum.

Madsen, T., 2009. Aalstrup – en boplads og systemgravsanlæg ved Horsens Fjord. In: A. Schülke, ed., *Plads og rum i tragtbægerkulturen. Bidrag fra Arbejdsmødet på Nationalmuseet, 22 September 2005*. Copenhagen, Det Kongelige Nordiske Oldskriftselskab: 105–138.

Manning, E. and Massumi, B., 2014. *Thought in the Act: Passages in the Ecology of Experience*. Minneapolis: Minnesota University Press.

Massumi, B., 1993. Everywhere You Want to Be: Introduction to Fear. In: B. Massumi, ed., *The Politics of Everyday Fear*. Minneapolis: University of Minnesota Press: 3–37.

Massumi, B., 2002. *Parables for the Virtual: Movement, Affect, Sensation*. London: Duke University Press.

Merleau-Ponty, M., 1964. *The Primacy of Perception and Other Essays on Phenomenological Psychology, the Philosophy of Art, History, and Politics*. Evanston, IL: Northwestern University Press.

Merleau-Ponty, M. [1962] 2002. *Phenomenology of Perception*. London: Routledge.

Metcalf, P. and Huntingdon, R., 1991. *Celebrations of Death: The Anthropology of Mortuary Ritual*. Cambridge: Cambridge University Press.

Midgley, M. S., 1992. *TRB Culture. The First Farmers of the North European Plain*. Edinburgh: Edinburgh University Press.

Nielsen, P. O., 1999. Limensgård and Grødbygård. Settlements with house remains from the Early, Middle and Late Neolithic on Bornholm. In: C. Fabech and J. Ringtved, eds, *Settlement and Landscape: Proceedings of a Conference in Århus, Denmark, May 4–7 1998*. Aarhus, Aarhus University Press: 149–165.

Nordman, C. A., 1917. Studier över gånggriftkulturen i Danmark. *Aarbøger for Nordisk Oldkyndighed og Historie*, 1917: 269–332.

Nordman, C. A., 1918. *Jættestuer i Danmark. Nya Fund. Nordiske Fortidsminder.* Copenhagen: Munksgaard.

Persson, P. and Sjögren, K.-G., eds, 2001. *Falbygdens gånggrifter. Undersökningar 1985–1998.* Göteborg: Göteborgs Universitet.

Poyil, M., 2009. Farewell Ritual and Transmigrating Souls: Secondary Funeral of the Attappadi Kurumbas. *Anthropologist*, 11(1): 31–38.

Quinn, C. and Kuijt, I., 2013. Biography of the Neolithic Body: Tracing Pathways to Cist II, Mound of the Hostages, Tara, Ireland. In: M. O'Sullivan, ed., *Tara – From the Past to the Future.* Bray, Co. Wicklow, Wordswell and UCD School of Archaeology: 130–143.

Rebay-Salisbury, K., Sørensen, M. L. S. and Hughes, J., eds, 2010. *Body Parts and Wholes: Changing Relations and Meanings.* Oxford: Oxbow.

Richards, M. P., Price, T. D. and Koch, E., 2003. Mesolithic and Neolithic Subsistence in Denmark: New Stable Isotope Data. *Current Anthropology*, 44(2): 288–295.

Rosenberg, G., 1929. Nye jættestuefund. *Aarbøger for nordisk Oldkyndighed og Historie*: 189–262.

Runia, E., 2006. Presence. *History and Theory*, 45(February): 1–29.

Schuldt, E., 1972. *Die mecklenburgischen Megalithgräber. Untersuchungen zu ihrer Architektur und Funktion.* Berlin: Deutscher Verlag der Wissenschaften.

Shanks, M. and Tilley, C., 1982. Ideology, Symbolic Power and Ritual Communication: A Reinterpretation of Neolithic Mortuary Practices. In: I. Hodder, ed., *Symbolic and Structural Archaeology.* Cambridge: Cambridge University Press: 129–154.

Sheets-Johnstone, M., 2011. *The Primacy of Movement*, expanded second edition. Philadelphia, PA: John Benjamins Publishing Company.

Sjögren, K.-G., 2010. Anonymous Ancestors? The Tilley/Shanks hypothesis revisited. In: D. Calado, M. Baldia and M. Boulanger, eds, *Monumental Questions: Prehistoric Megaliths, Mounds, and Enclosures.* Oxford: Archaeopress: 111–118.

Sjögren, K.-G., 2015. Mortuary Practices, Bodies and Persons in Northern Europe. In: C. Fowler, J. Harding and D. Hofmann, eds, *The Oxford Handbook of Neolithic Europe.* Oxford: Oxford University Press: 1005–1022.

Skaarup, J., 1985. *Yngre stenalder på øerne syd for Fyn.* Rudkøbing: Langelands Museum.

Spinoza, B., 1996. *Ethics.* London: Penguin.

Strathern, M., 1988. *The Gender of the Gift.* Berkeley: University of California Press.

Sørensen, T. F., 2009. The Presence of the Dead: Cemeteries, cremation and the staging of non-place. *Journal of Social Archaeology*, 9(1): 110–135.

Sørensen, T. F., 2010. An Archaeology of Movement: Materiality, affects and cemeteries in prehistoric and contemporary Odsherred, Denmark. Unpublished doctoral thesis, Aarhus University.

Sørensen, T. F., 2014. Re/turn: Cremation, movement and re-collection in the Early Bronze Age of Denmark. In: I. Kuijt, C. Quinn and G. Cooney, eds, *Transformation by Fire: The Archaeology of Cremation in Cultural Context*. Tucson: University of Arizona Press: 168–188.

Sørensen, T. F., 2015a. More Than a Feeling: Towards an archaeology of atmosphere. *Emotion, Space and Society*, 15: 64–73.

Sørensen, T. F., 2015b. In Praise of Vagueness: Uncertainty, ambiguity and archaeological methodology. *Journal of Archaeological Method and Theory.*

Tarlow, S., 2002. The Aesthetic Corpse in Nineteenth Century Britain. In: Y. Hamilakis, M. Pluciennik and S. Tarlow, eds, *Thinking Through the Body: Archaeologies of Corporeality*. London: Kluwer Academic: 85–97.

Telban, B., 1998. Body, Being and Identity in Ambonwari, Papua New Guinea. In: V. Keck, ed., *Common Words and Single Lives: Constituting Knowledge in Pacific Societies*. Oxford: Berg: 55–70.

Thomas, J., 1993. The politics of vision and the archaeologies of landscape. In: B. Bender, ed., *Landscape: Politics and Perspectives*. Oxford: Berg: 19–48.

Tilley, C., 1991. Constructing a ritual landscape. In: K. Jennbert, L. Larsson, R. Petre and B. Wyszomirska-Werbart, eds, *Regions and Reflections (in Honour of Marta Strömberg)*. Lund: Almquist & Wiksell International: 67–79.

Tilley, C., 1996. *An Ethnography of the Neolithic: Early Prehistoric Societies in Southern Scandinavia*. Cambridge: Cambridge University Press.

Viveiros de Castro, E., 2004. Exchanging Perspectives: The Transformation of Objects into Subjects in Amerindian Ontologies. *Common Knowledge*, 10(3): 463–484.

Wagner, R., 1991. The Fractal Person. In: M. Godelier and M. Strathern, eds, *Big Men and Great Men: Personifications of power in Melanesia*. Cambridge: Cambridge University Press: 159–173.

Willerslev, R., 2007. *Soul Hunters: Hunting, Animism and Personhood among the Siberian Yukaghirs*. Berkeley: University of California Press.

Willerslev, R., 2009. The Optimal Sacrifice: A Study of Voluntary Death among the Siberian Chukchi. *American Ethnologist*, 36(4): 693–704.

Williams, H., 2004. Death Warmed Up: The Agency of Bodies and Bones in Early Anglo-Saxon Cremation Rites. *Journal of Material Culture*, 9(3): 263–291.

Chapter 4

Still in the Picture:
Photographs at Graves and Social Time

Anne Kjærsgaard and Eric Venbrux

At the End of Our Days?

Ultrasound images placed at a grave of a deceased future grandfather (see Figure 4.1a), together with his photograph, raise the question of what relation between death and time they entail.

The pictures link the unborn child with the passed away man. Both will undergo a change of social status, but they cannot be met in person yet or anymore, respectively. Absent is also the pregnant woman, who visited the grave, informing the ones who pass it about her impending motherhood. Her father has already

Figure 4.1   **a) Ultrasound images placed at a grave with a photograph of the (deceased) grandfather-to-be, 2012; b) photograph of the new-born child placed at the same grave five months later, Nijmegen region, the Netherlands, 2013**

Source: Photos by Nicole Schubert and Eric Venbrux.

passed from this world and her child has yet to enter it. The images of the foetus point to a childbirth in the near future of which the dead man apparently should not be unaware. When we visited the grave five months later, the ultrasound images had been replaced by a photo of a new-born child (Figure 4.1b). The dead man now had a granddaughter. At another grave in the same cemetery near Nijmegen, the Netherlands, there was, similarly, a photograph of a baby substituted for a framed ultrasound image.

In Denmark, too, we came across examples of the dead being kept posted about high points in the life of the family. After her wedding, for instance, a bride placed her bridal bouquet on the grave of her deceased father. We were told it was customary when there was a deceased parent, especially a dead father, who should have walked his daughter down the aisle. The woman's sister visited the grave with her baby daughter later on, photographing the child sitting on her grandfather's grave (photographs in the possession of the authors). She sent the photo to the first-mentioned sister living elsewhere to assure her that their father's grave was being looked after well. Like the photograph of the bridal bouquet on the grave it attests to the dead man's inclusion in the ongoing life of the family. This ongoing life beyond the day of death of the *pater familias* also comes to the fore in a Danish example we will discuss further below: the celebration of the man's birthday with his family gathered around the grave; this event too was photographed (Figure 4.2). The posthumous birthday party suggests that his days did not end on the day that he died.

This does not sit well with the idea – derived from Protestant theological discourse – that cemetery visits are mainly to honour the *memory* of the dead. Graves attesting to the celebration of birthdays can also be found in other seemingly secularized countries, such as Switzerland and The Netherlands. And as the Dutch case of the ultrasound images clearly shows, the pictures do not necessarily point to the past but can also point towards the future. Do photographs in connection with the grave enable people to 'transcend the reality of biological death'? (Astuti 2007: 227).

'Photography is the inventory of mortality', according to Sontag ([1977] 1990: 70). The different images made over time demonstrate that we inevitably grow older – and eventually die, an irreversible passage of time. Certainly, the close relationship between photography and mortality has often invited attention or scrutiny (cf. Barthes 1981; Metz 1985; Venbrux and Jones 2002; Grimes and Venbrux 2010): 'In a sense, photography kills what it captures in rendering it inanimate and devoid of life' (Shaw 2009: 257). Conversely, photographs fixed onto a headstone might tell us that the person depicted is dead, but for the survivors it may simultaneously keep that person alive.

'Photography's peculiar temporal characteristics, in particular its ability to bring past and present together in one visual experience', meant that at the time of its emergence it was often associated with necromancy or communication with the dead (Batchen 1999: 92). The belief that a photograph – not unlike a reflection in a mirror, which is covered after a death – could capture one's soul dates back

Graven den 8/11.08

Nogle af dine børn, svigerbørn og barnebarn siger tillykke til dig

Figure 4.2   Photograph of a posthumous birthday celebration at a grave uploaded with a text on a memorial website, Denmark, 2008

Source: Screenshot by Anne Kjærsgaard. Reproduced with permission.

to the early days of photography. This belief vanished as photography became more common and familiar. 'Nevertheless, the underlying assumption that the photograph stands in a direct causal and mimetic relationship with its referent has continued to condition the ways photographs are viewed and understood' (Rojas 2009: 208). Furthermore, there might be a striking subjective element in the picture that evokes the known person's presence, as Barthes (1981) reports with regard to a childhood photo of his recently deceased mother. Mitchell (2005: 10–11) speaks of a 'double consciousness' with regard to photographs. 'Everyone knows that a photograph of their mother is not alive, but they will still be reluctant to deface or destroy it. No modern, rational, secular person thinks that pictures are to be treated like persons, but we always seem to be willing to make exceptions for special cases' (ibid.: 31). Especially when the persons in question have passed away, photographs can bring them near (Walton 1984: 251–253). This feeling might be even more heightened with photos at graves.

Graves are contact points between the living and the dead (Wartmann 1986). In their research in London cemeteries Francis, Kellaher and Neophytou found that grave visits attest to a 'social interdependency across time and death' (2000: 46). Graves happen to be loci for exchange between the living and the dead (Francis, Kellaher and Neophytou 2005: 144), indicating that a death does not annihilate the bond. 'The current use of photographs at the site of graves embeds them within an unfolding set of material relations and exchanges which sustain the dead as socially living persons', according to Hallam and Hockey (2001: 152). But what do these photographs contribute to the process of transcending physical death? And what kind of time characterises this dealing with the dead?

Writing on death and time, Humphreys remarks that a 'study of the use of photographs by mourners is badly needed' (1981: 272; but see Riches and Dawson 1998). While mortality puts the time in the life of an individual in perspective (May 2009), those who stay behind after a death have a need to not be constrained by the limits of the deceased's lifespan. They act, we argue, from within a different time frame. In our view, photographs at graves can be best perceived in terms of social time, such as time related to the life of the family rather than the individual. Following Bourdieu ([1965] 1990: Chapter 2), photography – being widely introduced in the decade before the Great War – obtained the important function and meaning of 'an index and instrument of the integration' of the family or social group. We will draw on Bourdieu in our discussion, and will show that his argument can be extended to photographs in relation to graves.

In this chapter we focus on the role of this technology in blurring the boundary between the living and the dead. Placing photos at graves as well as the act of photographing grave visits are part and parcel of a wider set of practices, including the widespread one of talking to the dead (Schmied 2002; Bachelor 2004: 110–111; Francis, Kellehar and Neophytou 2005; Stringer 2008a, b), in which the living consider themselves to be in touch with the dead and by which they continue their relationship and communication with the dead. As Walter (2009: 219) notes, 'communications with the dead can be seen as, in the broadest sense, religious experiences'. Stringer (2008a, b) takes a similar view. When people do not consider physical death as the end, we may safely assume that we are dealing with religiosity. We therefore regard the practices with photographs at graves as telling us about the limits of secularization.

Photos on Graves

Pictorial representations of the dead have been applied in memorial settings long before the invention of photography; and the history of painted and sculpted portraits is deeply connected with death (see Belting 1990). 'There is a direct relation between the portrait and death', according to Ariès ([1973] 1983: 261). Ariès notes that when, early in the nineteenth century, the grave became 'a place for family pilgrimage', sculptures displaying family unity could be seen at the resting places of the more wealthy citizens. From the mid nineteenth century onwards, however, photographs, depicting the deceased, on the mass-produced headstones of the middle classes, expressed the same idea 'of a family presence' (Ariès 1985: 260).

The invention of the technology of photography, in 1839, thus led in due time to an availability of portraits that was no longer restricted to the happy few. Professional photographers became memory-makers *par excellence*, taking pictures of the living as well as the dead to fulfil this purpose. Post-mortem photos comprised an important part of the photographers' business from very early on; the same goes for photographic portraits that could end up at gravestones and depictions of gravesites (Spira 1981; Ruby 1995; Linkman 2011; Kragh 2003: 124–126).

Already, from the 1840s onwards, photographs were placed on gravestones in the USA; in Europe this occurred at least from the 1860s (Ruby 1995: 143; Linkman 2011: 119). The challenge was to find a way to fix photos in a waterproof and durable way to the stone. Initially glass frames were used to solve the problem (the first American patent dates from 1851, cf. Matturri 1993: 23), but soon photoceramic technology was developed (in 1855 in France, cf. Christen 2010: 117), allowing photographs to be baked onto porcelain or enamel. While photoceramics is still widely employed, new techniques, such as laser etching, to reproduce photos directly onto the headstone, also came into use in the late twentieth century (Ruby 1995: 142ff; Linkman 2011: 120–121; Reynolds 2012: 42–43).

Notwithstanding the techniques to make photos more durable and less fragile than ever, more and more people are placing unprotected or barely protected photographic prints on graves. These involve low costs and can easily be reproduced and replaced. Whereas previously formal portraits made by professional photographers were fixed upon the headstone, people now increasingly place informal snapshots taken by themselves at the grave, which reflects how this type of photography has come to dominate family collections (Linkman 2011: 121–122) and the grave sites are conceived of as an increasingly personalised space (Hallam and Hockey 2001: 147; Worpole 2003: 93).

The presence of photographs on gravestones varies greatly over space and time. In some places there are quite a few, in other places they are almost absent. In the cemetery of Westmalle, Belgium, 20 per cent of the headstones dating from the 1970s and 1980s had a photograph; in the 1990s this increased to 25 per cent of the graves, according to Bleyen, which was still relatively less than in other places in Flanders and also remarkably less than in the Westmalle columbarium where a photograph was counted in 50 per cent of the instances (Bleyen 2005: 177). The same would probably hold true in the Netherlands; in a place like Volendam a photographic portrait of the deceased is fixed to almost all headstones in the Catholic cemetery, and in Leur, near Wijchen, in the previously predominantly Catholic South of the Netherlands, quite a few Protestant graves also have a photo attached to the headstone.

In Lutheran Denmark such photos are rare. A stronger identification between the dead person and the headstone might take place instead, because in contrast to many other places it is not the area where the body lies that is marked and embellished, but the gravestone. Photos are, however, sometimes seen on gravestones in Denmark too, particularly in Zealand and in urban cemeteries (cf. Haakonsen 2011; Helweg 2010). First they appeared on graves of migrants. But during the last 10 to 15 years they can also be seen on the gravestones of ethnic Danes, albeit it is still an uncommon practice. Haakonsen (2011), for example, counted a mere 15 gravestones with photos in two cemeteries in Copenhagen in the autumn of 2009. But these are not without earlier antecedents. Figure 4.3a, for example, shows a photographic portrait on a gravestone in Tømmerby churchyard of a man who died in 1911. But such early examples of photographs on gravestones are rare.

In general, the practice is more widely spread in – culturally speaking – Catholic regions than in Protestant ones (cf. Worpole 2003: 113). Schmied (2002: 148) relates it to the Protestant aversion to imagery and preference for 'the Word'. In parts of confessional split Germany photographs on gravestones are common, in other parts they are not or are even forbidden (albeit sometimes condoned). In 1995 the court ruled that survivors were not allowed to put a photo of their loved one on a gravestone, in an Evangelical cemetery in Lüneburg, because it was considered inappropriate (Schmied 2002: 148). This stands in sharp contrast to the popularity of having photographs on headstones in non-Protestant Southern and Eastern Europe (Linkman 2011: 116).

In the predominantly Catholic, Swiss Canton of Ticino they are also a common sight. Visiting cemeteries there, Starck observes that there are so many photographs that inevitably the looks of the living and the dead intersect. Not only do they add something personal to the tombs, but it is also much easier to have silent dialogues with faces rather than with writings on bare stones (Starck 2013: 5). A photo of the deceased on a gravestone, as Starck points out, gives the dead person a face.

Sooner or later the memory of what a dead person's face looked like might be lost unless we resort to photographs. We tend to read a lot from faces (Jeggle 1986), but due to the conventions of social interaction it is very hard for us to remember a face in full, even of someone we know intimately, as Elkins (1997: Chapter 5) reminds us. Characteristic details come to mind, often in train with emotions, rather than the face as a whole, because in order to avoid intrusive staring we fail to see it as such. Yet, 'a face is a place where looking and feeling are very closely allied' (ibid.: 181). Hence, depending on the context, photographic portraits can evoke the feeling of the presence of a deceased relative or partner. Barthes (1981) attributes this to subjective elements. And it is precisely the characteristic details, which are hard to pinpoint, that allow us to recognise others over time. 'The force of a photograph is that it keeps open to scrutiny instants which the normal flow of time immediately replaces', Sontag notes ([1977] 1990: 111). Besides the all-too-obvious transience, we contend that the bereaved see in the photographic portraits of their loved ones emotionally touching signs of permanence. Or, as Bourdieu puts it, 'while seeming to evoke the past, photography exorcizes it by recalling it

Figure 4.3   a) Photographic portrait attached to a headstone in Tømmerby churchyard, western Jutland, Denmark; b) Framed hairwork with photographic portrait, dating from 1943 (kept at the Limburgs Museum, Venlo, the Netherlands)

Source: a) Courtesy of Klaus Bertelsen; b) Photo by Eric Venbrux.

as such' ([1965] 1990: 31). To our mind, the subjective, characteristic details of recognition are lasting.

What is special about photography, Walton (1984: 251) argues, is that 'it gave us a new way of seeing', a manner of looking that negates the passage of time: 'We see long deceased ancestors when we look at dusty snapshots of them' (Walton 1984: 251). For Walton, 'Photographs are *transparent*. We see the world *through* them' (ibid.). Or as Barthes puts it, 'Whatever it grants to vision and whatever its matter, a photograph is always invisible, it is not what we see' (1981: 6). Walton claims that '… we *see*, quite literally, our dead relatives themselves when we look at photographs of them' (Walton 1984: 252). This seeing (and it can be distorted, like seeing with the real eye or in a mirror) has to be distinguished from seeing the object of the photograph. The seeing through photographs is 'a way to find out about the world'; in that sense what matters is that 'we can *see* our loved ones again' (ibid.: 253). Walton's point is that due to the photographs' transparency – our seeing via photographs – we are in *perceptual* contact with them. To many this photographic realism makes sense.

The manner in which photographs of the dead are perceived and experienced is of course also influenced by religious tradition. Matturri (1993: 20–27) discusses the photographs of the deceased on gravestones in Italian-American cemeteries up until the 1940s. In this Roman Catholic context the survivors considered them 'windows' through which they could communicate with the dead. 'Like religious images and relics, they served to establish a cultural space in which the earthly and spiritual realms could intersect'; the photographs thus helped to maintain 'a continued relationship between the living and the dead' (Matturri 1993: 27).

The Greek Orthodox, too, make use of photographic portraits of the dead. Sometimes mention of the practices with photographs is made in ethnographic reports. Danforth (1982: 10, 44–45) describes how in the mid 1970s women in rural Greece used to take a photograph of the deceased from the house of mourning to the grave on the eve of the fortieth day after the death of the person in question. Together with a lamp it was placed in a box at the newly made grave monument. The time taken for the territorial passage of the photograph coincides with the 40 days that lapsed between Christ's resurrection and ascension. For between three and five years the women would visit the graves of their dead on a daily basis. They looked at the photographs placed at the graves, wailed and sang laments (1982: 11–12, 16). Finally, the bones were exhumed and, together with the photograph, placed in the ossuary (Danforth 1982: 11, 20, 22). Seremetakis (1991: 108–111) relates how in the 1980s a photograph and a box with the bones of the son were placed next to the corpse of a woman, laid in state, in a house of mourning in Inner Mani (southern Greece). It indicated that this particular lineage had died out. The photograph, according to Seremetakis, 'expressed the separation of soul from body' (ibid.: 111).

As mentioned, the Protestant attitude to headstone-photographs and placing photographs at graves in general differs greatly from the Catholic and Orthodox stance and practices such as those described above are often anathema to them. After the Reformation, the 'dead were becoming a part of history' (Koslofsky 2002: 30). All that remained was the memory of their lifetime, because the teachings held that on the occasion of death the ties with the dead ought to be broken. Objections to intercessions had already been raised by earlier reformers, according to Goody and Poppi, 'from the Waldensians onwards' (1994: 195). Protestant Christianity 'bans relationships with the dead', whereas 'secularism considers such relationships impossible' (Walter 2013: 13). Although proscriptions are not always in accordance with the actual practices of the adherents (ibid.), in theory, the living can only deal with the memory of the deceased.

The official religion of Lutheranism in Denmark professes that due to the personal relation with God, the survivors cannot do anything for the dead in the other world (Kjærsgaard Markussen 2013). As the recent exhibition *De dødes liv* ('The Dead Live') at the Moesgaard Museum (in Aarhus, Denmark) shows, however, the dead are not entirely absent for some Danes (Høiris, Otto and Rolsted 2014); the intricate links that Danish people maintain with their dead have been further documented by Trap (2013). Just to mention a few examples involving photographs: A woman attached a photographic portrait of her deceased father to her bridal bouquet so that he would still accompany her when she walked down the aisle (ibid.: 86–87). A man had a photographic portrait of his daughter, who died at the age of 24, tattooed on his chest (ibid.: 58–59). And a woman decorated her Christmas tree with a small, framed photographic portrait of her deceased mother (ibid.: 64–65). Others opt for the grave as a place for maintaining 'a living connection with the dead' (*en levende forbindelse til den døde*; Trap 2013: 70). An extension of these practices – with ample use of photography – is performed on memorial websites, such as Mindet.dk (as we will discuss further below).

In a region such as Brittany, France, that used to be predominantly Catholic, the official religion did not completely erase the still widespread common people's view of the afterlife. In this Breton view, as Badone makes clear, the cemetery is 'the locus for the continued existence of the dead' (1989: 156). Rather than being separated, 'the body and soul remain together in the tomb' (ibid.: 132). The deceased is thus seen as '*homo totus* at rest in the tomb' (ibid.: 133). Badone attributes this to the local familiarity with death and the importance of the collective, although changes are underway towards an increased importance of the individual (ibid.: 133–134). This can hardly be a sufficient explanation, however, for in the Portugese region of Minho exists the same familiarity with death and appreciation of the collective, but in fact the people believe in the separation of soul and body (de Pina-Cabral 1986: Chapter 6). It is our belief, however, that generally speaking the bodily remains will somehow remain associated with the living person as a feature of the usually unacknowledged magical thinking in our societies. Plaques with photographs of the deceased can be seen placed on the Breton graves (see the photo in Badone 1989, figure 9 following on p. 130), but unfortunately Badone does not comment on them.

Christen, referring to German-speaking areas, notes that such durable photos – in spite of the subterranean decay of the corpses – visually suggest the continued existence of the persons in question. Moreover, the placement of the photographic portraits of both husband and wife on the couple's joined grave demonstrates that their bond of marriage extends into death (Christen 2010: 120). Social relations continue between the dead, but also between the living and the dead, for the photographs allow the survivors to encounter the familiar faces of their dead whenever they visit the graves. The images make sure that the dead stay in the picture.

The experience of the deceased's presence, however, varies with the type of relationship and changes over time. Bennett and Bennett point out that it also varies in intensity: 'At its weakest this is a feeling that one is somehow being watched; at its strongest it is a full blown sensory experience' (2000:139). Actually, it is quite common that people report seeing, hearing or feeling the presence of close friends or family members who have died (Sanger 2009), especially when it concerns their deceased spouse (Greely 1987; Rees 1971). For parents with stillborn children the 'realness problem' can become particularly acute, according to Layne (2000: 323). The possession of baby things bought for the baby-to-be such as baby blankets, clothes and toys helps to convince them and others of the child's existence and their own parenthood. What is more, ultrasound images are often 'the only things available to testify to the fact that a "real baby" ever existed' (ibid.: 334). Bourdieu stresses that mainly 'social roles' are read in family photographs ([1965] 1990: 24). Photos of a new-born child are swiftly distributed to family and friends, because 'the arrival of the child reinforces the integration of the group' (ibid.: 26). As we have seen, this also applies to family members who are deceased – ultrasound images and subsequently photos of a new-born child were placed on the graves, making them part of the social time of the living.

We also have to take into account 'the materiality of images' (Edwards and Hart 2004) and the qualities of photographs as sensory objects (Barthes 1981; Edwards 2012). Edwards (2012) has recently described them as 'objects of affect' and also draws attention to the matter of 'placing', the role of photographs in assemblages of objects. She argues that 'photographs cannot be understood through visual content alone but through an embodied engagement with an affective object world, which is both constitutive of and constituted through social relations' (ibid.: 221). In relation to this, it is important to note that the way in which a photograph is seen depends on 'where it is inserted' and on the context of its use (Sontag [1977] 1990: 105–106). Furthermore, as Riches and Dawson argue, 'photographs can provide an important prop both as an object of personal internal conversation *with* the deceased and as a vehicle for conversations between surviving relatives and others *about* the deceased' (1998: 124; for a Danish example, see Trap 2013: 102–103). For Sontag, a photograph 'is also a trace, something directly stenciled off the real, like a footprint or a death mask' ([1977] 1990: 154). Photography has something magical about it, she explains. In her view, 'a photograph is not only like its subject' but also 'part of, an extension of that subject; and a potent means of acquiring it, of gaining control over it' (ibid.: 155). It is somewhat akin to a relic. Frazer's laws of contagion and similarity seem to apply to these magical properties (Frazer 1922: 11). One can get in touch with the deceased by means of the photograph due to the lifelike image as well as 'the physical proximity' (Hallam and Hockey 2001: 143) or contact with the portrayed person at the moment it was taken. In this sense, the photograph has the characteristics of a contact relic.

Photographs fixed upon gravestones have a particularly 'relic-like quality' (Matturri 1993: 20). While these photographs themselves can be perceived as remains, the direct association of these 'ghostly shadows' (Sontag [1977] 1990: 9) with the actual bodily remains in the grave increases their efficacy as relics. According to Hallam and Hockey, the durable gravestone – as perceived or experienced – substitutes for the corpse; and the photograph attached to the headstone consolidates the association at the same time as it animates the stone (2001: 146–147). An analogy can be seen with memorial hairworks that include photographs of the deceased (Figure 4.3b). The addition of hair – bodily remains – strengthens their effect. Hairworks with photographs are mostly framed, in a medallion to carry around or in a frame behind glass to hang on the wall. The hair makes us aware of the sensory aspects (Batchen 2004a: 32–35), namely vision, touch and smell that apply likewise to objects such as old photo-prints and albums. Also, gravestones are also often touched; sometimes they are held, kissed and cared for by being wiped off or washed. With regard to the sensory experience there is thus also some resemblance between the hairworks with photographs and the gravestones with photographs of the once living attached. The grave provides another frame and contact point due to the bodily remains it contains, to which photographs have been added.

Whereas in some religious understandings a future *rendezvous* of relatives or marriage partners can be stressed, the practice of 'speaking to photographs' (Francis, Kellaher and Neophytou 2005: 90, 96) of the dead suggests an ongoing presence in whatever form. In the domestic context this presence is sometimes evoked by placing objects associated with the deceased, such as personal belongings, near the framed photographs (Batchen 2004b: 41; Parrott 2009: 136). The presence of the dead, however, appears to be sensed most strongly at the location of the bodily remains. So while talking to the dead can occur almost everywhere, people tend to visit the grave when it concerns a really important matter (see Miller and Parrot 2007: 157). The particular photographic portrait placed at the grave and encountered in recurring visits to the grave becomes emblematic of the deceased. Yet, 'a photograph is only a fragment, and with the passage of time its moorings come unstuck' (Sontag [1977] 1990: 71); it will acquire new meaning in association with the grave.

The very same photograph as the one attached to a gravestone would have often seen a wider distribution, in different circumstances (see Christen 2010). The image would have been used on other occasions and the picture itself may have been taken for a special occasion, such as a wedding. One can find it in a family album, at a house shrine or as a framed portrait in the living room. If cut from a portrait with two or more people, the social life of the photograph continues in its use and distribution on, for instance, a prayer card among Catholics in Switzerland. It might also be advertised with the death notice or distributed to family and friends after the death (see Christen 2010). Finally, it might be attached to a grave or placed in a columbarium, so one can get in touch with the person portrayed again. The media may differ but the image links social occasions at various points in time and gives substance to ties in a web of social relations. The photographs are passed around, passing the person who passed away back into the social realm.

The social life of the photographic images (Pinney 1997) is thus intertwined with the social life of the group. In the words of Bourdieu, such photographs have the function of 'reinforcing the integration of the family group' by 'solemnizing and immortalizing the high points of family life' ([1965] 1990: 19). Typically, photographic portraits attached to headstones show the deceased at his or her best, 'the idealized image' (Sontag [1977] 1990: 85). Moreover, they have often been taken at important occasions in the life of the family, such as rites of passage. With regard to photographs used on headstones, Matturri notes that 'particularly common are photographs taken at weddings, first communions, confirmations and graduations' (1993: 27). All are status passages, celebrated by the family. They mark moments of integration as well as the passage of social time. Leach writes, 'We talk of measuring time, as if time were a concrete thing waiting to be measured; but in fact we create time by creating intervals in social life' (1961: 135). Commonly celebrated rites of passage of family members and other occasions when families gather mark the intervals in family life, and so constitute its social time. This notion of time goes beyond the limited lifespan of the individual member. The family existed before the individual was born and will continue to exist after one's death. Intergenerational exchange at graves (Francis, Kellaher and Neophytou 2005) underscores the notion of ongoing family life. The photograph on the headstone, being 'an almost temporally transparent image' (Matturri 1993: 20), mediates the relationship between the living and the dead. Let us now turn to how photography also brings the dead and the living together.

Integration of the Dead and the Living

While for a long time it was photos of the deceased that were most often seen, we now observe photographs of the living appearing more and more at graves and in columbariums in the Netherlands. They are placed alongside pictures of the dead. Some are laminated or covered with transparent plastic to protect them against the weather. Seemingly, graves and niches with urns are increasingly considered domestic spaces. Furthermore, the dead are increasingly welcomed 'home' by the living, rather than thought to vanish to a distant other world (cf. Heessels 2012). The this-worldly perspective and their reintegration is emphasised by placing photos of the living along with those of the dead. The boundary between the living and the dead has been blurred (cf. Heessels, Poots and Venbrux 2012); the photos of the living are there to comfort the dead. A nice example is the photograph of two grandchildren on a tile placed at a headstone in the cemetery of Someren, the Netherlands. The text on the tile reads: 'Dear grandfather, in this way we are still somewhat with you'.

We encountered another similar example in a cemetery in Nijmegen. On the headstone, which is in the shape of a heart, there is a photograph of a 26-year-old man looking over his shoulder. Below the photo the text reads: 'As often as you see my image/in the name of heaven forget me not'. Next to it is installed a photograph of three children, two daughters and a baby. Although the man died 36 years earlier, a boat-shaped box planted with succulents was placed on the grave to celebrate his birthday. An accompanying card says 'heartfelt congratulations'. It is as if in the understandings of the survivors the man's life somehow continued and, although deceased, he was still amongst them. Bringing the photographs of the living and the dead together at the grave increases the impression of that presence.

Perhaps not so common at graves, the practice is widespread in the interior of people's homes, where portraits of the dead and the living hang jointly on the wall or stand on a mantelpiece or cabinet. Sometimes graves are associated with the home and/or garden (e.g. Venbrux 1991; Hallam and Hockey 2001: 147). In the case of an 'untimely' death the need for the ensemble at the grave might be more pressing, stressing continuing bonds in time that otherwise would have been spent together. And if cremation is a more transient way of bodily disposal, it is understandable that one can encounter more photographic ensembles of the dead and the living at columbariums. The pigeon-holes in the Dutch case are more akin to the home memorials that almost always contain photos of the dead (cf. Wojtkowiak and Venbrux 2010). Across Europe, many graves or places where urns are kept have photographs of the deceased. Sometimes ensembles of photos of dead relatives are created, with flowering plants signalling the visits of the living. These are places where the living can converse with their dead kin. The imaged and imagined co-presence contributes to a sense of belonging, surpassing the boundary between life and death.

As Morgan notes, 'Protestants have generally avoided free-standing imagery' (1999: 236). Therefore, one would expect relatively less photographs at graves in areas that are or used to be predominantly Protestant: Not only photos of the dead but also those of the living considered to be in bad taste. For example, Hauser reports that in the Swiss city of Zurich photos of the bereaved were no longer allowed on gravestones because, as the responsible officer put it, 'we want a tomb culture, not a photo album at the cemetery' (1994: 283). Haakonsen (2011: 40) refers to a case in Denmark in which the friends of a deceased girl brought photographs to the grave, but her parents did not approve of it. As we have seen, photographs at graves are rare in Lutheran Denmark. However, at the memorial web site Mindet.dk, run by the newspaper *Kristeligt Dagblad* (Christensen and Sandvik 2013: 101), the bereaved upload many photos of graves and grave visits. These pictures are integrated with text and, therefore, probably less prone to offending religious sensibilities (cf. Morgan 1999: 236).

A montage of images of the deceased in photographs of their living kin offers another way of placing them together, against the odds of time. Their individual lifetime has passed, but the dead are presented as still amongst the living. The fact of their demise is thus erased in family photographs taken at some point after their passing away. Figure 4.4 shows a portrait of a Danish family from northern Jutland in which an older photographic image of a dead child has been pasted in. In the background of another, from the album of the same family, photographic portraits of relatives, dead and alive, are displayed on the wall. Assembling kin by means of placing photographic portraits together or employing photo-editing technology defies spatiotemporal separation.

Christen (2010: 158–161) relates how a Swiss family that went to a photo studio with a stand-in two decades after a family member, since deceased, had had a portrait made in the very same studio. The face of the latter was retouched on the substitute person in the newly made family portrait with the parents, two brothers and three sisters (ibid.: 159, 161, figures 96 and 97). The manipulated portrayals help in 'imagining the intangible' (Whincup 2004). The practice might seem odd but, historically speaking, family portraits had their origin in painted portraits of both the living and dead members (Ariès [1972] 1983: 257). Historical epitaph

**Figure 4.4   Family photograph, including the image of a dead child,
                 northern Jutland, Denmark, 1930s**

Source: Courtesy of Niels Peter Vistisen.

paintings of notables and their families that are still on display in churches in
Denmark portray the living as well as the dead (cf. Kragh 2003: 122; Jørgensen
1987: 61).

Montage and assemblage also points to another form of bringing the dead
and the living together by means of photography, namely photos made of
representations of non-existent others and living persons. Gibson (2004: 293–296)
tells how she showed her dying father an ultrasound image to inform him about the
future grandchild, Joshua, who he would never see in real life, an event of which
a photo was taken. She notes, 'Joshua and Dad have only met each other through
a photograph. My father is with Joshua for the first and last time, in the only
way that is possible. They were in the same photograph at completely different
stages in life, and yet existentially they were close to each other' (ibid.: 296).
Photography here provides the technology of 'meeting' like it probably did for
those who placed ultrasound images at Dutch graves (Figure 4.1). However, in
Gibson's case we know that a photo was taken of the event, which is also used in
another way to keep the absent person socially alive. What Gibson actually did
was to take a family photograph, like she would have done of grandfather and
grandchild together when the child had been born. In this way the very act of

making the photo constructs the family for the future as consisting of both those absent and those present.

The photograph would most likely end up in the family album. According to Bourdieu, 'there is nothing more decent, reassuring and edifying than a family album' ([1965] 1990: 31). Family photographs obtain a 'sacred character' because they evidence the continuing history of the family and thereby 'consecrate its social identity, always inseparable from permanence over time' (ibid.: 31). In other words, the photographs assembled in the album enable the family to draw 'confirmation of its present unity from its past' (ibid.). Both dead and living members are commonly represented in the family album. 'Through photographs, each family constructs a portrait-chronicle of itself – a portable kit of images that bears witness to its connectedness', says Sontag ([1977] 1990: 8). She continues by saying, however, that right when photography became 'a family rite' in Europe and America the extended family was losing ground to the new phenomenon of the nuclear family. Nevertheless, the photograph album was to convey an image of the extended family, albeit no longer rooted in reality (ibid.: 8–9). The inclusion of photographs of more distant and absent relatives along with the dead upheld the idea of a larger family unity.

Like Gibson (2004), Anne Kjærsgaard, one of the authors of this chapter, has also looked at her family's photographs. She went through the photograph albums made by her mother in Denmark. She found an amazing number of family photos that confirmed Bourdieu's understanding of them as an index of the integration of the family ([1965] 1990: Chapter 2). The photographs chronicled the history of the family, not just the nuclear family but also the moments of gathering with other relatives and friends over time. In the family album, as Bourdieu puts it, 'the common past, or, perhaps, the highest common denominator of the past, has all the clarity of a faithfully visited grave' (ibid.: 31). Actually, although Bourdieu does not refer to photographs of the dead, there were photos of people now deceased, grandparents' funerals, their fresh graves covered with flowers, family reunions at the grave and of grave visits that took place on memorable days, such as birthdays, Christmas and Mother's Day.

Figure 4.5a shows one of these visits, picturing Anne Kjærsgaard, her siblings, mother and grandfather, together with her (dead) grandmother who is represented by the gravestone. The visit was made on the anniversary of the grandmother's (*mormor*, mother's mother) death. Although most of the photographs in the albums were taken by Kjærsgaard's mother, her father (who is clearly without practice) took this one at the request of her mother, who is the one who generally takes responsibility for maintaining the relations with the dead (and more particularly in this case because it concerns her own mother). So on her initiative, a photograph was also taken years later at the same grave on the day of the deceased's birthday, but now it included a member of another generation, the dead woman's great-grandson. Figure 4.5b shows Kjærsgaard with her mother and son at the grave, where Kjærsgaard likewise was photographed as a child. Her grandfather, who had died in the meantime, is also made present by the gravestone that is now inscribed

Figure 4.5   a) Photograph of three generations visiting the grave of a
deceased wife/mother/grandmother, 1986; b) Photograph of
the same family making a three-generation visit at the grave
one generation later, 2011, both in northern Jutland, Denmark
Source: Photos by Ole Kjærsgaard.

with the names of both grandparents. The family album contains photographs of
every birthday celebration within the family, and no difference is made between
those of the living and the dead. The practices of celebrating a dead person's
birthday, taking photographs of descendants at the grave and placing them in the

album amongst other family photographs blur the boundary between the living and the dead. It conveys the message that the dead are still members of the family, regardless of their demise. They live on as social persons.

Digital photography, according to Ennis, has resulted in vernacular post-mortem photographs being kept private and secret, restricted to intimates (2007: 18–19). It could therefore be expected that the family photos at the grave would become more restricted than is already the case. Digital and digitalized photographs, however, can also easily be distributed and graveside photographs do appear on memorial websites. In contrast to the digital post-mortem ones, the digital graveside photographs are made public.

On the Danish website Mindet.dk people write about and to the dead person. People also upload a lot of pictures that document the grave in its various stages, freshly made and covered with flowers, or with the headstone and ornaments placed, and so forth. They also document their visits to the grave with *in situ* photographs and often write about the context of the visit. Because photography fulfils a social function with regard to the family, it is, according to Bourdieu, 'dependent on the rhythms of the group' ([1965] 1990: 31). In other words, it reflects and marks the group's social time.

Like in family albums, we find photos of grave visits on special days, such as the anniversary of death, the dead person's birthday, the wedding anniversary and Christmas and Easter when the family normally meets. Confirmation, a wedding or other rites of passage of close relatives give further reason to visit the grave. Figure 4.2 provides a nice example of a birthday celebration at the graveside, photographed by the widow (whose shadow can be seen), complete with the customary Danish flag, coffee and the favourite cake of the one having his birthday. The photo caption reads: 'Some of your children, children-in-law and grandchild congratulate you [on your birthday]' (Figure 4.2). The dead person is addressed as if he were still alive.

Website memorials demonstrate that taking photographs of people at the graves of their dead is a very common practice in Denmark. However, the memorials on Mindet are mainly made for people who met an 'untimely' death (disruptions of what is perceived or experienced as the normal course of time of the member's participation in the social group). This might suggest that grave-visit photography more often takes place in cases of an untimely death. Other evidence, however, indicates that this type of relationship with the dead is not fostered with all the deceased members of the family. It has more to do with the relation that was maintained with the dead persons when they were alive than with the mere fact of an untimely death. Schmied (2004: 226–227) found that this applied equally to the care for the actual grave: some felt obliged to and others did not.

Moreover, the practice of talking to the dead at the grave frequently appeared to be a continuation of the conversations one had with the deceased during the latter's life (Schmied 2004: 332). One of us (Eric Venbrux) is acquainted with a man who paid daily visits to the grave of his mother at a cemetery in Lucerne, Switzerland. The woman had been ill and in a wheelchair for 30 years and her son had nursed her during that time. His care was now directed to the grave. The state of the unblemished grave – with a colourful pattern of different types of flowering plants, candles, and an elevation he described as an 'altar'– reflected his devotion. The man brought her a bunch of fresh flowers (often roses) every week, as he used to do when she was alive, and he spoke to her as well as to her dead friends at their graves in the same cemetery, assuring them that everything (meaning the grave) was alright. Like the memorials on the Danish website Mindet, his actions illustrate that the relations between the living and the dead tend to be extensions of the relationship that existed before the death occurred. The same accounts for the man's younger brother, who had sporadic contact with their mother. Subsequently, he rarely visited her grave.

The nature of the relationship can also be contested. Family conflicts are played out in relation to the care of the grave (Schmied 2002: 226–227) as well as entitlement to the grave. In the latter case, graveside photography can be a powerful means to (re)establish links. We have seen that children born after the death of an ancestor are often introduced to their ascendants by either placing photographs at the graves or photographing them in person at the grave. Simultaneously, the photographs attest to the relation of kinship, a relationship that transcends the boundary between life and death, and suggest that the deceased forebear lives on in the living descendants.

On an autumn day in the old cemetery of Kolding, Denmark, Kjærsgaard encountered a woman who was taking pictures of her daughter next to the family grave, using her mobile phone. It turned out that the woman took the photographs to link her young daughter to her grandmother, with whom she had a very close emotional bond. Living in another part of Denmark, she usually visited the grave every second month, but on this special occasion, around the anniversary of her grandmother's death, she had brought her daughter. The grandmother died at the age of 96. In spite of a family conflict, she was buried in the family grave. As a granddaughter, the woman encountered had no say in the decision making and the ashes had been put in a corner of the grave. Although the other part of the family tolerated the interment of the ashes, they did allow a headstone – next to the three already installed – to be placed there. They had been paying for the family grave for decades, refused the woman's offer of reimbursement, and did not accept any further 'invasion' on their entitled grave. It was like moving into an apartment rented by others, the woman explained. She had not liked the other dead when they were still alive. And, as we later learned from her blog, even her relationship with her mother had been troubled, so she tried to emulate her grandmother (instead of her mother) when raising her daughter. The woman claimed the grandmother had kept the family together. The latter's husband was in an anonymous grave (see also Sørensen 2009). The woman never visited him, because she had not known him, being only four years of age when he died. But the relationship with her grandmother was of great emotional significance to her, and was the reason why she wanted to assure a similar connection with her daughter by means of photography. The inscriptions on the grave gifts they brought – *mormor* (mother's mother) and *olde mom* (meaning *oldemor* or great-grandmother) – further attested that they belonged together. The daughter, however, did not 'belong' to the other dead of the family. The woman told Kjærsgaard that she turned the camera away from the headstones on the family grave on purpose. These were left out of the picture.

Lifton and Olson, who recognised the idea of the dead living on in their progeny as 'biological immortality', note that it 'is never purely biological' but 'experienced emotionally and symbolically' and may not be restricted to 'one's own biological family' (1974: 60–61). Mindet also reveals that there have been strong emotional bonds between the dead and those who construct this mode of 'symbolic immortality' (ibid.) on the website by producing memorial pages rich in photography. Photographs and the accompanying texts tell about the deceased's association with relatives and friends during the course of their life. They stress their social integration and connectedness. The photos are frequently taken on celebrations, especially in connection with rites of passage, and highlight family unity at those pivotal moments (cf. Bourdieu [1965] 1990: 19, 24, 26). For example, the recurrent photograph of a grandmother holding the grandchild in baptismal dress (when either one of them or both have died) emphasises the continuity of the line, intermingling the transitions to death and life. The contributions to Mindet seem to suggest that, in spite of a death, the relationships between those portrayed endure. Strikingly, women play a major role in making the contributions, and thereby in keeping up the image of prevailing relationships with the dead, both of themselves and of other surviving family members.

Their use of photography displays what Drazin and Frohlich have dubbed 'good intentions' (2007). The imagined, ongoing bonds with relatives who might be dispersed or never be seen again as a result of death draw heavily on the technology of photography. An ideal picture is produced. As Sontag reminds us, 'reality has come to seem more and more like what we are shown by cameras' ([1977] 1990: 161). Hence, photographic images are a 'potent means for turning the tables on reality' (ibid.: 180). Furthermore, photographs, as we have seen, can refer to emotional attachments. The sentiments concerning the proper context for their use have to be taken into account. The deceased can get a photograph of the spouse in the coffin (Vermeule 1979: 211, note 4), whereas others might consider keeping photographs on the grave as 'too intimate' (Kellehar, Prendergast and Hockey 2005: 243). In contrast to the actual Danish graves, the memorial website Mindet does provide a context for the display of numerous photographs, including photographs depicting the dead, as well as of graves and visits to graves.

Conclusion: Death and Social Time

Biological death terminates an individual's lifetime, but does not necessarily coincide with that person's social death. From the perspective of the survivors, as Humphreys points out, 'becoming dead' is a process that 'takes time' (1981:

263; see also Hertz 1960). She writes, 'The process of dying, in its widest sense, stretches from the decision a person is "dying" (as opposed to being temporarily unconscious, or seriously ill, but with chances of recovery) to the complete cessation of all social actions directed towards their remains, tomb, monument or other relics representing them' (Humphreys 1981: 263). We have dealt with the use of photography in this process of passing during which the survivors stave off the social death of persons who are biologically dead.

Biological death is transcended with help of the technology. Following Hubert and Mauss (1909), Leach considers the related mingling of two experiences in terms of time a religious move. Equating the experience of events that are repetitive (e.g. recurring seasons and rites) with those that are non-repetitive and irreversible (we grow older and eventually die) implies a denial of death (Leach 1961: 125–127). As we have seen, the photos related to repetitive events (such as rites of passage), reflecting 'the rhythms of the group' (Bourdieu [1965] 1990: 31; cf. Munn 1992: 96), mark the family group's social time. We also found that Bourdieu's thesis of photography as 'both an index and instrument of integration' ([1965] 1990: 40) of the family or social group was confirmed with regard to photographs in relation to graves. Both the living and the dead were part of the image projected of the ongoing life of the family. The sense of continuity was further supported by emotional attachments and the practices with photographs we described as well as the materiality and 'relic-like quality' of the photographs. By integrating the deceased with the social time of the bereaved they were no longer out of synchrony and thus transcending biological death. They stayed in the picture, socially alive, even more so because photographs have come to be seen as depicting the 'really real' (Geertz 1973: 112). As we have seen, the photography provided an ideal picture of social connection and continuity. In that sense, it is perhaps not that far removed from the 'model for reality' (Geertz 1973) found in religious worldviews. As a technique of modernity photography paradoxically has contributed to a re-enchantment of the dead.

References

Ariès, P. [1973] 1983. *The Hour of Our Death*. Harmondsworth: Penguin.

Ariès, P., 1985. *Images of Man and Death*. Cambridge, MA: Harvard University Press.

Astuti, R., 2007. What happens after death? In: R. Astuti, J. Parry and C. Stafford, eds, *Questions of Anthropology*. Oxford: Berg, pp. 227–247.

Bachelor, P., 2004. *Sorrow and Solace: The Social World of the Cemetery*. Amityville, NY: Baywood.

Badone, E., 1989. *The Appointed Hour: Death, Worldview and Social Change in Brittany*. Berkeley: University of California Press.

Barthes, R., 1981. *Camera Lucida: Reflections on Photography*. New York: Hill and Wang.

Batchen, G., 1999. *Burning with desire: The conception of photography.* Cambridge, MA: MIT Press.

Batchen, G., 2004a. *Forget Me Not: Photography and Remembrance.* New York: Princeton Architectural Press.

Batchen, G., 2004b., Ere the substance fade: Photography and hair jewellery. In: E. Edwards and J. Hart, eds, *Photographs Objects Histories: On the Materiality of Images.* London: Routledge, pp. 32–46.

Belting, H., 1990. *Bild und Kult. Eine Geschichte des Bildes vor dem Zeitalter der Kunst.* München: C. H. Beck.

Bennett, G. and Bennett, K. M., 2000. The presence of the dead: An empirical study. *Mortality*, 5(2): 139–157.

Bleyen, J., 2005. *De dood in Vlaanderen. Opvattingen en praktijken na 1950.* Leuven: Davidsfonds.

Bourdieu, P. [1965] 1990. *Photography: A Middle-Brow Art.* Cambridge: Polity Press.

Christen, M., 2010. *Die letzten Bilder. Tod, Erinnerung und Fotografie in der Zentralschweiz.* Baden: hier+jetzt.

Christensen, D. R. and Sandvik, K., 2013. Sharing death: Conceptions of time at a Danish memorial online site. In: D. R. Christensen and R. Willerslev, eds, *Taming Time, Taming Death: Social Technologies and Ritual.* Farnham: Ashgate, pp. 99–118.

Danforth, L. M., 1982. *The Death Rituals of Rural Greece.* Princeton, NJ: Princeton University Press.

de Pina-Cabral, J., 1986. *Sons of Adam, Daughters of Eve: The Peasant Worldview of the Alto Minho.* Oxford: Clarendon Press.

Drazin, A. and Frohlich, D., 2007. Good intentions: Remembering through framing photographs in English homes. *Ethnos*, 72(1): 51–76.

Edwards, E., 2012. Objects of affect: Photography beyond the image. *Annual Review of Anthropology*, 41: 221–234.

Edwards, E. and Hart, J., 2004. *Photographs Objects Histories: On the Materiality of Images, Material Cultures.* London: Routledge.

Elkins, J., 1997. *The Object Stares Back: On the Nature of Seeing.* San Diego: Harcourt.

Ennis, H., 2007. *Reveries: Photography and Mortality.* Canberra: National Portrait Gallery.

Francis, D., Kellehar, L. and Neophytou, G., 2000. Sustaining cemeteries: The user perspective. *Mortality*, 5(1): 34–52.

Francis, D., Kellehar, L. and Neophytou, G., 2005. *The Secret Cemetery.* Oxford: Berg.

Frazer, J.G., 1922. *The Golden Bough: A Study of Magic and Religion.* New York: Macmillan.

Geertz, C., 1973. Religion as a cultural system. In: *The Interpretation of Cultures: Selected Essays.* New York: Basic Books, pp. 87–123.

Gibson, M., 2004. Melancholy objects. *Mortality*, 9(4): 285–299.

Goody, J. and Poppi, C., 1994. Flowers and bones: Approaches to the dead in Anglo-American and Italian cemeteries. *Comparative Studies in Society and History*, 36(1): 146–175.

Greely, A. M., 1987. Hallucinations among the widowed. *Sociology and Social Research*, 71(4): 258–265.

Grimes, R.L. and Venbrux, E., 2010. Shooting embalms. In: D. Gross and C. Schweikardt, eds, *Die Realität des Todes. Zur gegenwärtigen Wandel von Totenbildern und Erinnerungskulturen.* Frankfurt: Campus Verlag, pp. 63–75.

Haakonsen, M., 2011. Mindekulturens visuelle genkomst: om fotografi på nutidens danske kirkegårde. *Kirkegårdskultur*, 2010–11: 31–42.

Hallam, E. and Hockey, J., 2001. *Death, Memory and Material Culture.* Oxford: Berg.

Hauser, A. 1994. *Von den letzten Dingen. Tod, Begräbnis und Friedhöfe in der Schweiz 1700–1990.* Zürich: Verlag Neue Züricher Zeitung.

Heessels, M. 2012. *Bringing Home the Dead: Ritualizing Cremation in the Netherlands.* PhD Thesis. Radboud University, Nijmegen, the Netherlands.

Heessels, M., Poots, F. and Venbrux, E., 2012. In touch with the deceased: Animate objects and human ashes. *Material Religion*, 8(4): 466–489.

Helweg, S. 2010. *Tidstypiske grave på Assistens Kirkegård 1760–2010.* København: Københavns Kommune.

Hertz, R. [1907] 1960. A contribution to the collective representation of death. In: *Death and the Right Hand.* London: Cohen and West, pp. 27–86.

Hubert, H. and Mauss, M., 1909. Étude sommaire de la représentation du temps dans la religion et la magie. In: H. Hubert and M. Mauss, eds, *Mélanges d'histoire des religions.* Paris: Alcan, pp. 189–229.

Humphreys, S. C., 1981. Death and time. In: S. C. Humphreys and H. King, eds, *Mortality and Immortality: The Anthropology and Archaeology of Death.* London: Academic Press, pp. 261–283.

Høiris, O., Otto, T. and Rolsted, A.B., eds, 2014. *De dødes liv.* Aarhus: Moesgaard Museum/Aarhus Universitetsforlag.

Jeggle, U., 1986. *Der Kopf des Körpers. Eine volkskundliche Anatomie.* Weinheim: Quadriga.

Jørgensen, T., 1987. Skt. Nikolaj kirke i nyere tid. In: T. Jørgensen, V. Jensen and P. Dedenroth-Schou, eds, *Skt. Nikolaj kirke Kolding.* Kolding: Konrad Jørgensens Bogtrykkeri, pp. 61–104.

Kellehar, L., Prendergast, D. and Hockey, J., 2005. In the shadow of the traditional grave. *Mortality*, 10(4): 237–250.

Kjærsgaard Markussen, A., 2013. Finding consolation on churchyards in Lutheran Denmark. *Nederlands Theologisch Tijdschrift*, 68(1/2): 101–119.

Koslofsky, C. M., 2002. From presence to remembrance: The transformation of memory in German Reformation. In: A. Confino and P. Fritzsche, eds, *The Work of Memory.* Urbana: University of Illinois Press, pp. 25–38.

Kragh, B., 2003., *Til jord skal du blive. Dødens og begravelsens kulturhistorie i Danmark 1780–1990* (Skrifter fra Museumsrådet for Sønderjyllands Amt 9). Sønderborg: Aabenraa Museum.

Layne, L. L., 2000. 'He was a real baby with baby things'. *Journal of Material Culture*, 5(3): 321–345.

Leach, E. R., 1961. Two essays concerning the symbolic representation of time. In: *Rethinking Anthropology*. London: Athlone, pp. 124–136.

Lifton, R. J. and Olson, E., 1974. *Living and Dying*. New York: Praeger.

Linkman, A., 2011. *Photography and Death*. London: Reaktion Books.

Matturri, J., 1993. Windows in the garden: Italian-American memorialization and the American cemetery. In: R. E. Meyer, ed., *Ethnicity and the American Cemetery*. Bowling Green: Bowling Green State University Popular Press, pp. 14–35.

May, T., 2009. *Death*. Stocksfield: Acumen.

Metz, C., 1985. Photography and fetish. *October*, 34: 81–90.

Miller, D. and Parrott, F., 2007. Death, ritual and material culture in South London. In: B. Brooks-Gordon, F. Ebtejehai, J. Harring, et al., eds, *Death Rites and Rights*. Oxford: Hart Publishing, pp. 147–162.

Mitchell, W. J. T., 2005. *What Do Pictures Want? The Lives and Loves of Images*. Chicago: University of Chicago Press.

Morgan, D., 1999. *Protestants and Pictures: Religion, Visual Culture, and the Age of American Mass Production*. New York: Oxford University Press.

Munn, N., 1992. The anthropology of time: A critical essay. *Annual Review of Anthropology*, 21: 93–123.

Parrott, F. R. 2009. Bringing home the dead: Photographs, family imaginaries and moral remains. In: M. Bille, F. Hastrup and T.F. Sørensen, eds, *An Anthropology of Absence: Materialisations of Transcendence and Loss*. New York: Springer Press, pp. 131–146.

Pinney, C., 1997. *Camera Indica: The Social Life of Indian Photographs*. London: Reaktion Books.

Rees, W. D., 1971. The hallucinations of widowhood. *British Medical Journal*, 4: 37–41.

Reynolds, P. L., 2012. *Temporal Trends in Grave Marker Attributes: An Analysis of Headstones in Florida*. Honors Thesis. University of Central Florida, Orlando, Florida, USA.

Riches, G. and Dawson, P., 1998. Lost children, living memories: The role of photographs in processes of grief and adjustment among bereaved parent. *Death Studies*, 22(2): 121–140.

Rojas, C., 2009. Abandoned cities seen anew: Reflections on spatial specificity and temporal transience. In: R. C. Morris, ed., *Photographies East: The Camera and its Histories in East and Southeast Asia*. Durham: Duke University Press, pp. 207–228.

Ruby, J., 1995. *Secure the Shadow: Death and Photography in America.* Cambridge, MA: MIT Press.

Sanger, M., 2009. When clients sense the presence of loved ones who have died. *Omega,* 59(1): 69–89.

Schmied, G., 2002. *Friedhofsgespräche. Untersuchungen zum 'Wohnort der Toten'.* Wiesbaden: Springer.

Schmied, G., 2004. Der Friedhof als Aspekt der Familienkultur. *Sociologia Internationalis,* 42: 221–241.

Seremetakis, C. N., 1991. *The Last Word: Women, Death, and Divination in Inner Mani.* Chicago: Chicago University Press.

Shaw, D. B., 2009. Technology, death and the cultural imagination. *Science as Culture,* 18(3): 251–260.

Sontag, S. [1977] 1990. *On Photography.* New York: Anchor Books/Doubleday.

Spira, S. F., 1981. Graves and graven images. *History of Photography,* 5(4): 325–328.

Starck, N., 2013. *Unter der Tessiner Sonne – ein Führer zu besonderen Grabstätten.* Ascona: Porzio.

Stringer, M. D., 2008a. *Contemporary Western Ethnography and the Definition of Religion.* London: Continuum.

Stringer, M. D., 2008b. Chatting with Gran at her grave: Ethnography and the definition of religion. In: P. Cruchley-Jones, ed., *God at Ground Level: Reappraising Church Decline in the UK through the Experience of Grass Roots Communities and Situations.* Frankfurt/New York: Peter Lang, pp. 23–39.

Sørensen, T. F., 2009. The presence of the dead: Cemeteries, cremation and the staging of non-place. *Journal of Social Archaeology,* 9(1): 110–135.

Trap, L., 2013. *Hjertebånd – at leve med sine døde.* Frederiksberg: Alfa.

Venbrux, E., 1991. A death-marriage in a Swiss mountain village. *Ethnologia Europaea,* 21(2): 193–201.

Venbrux, E. and Jones, P., 2002. 'Prachtaufnahmen': Police Inspector Paul Foelsche's anthropometric photographs of Aborigines from Northern Australia, 1879. In: L. Roodenburg, ed., *De bril van Anceaux/Anceaux's Glasses: Anthropological Photography since 1860.* Leiden: Rijksmuseum voor Volkenkunde, pp. 116–127.

Vermeule, E., 1979. *Aspects of Death in Early Greek Poetry and Art.* Berkeley: University of California Press.

Walter, T., 2009. Communicating with the dead. In: C. D. Bryant and D. L. Peck, eds, *Encyclopedia of Death and Human Experience,* vol. 1. Los Angeles: Sage, pp. 216–219.

Walter, T., 2013. *Do Modern Societies Comprise the Dead as Well as the Living?* CDAS (Centre for Death and Society) Working Paper series – January 2013. Bath: CDAS, University of Bath.

Walton, K. L., 1984. Transparant pictures: On the nature of photographic realism. *Critical Inquiry,* 11(2): 246–277.

Wartmann, M., 1986. Leben auf Züricher Friedhöfen: Impressionen, Gespräche, Beobachtungen. *Schweizerisches Archiv für Volkskunde*, 86(2): 30–40.

Whincup, T., 2004. Imaging the intangible. In: C. Knowles and P. Sweetman, eds, *Picturing the Social Landscape: Visual Methods and the Sociological Imagination*. London: Routledge, pp. 79–92.

Wojtkowiak, J. and Venbrux, E., 2010. Private spaces for the dead: Remembrance and continuing relationships at home memorials in the Netherlands. In: A. Maddrell and J. D. Sidaway, eds, *Deathscapes: Spaces for Death, Dying, Mourning and Remembrance*. Farnham: Ashgate, pp. 207–221.

Worpole, K., 2003. *Last Landscapes: Architecture of the Cemetery in the West*. London: Reaktion Books.

PART II:
Transition: Detachment and Continuing Bonds

Chapter 5

Understanding Self-Care: Passing and Healing in Contemporary Serbia

Maja Petrović-Šteger

The so-called Yugoslav Wars ended in 1999. To what extent has the post-war period brought healing and to what extent has the war fully 'passed'? How is the transition to a post-conflict society understood in Serbia? How can we register – ethnographically but also through narrative and metaphor – the persistence of states of mind associated with the war and with attachments not extinguished by the war ending?

The word 'post-conflict' typically evokes images of a shattered human environment, whose strewn bodies denote a bruised social psyche in sore need of mending and healing. Following the 1990s wars, the international community insisted that the witnesses to, and perpetrators of, war crimes could only reconcile themselves to a post-war polity, and start on a course of healing, on the condition of their facing up to the evidence of their wrongs. The assumption was that it would be possible to create, or indeed restore, a 'healthy' civil society only through people spontaneously saying what they thought politically, as they cooperated with locally and internationally run programmes of interstate reconciliation.[1] Through framing the terms of Serbia's role in the wars, and its relation to Europe and the world, Serbia would be able to consolidate itself democratically, reduce any stigma associated with looking backward, and symbolically attenuate inequalities and tensions among its population. Yet the terms of Serbs' participation in these programmes – regarding their culpability for events in their recent past – were not uncontentious. Political, civil society organisations and NGOs in fact clashed over Serbia's role in the wars and how this should relate to the work of the agencies dealing with war's human fallout.

Numerous anthropologists have examined the impacts that radical social and political change, economic hardship, structural violence, humanitarian interventions and conflict have on health (see, for example, Adams 1998; Asad 2011; Briggs and Mantini-Briggs 2003; Brotherton 2008; Farmer 2003; Fassin 2005, 2008; Gibson 2001; Kleinman, Das and Lock 1997; Petryna 2013; Scheper-

---

1   For an excellent analysis of the significance of psycho-social intervention as a new form of 'therapeutic' international governance based on social risk management, see Pupavac 2001, 2005.

Hughes 1992; Tapas 2006).[2] This chapter takes its cue from this scholarship, but focuses distinctively on the body and on health as the sites of medical and humanitarian intervention. It traces debates over whether Serbia is healthy, not only in the sense of being reconciled with its neighbours but more literally – does Serbia's post-conflict social health apparatus actually function? Examining practices through which people monitor and manage their bodily conditions and health as forms of medical and humanitarian intervention and production, my analysis shows how certain personal and social aspirations towards societal changes in Serbia are transacted through biomedical and political categories of healing. It also complicates certain representations of Serbia as an emotionally dysfunctional society, asking whether such a depiction and such an intervention serves to rehabilitate or further pathologise the society in question. The discussion of a range of practices, desires and agencies relating to conceptions of health also illuminates some of the modes by which ideas of Serbia's post-conflict and post-socialist transition or passing are publicly understood. This chapter is based on intermittent fieldwork in Serbia between 2004 and 2009 and builds off an ethnographic data encompassing extended interviews and close interactions with more than a hundred respondents (including patients and doctors) from various sections of Serbian society.

Health in Pre- and Post-War Serbia

The transition of post-conflict states is often captured in statistical indicators such as GDP per capita, people's access to health, education, and other measures tracking the development of a civil society. In the early 2000s these indicators marked undeniable progress for Serbia. Today, however, over 15 years after the last of the 1990s wars, the country seems to have returned to a state of dissatisfaction and uncertainty – the economy is faltering, living standards are poor and levels of public health are worryingly low. In such a situation, providing conditions for politics of accounting, economic investment and humanitarian assistance in medical resources and equipment has become an important marker of international willingness to speed the country's recovery, as (possibly) compelled by a notion on the world community's part of its obligations and of the value of reconciliation in Serbia.

This form of international justice, typically and increasingly articulated in the language of healing, has in the former Yugoslavia attached itself closely not just to

---

2   There is a copious literature analysing the influence of conflict on public health. For interesting sociological, medical, epidemiological, human rights and security specialists' research relating to former Yugoslav territories, see Banatvala and Zwi 2000; Cardozo et al. 2000; Hjelm et al. 1999, Hjelm et al. 2005; Jones et al. 2006; Kunitz 2004; Luta and Dræbel 2013; McCarthy 2007; Nelson et al. 2003; Pupavac and Pupavac 2012; Thoms and Ron 2007; Toole, Galson and Brady 1993; Vlajinac et al. 2008.

questions affecting the health of the living but also to human remains and to claims made in their name. Estimating that more than 40,000 persons remain unaccounted for after the Yugoslav Wars, various organisations, most notably the International Commission on Missing Persons, have established, under a 'strictly humanitarian mandate', a 'mission to bring relief' to the families of the missing (both former combatants and civilians), regardless of families' religious, national or ethnic identity.[3] The recovery of bodily remains, and their return to the bereaved families, has thus been identified as crucial to restorative and reconciliatory processes. In ambiguous ways, the project came to signify ideas of modernity, Europeanness, and of health and rehabilitation at a societal level (see Petrović-Šteger 2009).

Besides the financial and infrastructural support tied to the identification of human remains, Serbia has over the last 15 years or so received hundreds of millions of euros' worth of international aid earmarked for the housing, healthcare and psycho-social support of refugees, displaced persons and the relatives of the war missing.[4] During the war, a sudden influx of internally displaced people placed a heavy burden on primary healthcare centres already struggling with staff shortages and unreliable supplies. This help has thus proved essential for a vast number of people, especially given that in the post-war period the health of Serbia's population has visibly worsened. Life expectancy is falling and the incidence of cardiovascular diseases, various forms of cancer, stroke, depression and suicide rate is on the rise (Institute of Public Health of Serbia 2009; see also Marković 2010). The quality of healthcare has also deteriorated dramatically.

---

3   The Commission has mounted a major public health campaign involving the DNA-sampling of the population as a precondition for the identification of remains exhumed from mass gravesites. In the hope that a secure method of attribution would stimulate people to exchange information concerning missing people with more speed and candour, the proponents of national reconciliation have styled DNA in public discourse as a figurative basis on which people previously at loggerheads could be brought together. The effect of these campaigns and, most of all, of identification results, was to give rise to a notion that one could cope with the loss of loved ones, and attempt to secure justice on their behalf, by searching for them on the molecular level of their DNA profile. If atavism and conflicts had torn Yugoslavia apart, science would, as it were, put it back together again.

4   The EU is the main international donor to Serbia. Through programmes managed by the European Agency for Reconstruction, the support that came from the EU for the Serbian health sector, from 2000 to 2007, has totalled almost €100 million. Further, the US Agency for International Development (USAID) represents the largest bilateral donor. Other donors and agencies providing assistance to the health sector include the World Bank, World Health Organization, United Nations Children's Fund, United Nations Development Programme, International Committee of the Red Cross, UK Department for International Development, Canadian International Development Agency, South African Development Community and Government of Germany (as listed in the DFID Health System Resource Centre Report on Serbia and Montenegro Health profile 2003, London). See also http://ec.europa.eu/enlargement/archives/ear/sectors/main/documents/HEALTH_SERBIA_EN.pdf (accessed 21 July 2015).

This reduction in the quality of Serbia's healthcare system, along with the development of an unofficial health economy incubated by discrimination and corruption in public healthcare provision, has reduced people's incentives to cash in their state-run health insurance, and likewise to make their social contributions, thereby substantially undermining the public's previous relationship of trust with state healthcare.

The current situation of public healthcare in Serbia, then, is a far cry from that which prevailed before the 1990s conflicts. Under the socialist regime, the Yugoslavian healthcare system was not financed, as in the rest of Eastern Europe, through a Health Ministry Budget, but rather drew on a social insurance fund modelled on the Bismarck system (as opposed to a British-style welfare state arrangement). The system made contributions compulsory for all employees who, together with their families, benefited from insurance. Those unemployed came under a separate system financed out of the state budget. Healthcare – that is, treatment, medicine and prosthetic interventions – was free at the point of delivery, and regarded by Serbia's public as highly efficient and trustworthy.[5] The collapse of Yugoslavia, leading to Serbia's impoverishment, and the destruction of its middle class under a series of wars and the embargo, has hugely changed the landscape of which the healthcare system formed a part. Internationally renowned institutions, such as the Torlak Institute of Immunology and Virology, a major vaccine producer, for example, lost their external markets. The then government under Slobodan Milošević re-centralised the system, but did not re-size or reform it, leaving a painful incongruity between an unwieldy legacy structure of the communist era and any realistic possibility of financing (FIDH 2005: 5).

Further, during the early war years, a number of highly qualified doctors left the country, creating a supply–demand imbalance that even in a managed system pushed costs up to the highest level, for patients, in the region. Although the situation has changed somewhat over the years, leaving health institutions over-resourced in terms of locally educated personnel, those medical practitioners who could get jobs (in 2005, around 25,000 in Serbia) attested in the media to poor working conditions, wrecked facilities,[6] supply shortfalls and a constant need to appeal for money. An inadequately supervised and regulated private healthcare sector emerged, with members of what is perceived as a *nouveau riche* class bankrolling

---

5   The healthcare system in Serbia is still mainly financed through a network of employee contributions to a centralised social security system. Total expenditure on health per capita amounted in 2007 to $899 and in 2011 to $1,195, of which general government expenditure per capita in 2007 was $665 (see Marković 2010 and WHO 2011).

6   The ratio of hospital beds to patients is very low (1 bed for 184 patients), yet they are under-utilised (70 per cent) because of inefficiency. A 2002 European Agency for Reconstruction study further found that only a third of hospitals had functioning sterilisation equipment and 75 per cent of the medical equipment in health facilities was more than 10 years old. Patients had to buy their own hospital supplies out of their own pocket, even items such as bandages and catheters (McCarthy 2007).

a number of expensive gynaecological, reproductive, aesthetic, dental and other clinics to serve a wealthy minority. The state health apparatus has also fallen prey to massive corruption, with many documented cases of the misappropriation of funds. Poorly paid doctors, many with family obligations, began to take on additional work in private clinics, often referring patients who came to see them in the morning to their private clinics in the afternoon.[7] Those patients who could pay frequented these clinics because, as in the words of one respondent, 'they were sick of waiting and of the unreliable diagnoses of time-pressed state practitioners'. Medical equipment in state hospitals was often broken (or said to be broken), forcing those in need of ultrasound scanners, ECG exams or X-rays into the hands of the private clinics. Despite a formal prohibition on private clinics' contracting with the state for reimbursement of patients' social insurance, those able to pay for exams and treatment typically abandoned the state sector. This move was hastened by instances of the habit, even of eminent doctors', of asking for cash-in-hand payment (so-called 'red-handing'), as repeatedly exposed in the media. Even if the corruption in healthcare was not necessarily or systematically more prevalent than in other professional fields such as customs, shipping, the judiciary, the universities and accountancy, it was sufficiently marked and documented to figure as one of the major factors preventing rationalisation of the health system (Gredelj, Gavrilović and Šolić 2005: 24). My fieldwork interviewees would repeatedly tell me they simply could not afford to get ill.

My field notes from 2008 of a middle-class conversation in Belgrade illustrate the contempt in which all forms of healthcare, private and public, are held in contemporary Serbia:

> It's a Sunday morning in December and the Belgrade streets are full of people wearing thick coats, fur collars swaddling their necks, heads, and hands to protect them from the wind and biting cold. Their heavy boots and high heels crunch on the icy, snowy pavements. I'm on my way to a children's birthday party hosted by Marina, who is four, and her parents, in their early thirties. He's an investment banker and she an economist with an exceptionally successful career. The house – a children's play and party centre they've hired especially for the occasion – smells festively of winter foods, cinnamon and chocolate. On the upper floor, the children's playrooms are spilling over with soup, fruit, yoghurt, pastry, and puddings. The grown-ups party downstairs, tucking into lamb, different kinds of beans, peppers, potatoes, cheese and salads. Two vegetarian guests are sent upstairs, with the remark that food there might be healthier. A woman responds by bemoaning her child's newly developing food allergy and is consoled by two other women, whose kids similarly suffered from illnesses, infections and intolerance. Their conversation depicts the city's

---

7   In 2000, the average monthly salary for a doctor was €130 and for nurses €90, compared with the national monthly average of €176, according to the World Bank (McCarthy 2007).

kindergartens as breeding-grounds for bacteria. Since all the women speaking are employed, they see nursery care for their children as a necessary evil. The boy with a food allergy is summoned from upstairs. His back and his hands are covered with tiny red marks of inflammation. All the women in the circle come closer and start weighing in on the causes of the boy's rash, though none has any medical background. One prescribes a Swiss antihistamine, another the restorative properties of honey; a mother of three hopes that quails' eggs and thyme tea could clear the problem up. The addresses of health food shops selling gluten-free food are written down, even as the boy's mother denies that her child suffers from coeliac disease. Somebody inquires about the level of the boy's erythrocytes. The mother answers that his latest check-up came up perfect. Another woman asks about the paediatrician's diagnosis and how many allergy tests the hospital ran on the child. Rolling back the child's jumper and sending him to rejoin his friends, the mother raises her eyebrows, gives a quick, ironic smile and says that the paediatrician in their local hospital is a joke. He is always endlessly kind, but ceaselessly apologetic, saying that he cannot run any tests as the hospital laboratory is out of reagents. She suspects he is lying, aiming to lure her family to his private practice. They wouldn't object in principle to going private, but have heard that the clinic where he works is no good. The alternative specialist found by her husband has as yet been unable to pinpoint their child's exact food allergy. Everybody nods and empathises. The hostess of the party, Andrijana, offers to make a phone call to their family doctor who is also an immunologist to check whether the child can be seen to at once. In a courteous but business-like tone, she asks to speak to doctor Lidija. From what we can hear the doctor and Andrijana exchange pleasantries in the most polite language. Andrijana apologises for phoning on a Sunday morning in the festive season, and makes an appointment for the mother and child to see the doctor the very same day, Sunday. The mother is excited, grateful and ready to leave for the private clinic at once. Andrijana says: "Don't worry. They won't charge you much. I know them well. And you will be so pleased to send Nikola [the child] there. They have a beautiful, sparkling new clinic, done up with the most contemporary medical equipment brought from Belgium. You will like it, I know".

How to interpret this – in some ways not at all untypical – story? Many of my interviewees, regardless of their financial background, seemed obsessed with their health, with the stories of their scars, injuries and recovery. Elder respondents tirelessly informed me about their frail bodies, mounting varicose veins, bad circulation, high blood pressure, rheumatisms, water retention, kidney trouble and heart problems. They claimed that many of these problems were not related only to their age, and what some called 'embarrassingly old bodies', but were aggravated by their impoverished lives and inability to 'take proper care of themselves' due to the pitifully small pensions they were receiving. Wanting to show they were doing everything they could to take care of themselves, many made a point of how conscientiously they filled out diagnoses and prescriptions, offering printouts of diagnostic images and hospital discharge notices. They did this whether the medical establishment had pronounced them sick or well. Such heightened attention to health, though, did not extend only to parents and elderly people. My milieu in Belgrade was also one of younger people who casually but obsessively inspected and compared the level of their thrombocytes, red and white blood cell counts, protein profiles, haemoglobin and blood sugar levels, continually diagnosing each other, ascribing this or that condition, and discussing possibilities of therapy or remission. Women in their thirties and forties rarely lost an opportunity to discuss their levels of tyrosine and thyroid-stimulating hormone, exchanges that always saw me at a loss.

These conversations testified to an extraordinarily high level of specialised information among a section of the lay public. The situations in which I overheard the most apparently systematic 'knowledge' of healthcare dispensed were not (or not most usually) those of hospital waiting rooms, but were rather everyday interactions on public buses, in offices, between joggers or among the clientele of bars. The smart talk was all of the best aromatherapists and masseuses in the city. It was almost a mark of urban sophistication to be up to date on dietary supplements, restorative teas, melatonin intake, antioxidants, selenium, broccoli seeds, neem powder and various nutrition products – as if knowing these things was a sign of one's education, wealth and level of self-care. Indeed, the majority of my interviewees seemed constantly to bone up on newspaper articles on tips for a healthy life, reading books, consulting trusted doctors and on occasions becoming devotees of special teas and alternative treatments. Some utterly distressed people who were moneyed enough and open to alternative health practices saw their salvation in homoeopathy, apitherapy, aromatherapy, spiritual medicine, bioresonance therapy, quantum energy treatments[8] and many other healing methods. Those who could not pay for such treatments resorted to traditional and local herbal remedies made at home.

Pharmaceuticals and Humanitarianism

People's supposed knowledge of, and access to, healthcare tended to reflect their social status and aspirations. Their interest in monitoring the state of their health was most likely closely tied to their disillusionment with public healthcare and a sense that the envelope containing their pay cheque might never be fat enough to assure decent medical treatment. In consequence, it appears, many seem to have felt they have to educate themselves about their own conditions, populating the discomfort zone of illness with a host of reassuring health-indicator facts like hormonal and haemoglobin reports. More than disillusionment, however, was

---

8   Quantum energy treatments are known to many on account of their most famous practitioner – Dr Dragan Dabić, otherwise known as Radovan Karadžić.

involved in their desertion of the state system. Numerous people I had worked with simply seemed avidly fascinated with diagnostic laboratories.

Indeed, during the time the material for this research was collected (2004–2009), whether I thumbed through Belgrade's Yellow Pages or just walked through the city, I was astonished by the enormous number of private pharmacies and diagnostic and haematological laboratories, running into almost three figures, that together with scores of X-ray and ultrasound ambulances, systematically marked out the cityscape. These institutions sprang up in the 1990s with the collapse and isolation of the Yugoslav medicine market and state healthcare provision. The crisis in Serbia's 1990s, forced by United Nations Security Council sanctions, gave the go-ahead to a process of wild privatisation of healthcare and the public pharmaceutical sector, in which private companies were in some cases able to commandeer monopoly market positions and subdue the bargaining power of a highly educated class of chemists.[9] The government granted licences to pharmacies that had (as a sector) never been competently run or sufficiently well equipped. The argument went that a number of health-related laws formerly in force had to be cancelled, in order for the population to get access to medication. The founders of such pharmacies usually had good contacts abroad or were cash-rich enough to be able to buy in medicines from local pharmaceutical companies or drug wholesalers. Their drug stores were hard to differentiate from other aspirational shops, in stocking alongside medicine nutritional products, baby food, cosmetics, chocolates and perfume.

Pharmacies also prospered through their connection with international humanitarian help. During the wars and after, insulin, anaesthetics and medicine for treating infectious, endocrine and cardiovascular disease, psychosis, narcolepsy, kidney ailments and other organ failures were regularly shipped to Serbia and other ex-Yugoslav republics. Instead of ending up at branches of the Red Cross or local health institutes, some of those parcels were allegedly regularly diverted into the hands of those able to buy them for cash – that is, wealthy pharmacists or war profiteers.

Certain pharmacies, further, ran an endemically corrupt business. Public reports have alleged systematic over-prescription as a result of improper relationships between doctors and pharmacists, as well as cases of doctors' countermanding colleagues' diagnoses in order to push a particular line of medicaments with which they had some covert business relation. In this context, people's health increasingly depended on party or family connections, charitable help from humanitarian organisations, or access to the black market. During the war, smuggled drugs cost up to five times their normal price. Especially profitable were sales of Bensadine, Bromazepam and Diazepam, whose massive consumption suggested that the mental health of the population was parlous, with one in every two people in

---

9   The pharmaceutical industry in Serbia before the wars (with companies such as Hemofarm, Velefarm, Farmanova, Jugohemija, Farmalogist, Erma, Vetfarm, and so on) was small but nonetheless highly developed and profitable.

Serbia reliant on sedatives (Global IDP 2002). Further, according to some of my interviewees, some pharmacies sold a number of fake, unregistered and black-market drugs.

Despite health scandals and scares, for instance, over the degree to which parents had elbowed paediatricians aside in the care of their own children, and other 'portfolios of disasters' (Redfield 2006: 4) documenting patients' self-medication, people's concern to monitor their own health via various laboratory tests barely wavered. Those unable to afford regular check-ups from professionals would arm themselves with newspaper or internet research on trips to the chemist, often buying up antibiotics and other medicine in enormous quantities and an apparently hit-and-miss fashion.[10] Numerous people I spoke to voiced their scepticism about private healthcare's motives but would nevertheless regularly visit biochemical as well as DNA labs, some open 24/7, for self-diagnosis or simply to confirm doctors' examinations. Patients seemed to welcome this personalised approach to medicine and to labs' statistical representation of their health perhaps insofar as it has allowed them to develop their own 'aetiological vernacular'. The question put to Nikola's mother about the possible connection of his food allergy to his erythrocytes level in this sense conveys both care and some supposed, self-imputed medical knowledge. As a matter of fact, it often seemed to me that those particularly invested in healthcare were concerned to amass some sort of intellectual capital in, for example, recalling the provenance of medical equipment and drugs. Something of this can be seen in the pride with which Andrijana praised the Belgium medical technology of Dr Lidija's laboratory or in the manner her guests recommended a particular Swiss antihistamine. Within this framework, the pharmacies and diagnostic laboratories appeared to represent a sort of symbolic site of people's self-determination over their own health, and by extension over their lives.

Images of Medicine, Humanitarian Help and Europe

Although Serbia's health system was in the late 1990s and early 2000s almost entirely dependent on international help, this assistance was not always easy for Serbs to trust. After all, in the view of many NATO also intervened in the name of 'humanitarianism' in bombing Belgrade in 1999. Different international organisations thus faced the problem of how to foster trust in their medical provision. It is doubtless that these organisations have provided massive assistance to many internally displaced or otherwise affected by war. Along with

---

10   Contrary to the presumption that only wealthier social groups were able to enjoy the private health insurance options, research has shown that it was the middle-income class that used the private health sector most systematically. Nevertheless, private insurance coverage is still shown to be an exception rather than a common practice among the general population (see Marković 2010).

humanitarian health supplies, thousands of tonnes of food were distributed, with households benefiting from micro-credits, vocational training for young people and grants to buy tools, livestock and greenhouses. Government also directed international agencies to provide households with direct gifts of cash. The help, either routed through humanitarian agencies or through pharmacies and clinics, was much needed and therefore welcomed. But it was often also received as a cause for embarrassment among some sections of Serbian society. Western countries' public declarations of sympathy were almost always unanimously rejected. Especially those who denied that the country was at all at fault for the wars did not want a foot-up from 'the Americans'. People further turned against the presumptuousness of foreign largesse when they read local media reports that many medicines donated by humanitarian agencies had passed their sell-by date.[11] Humanitarian aid took over from private pharmacies in bearing the blame for importing and selling unregistered and knock-off medicine. The nation's Clinical Centre, for example, was vocal in complaining that the medicine it acquired in 1999 and 2000 from different humanitarian organisations was little better than some kind of pharmaceutical waste-product. These alleged 12 cubic metres of expired medicaments additionally burdened the hospital with disposal costs (see Derikonjić 2005).

This description of Serbia as the pharma-dump of Europe soured many Serbs against more obvious humanitarian interventions from the European Union and the West. For many, supposed humanitarian acts stank of hypocrisy. Something of this is suggested by the following conversation with a man in his 60s:

> Serbia is an autistic, pre-political, corrupt country, run by a kleptocracy. People respond to all sorts of fears and uncertainties, not in an educated way. Our problem was never the embargo or sanctions. Our problem is our own isolation. We have ruined all what we have had. Just look where we are now. Thirty years ago, Serbs were travelling all around the world. Our industry was good. Our kids were mouthing off that Belgrade was the first city in Eastern Europe to have opened a McDonald's. And where are we now? We're stealing from each other. We live in a corrupt country where people profiteer on each other's misery. One would maybe expect some corruption in the public finances, or in the police, in the customs, but it's the health sector that is most rotten here. [...] Do you know how much I paid for my granddaughter to be born [in 2002]? The tariff for a baby in Belgrade ranges from 300 to 500 EUR. I've heard that the price is calculated per weight – 100 EUR per kilo of a baby. For twins you get a discount. It's like they're selling you meat for grilling. Anaesthesiologists are particularly crazed for money ... . But I paid whatever they told me, and out of

---

11   Here are just two examples of numerous websites dedicated to fighting the corruption and mulfunctioning of the Serbian healthcare system: http://www.transparentnost.org.rs/ ts_mediji/stampa/2005/11NOVEMBAR/18112005.html and http://www.forum-srbija.com/ viewtopic.php?f=397&t=16138&start=80 (both accessed 21 July 2015).

sheer happiness I got such a beauty, I even sent coffee and sweets to the doctor. I was such a fool. That way I allowed these criminals to go on governing us ... . But don't believe for one moment that the West treats us any better. Nobody is kid-gloving us. In this country even the humanitarian agencies are corrupt. They nurture their egos imagining they are some sort of angel of the parish, whilst dumping old medicine on us and luring our people into shady clinical research trials. These clinical trials, I tell you, are catastrophic. Foreign pharmaceutical companies are literally abusing our people ... . But Serbia is drowning, and it needs somebody's help. It needs someone to grip her by the hair and fish her out of the dirt and mire.

For a somewhat different view, consider the following excerpt from an interview with a 43-year-old publisher:

Our society may indeed be gripped by apathy at the moment, but it is definitely not as fatalistic, pathological or corrupted as the media and foreign reports portray it. I actually feel safe here. My family and myself have always felt well cared for in the hospitals. I've lived for years in Austria and Belgium and have family all over Germany, and can tell you for sure that our doctors and nurses are far more devoted and kinder than theirs. Far more compassionate ... . My aunt has just come out from a hospital [she had spent couple of weeks there due to severe pneumonia]. She is a bit difficult, you know, slightly hypochondriac, on about every conceivable concoction you could think of. Kind of a high-maintenance woman, with awfully high standards when it comes to her health. She's gone through a lot in her life ... two wars, two divorces, all kind of bad experiences ... . But she praised the doctors and the treatment she had received in the hospital. Sure, the hospital was not a Hilton hotel, but what do you expect ... . To be honest she did pull a connection or two before checking in, but nothing too serious. She just wanted to make sure that she would be in good hands. One has to take good care of oneself ... . Serbia is in many ways a decayed place. But it is also a good, caring, humane place. Some doctors might be stuck-up sometimes. But expertise and sympathy are never denied here. Never.

Importantly, a number of respondents suggested to me that even when patients seek to establish contacts with doctors through informal channels (that is, through personal familiarity or through family, friends', partners' or acquaintances' connections) this should not be taken as a token of corruption, but rather as a sign of intimacy and care. On numerous instances I have heard people eulogising their physicians, oncologists, drug rehabilitation or mental health experts. These people were respected for their professionalism and for the personal care they had shown to their patients – which had led to many weaning themselves off previously unhealthy and destructive habits. Equally important to note is the fact that numerous medical personnel were also praised for publicly contesting systemic corruption.

My respondents in Serbia are not unanimous in their attitude towards the Serbian health system, nor towards the West, nor about the country's post-war transition or relationship with the European Union (and its versions of democracy). Many will call out domestic corruption, bullying and inefficiency when they see it. At the same time, they refuse to be stigmatised as pathological, backward or unhealthy. Health plays a key role in these discursive struggles over self-evaluation and any remaining power of Serbian self-determination. One of the stronger sentiments that shape such reactions, I believe, is a feeling of humiliation enforced by the comparison of an implicitly (or explicitly) healthy socialist past and diseased post-conflict present. One man half-jokingly, half-acidly explained why he refused to go to the former Yugoslav republic of Slovenia, now part of the EU, for surgery:

> No, no I can't do that to myself. That would be like knowing that you are going to bump into an ex-girlfriend on the street. You know for sure that she still looks great, is toned, healthy, well kept … obviously bourgeois. She would smile at your with her perfect teeth and ask you how you are whilst eyeing your bald patch, your beer belly, and grey complexion. What could you say? You would try to produce the most charming voice and say *I'm doing great, thanks*. But you would know that you have utterly embarrassed yourself!

Conclusion

In attending ethnographically to the pharmacies and biochemical and diagnostic labs flourishing across Belgrade, and to structural inequalities that have arisen in access to humanitarian medicine in the last 15 years or so, I have hoped to frame some theoretical terms for the analysis of a society both pervasively preoccupied with issues of bodily health and seen as needing psycho-social support. The chapter's aim has been critically to examine the psycho-social and cultural circumstances in which efforts are being made to establish a new political and physiological order in Serbia. My intention has not been to suggest a direct parallel between the health of Serbian citizens and the health (political and physical) of Serbian society. The sum of parts can often be different from the (presumed) whole. Neither have I proposed that those who recognise themselves as ill, or in need of medical assistance, are necessarily internalising the state of what is understood as a fractured society. Yet the ways in which the people I worked with narrate and practise their health concerns show that their bodies are often experienced as sites bearing palpable traces of the country's both conflictual and socialist past.

Moreover, the past (and the present) is often confronted through some form of bodily reckoning. This is not surprising, in that both the international community and local politics have focused on bodies and health as sites through which the past could be rectified. Both national and international agencies see bodily and healthcare interventions as able to ease social ills and re-knit social relations. Diverse actors impute different and heterogeneous assortments of ideas and values to health. Some feel the need to account for their bodily health as an index of certain personal and social aspirations to move towards a healthy post-war polity, a concept inflected with ideas of democratisation, political settlement and political emotions including (conceivably) pride, guilt and remorse. Other people took up positions in relation to their health that struck me as a sort of strategic autism, like that of the patient refusing to travel to Slovenia, even when they were expressed in a rhetoric of indignation. Talking about health, people made clear the gap that existed between themselves and supposedly richer people, and expressed the desire to close that gap. Indeed, many people's experiences of structural inequality in healthcare provision in post-conflict Serbia become analytically accessible[12] and emotionally describable through their practices, as these work out different emotional and political responses. The majority of my respondents understand health as an explicitly political and politicised category and experience healthcare as a commodity. Supposing a conception of this kind, some resist Western humanitarian help as a route to an ultimately better, or more sophisticated, version of democracy. When doctors are medically interventionist in accessing humanitarian aid, some respondents see this not as healing, or to be taken neutrally, but as politically invasive. Being or appearing dependent on Western healthcare is sometimes understood as shameful.

In spite of the discourse that portrays the management of personal and societal health as an essential means for traversing post-conflict conditions,[13] it is important to stress two things. First, the majority of the people I worked with do not recognise their self-care practices as particularly Serbian. Secondly, they do not experience the post-conflict period as truly a time of healing. Not yet. And maybe they never will. Some even claim that physically they feel worse than they felt in the 1990s. Yet they also seem to want to hold onto an equation between their personhood and their health, even as they reject any amelioration of their health as proposed, in part, by the symbolically therapeutic projects of the international community. These, indeed, are often received as infantilising and hypocritical (Pupavac 2005). Many, further, refuse to be understood in terms of the past – either as guilty for the war or dealing with or recovering from this guilt afterwards.[14]

---

12 Bearing in mind that all the 1990s conflicts took place outside of Serbia proper (except for the NATO bombing that destroyed a number of bridges, landmarks and public buildings inside the country), intervention for Serbians also served as an analytical framework to make sense of battles raging hundreds of kilometres away.

13 For rich and illuminating depictions of the moral landscapes of international humanitarianism, see Fassin 2011; Kennedy 2004; Redfield 2006. For analysis of similar struggles over narratives of modernity and backwardness in the vicinity of humanitarian interventions, see Fong 2007.

14 Some are visibly disgusted with what they understand as a situation where their right to healing is denied, because they are supposedly deemed undeserving. For an interesting discussion of the right to healing, see Petryna 2013.

Linked to these statements of personal independence, a number of my informants insist on their autonomy in taking care of their own body and health. They manage their conditions by excessively monitoring their health indicators and by naturalising their ailments through an assumption of (self-bestowed) authority in discussing them. Some project a particular sense of righteousness in criticising international humanitarianism on the one hand, while on the other embracing the potent language of haemoglobin level graphs and access to imported medical materials. The practices people describe of quasi-systematic self-monitoring and -measurement, using aetiological language and treating themselves, should not only be read as a form of healthcare in the last resort (as people lacking access to formal medicine) but also as forms of self-discipline and a particular form of contemporary culture of self-care in Serbia.[15]

Registering various tensions in health work, including forms of attention to the dead and ailing body in transitional Serbia, this chapter has argued that various practices of monitoring one's physiology mark the passing of time since the end of the wars. Some people I have described use their awareness of their health to 'pass through', or traverse, previous social and political identifications; this is often a matter of their insisting they are well (even when they are possibly not), and so making a claim to their autonomy, continued integrity or survival. The notion of good health translates into a range of different ideas: of entrenched inequalities among the population, of physical or social capital, of feelings of suspicion and indignation, and of other personal and social values and expectations. People both act on their expectations vis-à-vis and construct these as conceptual resources, since it is through the circulation of biomedical and political categories of health that people sometimes keep tabs on public modes of post-socialist and post-conflict temporality. Sometimes lacking healthcare, sometimes refusing it in the terms it is offered, people adopt a particular interpretive language of the body in such a way that it grants them authority over their bodies as knowable entities. Their aetiological language, compulsive checking of health indicators, naturalisation of ailments and general self-care are not only healthcare in extremis but may stand for a mode of self-discipline that aspires to record the nation's historical passage as this is irregularly inscribed on the body.

Acknowledgements

Different versions of this paper were presented at the Legal Knowledge and Anthropological Engagement conference in Cambridge (2008), at the London

---

15   These practices resisting or palliating medicalising conditions of the self, or the body, certainly recall the notion of 'biological citizenship' (Petryna 2002; Rose and Novas 2005). Yet people's eagerness to participate in social constructions of their own health is not always motivated by a desire to take part in 'global corporate or pharmaceutical citizenship' (see Dumit 2010; Ecks 2005; Hayden 2003; Van der Geest 1984a, 1984b).

School of Hygiene & Tropical Medicine (2010) and at the Materialities of Passing workshop, organised at the Museum of Cultural History in Oslo (2013). My sincere thanks to the organisers of these events and for their comments. I am especially grateful to the volume editors Peter Bjerregaard, Anders Emil Rasmussen and Tim Flohr Sørensen for their generous attention and insights. Warm thanks also to Tanja Petrović for her close reading of the chapter. The research on which this chapter is based was funded by the Wenner-Gren Individual Research Grant and Peterhouse Fellowship.

References

Adams, V., 1998. *Doctors for Democracy: Health Professionals in the Nepal Revolution*. New York: Cambridge University Press.

Asad, T., 2011. Thinking about the secular body, pain and liberal politics. *Cultural Anthropology*, 26(4): 657–675.

Banatvala, N. and Zwi, A. B., 2000. Conflict and health. Public health and humanitarian interventions: Developing the evidence base. *British Medical Journal*, 321(7253): 101–105.

Briggs, C. L. and Mantini-Briggs, C., 2003. *Stories in the Time of Cholera: Racial Profiling during a Medical Nightmare*. Berkeley: University of California Press.

Brotherton, S. P., 2008. 'We have to think like capitalists but continue being socialists': Dedicalized subjectivities, emergent capital, and socialist entrepreneurs in post-Soviet Cuba. *American Ethnologist*, 35(2): 259–274.

Cardozo, B. L., Vergara, A., Agani, F. and Gotway, C. A., 2000. Mental health, social functioning, and attitudes of Kosovar Albanians following the war in Kosovo. *The Journal of the American Medical Association*, 284: 569–577.

Derikonjić, M., 2005. Snadbevali VMA starim lekovima. Podignuta optužnica protov dva oficira. *Politika*, 18 November.

Dumit, J., 2010. Normal Insecurities, Healthy Insecurities. In: H. Gusterson and C. Besteman, eds, *The Insecure American: How We Got Here and What We Should Do About It*. Berkeley: University of California Press, pp. 163–181.

Ecks, S. 2005. Pharmaceutical citizenship: Antidepressant marketing and the promise of demarginalization in India. *Anthropology & Medicine*, 12(3): 239–254.

Farmer, P., 2003. *Pathologies of Power: Health, Human Rights, and the New War on the Poor*. Berkeley: University of California Press.

Fassin, D., 2005. Compassion and repression: The moral economy of immigration policies in France. *Cultural Anthropology*, 20(3): 362–387.

Fassin, D., 2008. The humanitarian politics of testimony: Subjectification through trauma in the Israeli–Palestinian conflict'. *Cultural Anthropology*, 23(3): 531–558.

Fassin, D., 2011. *Humanitarian Reason: A Moral History of the Present*. Berkeley: University of California Press.

FIDH (International Federation for Human Rights), 2005. *International Fact-finding Mission. Alternative Report in the Application of the ICESCR. Serbia: Discrimination and Corruption, the Flaws in the Health Care System.* April 2005, 416(2). Paris: FIDH. http://www.ifhhro.org.

Fong, V., 2007. SARS, a shipwreck, a NATO attack, and September 11, 2001: Global information flows and Chinese responses to tragic news events. *American Ethnologist*, 34(3): 521–539.

Gibson, D., 2001. Negotiating the new health care system in Cape Town, South Africa: Five case studies of the acutely chronically ill. *Medical Anthropology Quarterly*, 15(4): 515–532.

Global IDP, 2002. *Profile of Internal Displacement – Yugoslavia (Federal Republic of). Compilation of the Information Available in the Global IDP Database of the Norwegian Refugee Council.* http://www.idproject.org.

Gredelj, S., Gavrilović, Z. and Šolić, N., 2005. *Profesija (i) korupcija. Aktiviranje profesionalnih udruženja u borbi za integritet pro fesije i protiv korupcije.* Beograd: Centar za monitoring i evaluaciju.

Hayden, C., 2003. *When Nature Goes Public: The Making and Unmaking of Bioprospecting in Mexico.* Princeton and Oxford: Princeton University Press.

Helsinki Committee for Human Rights, 2001. *Survey of Serbia's Health Service.* Helsinki: Helsinki Committee for Human Rights.

Hjelm, K., Nyberg, P., Isacsson, A. and Apelqvist, J., 1999. Beliefs about health and illness essential for self-care practice: A comparison of migrant Yugoslavian and Swedish diabetic females. *Journal of Advanced Nursing*, 30(5): 1147–1159.

Hjelm, K. G., Bard, K., Nyberg, P. and Apelqvist J., 2005. Beliefs about health and diabetes in men of different ethnic origin. *Journal of Advanced Nursing*, 50(1): 47–59.

IPHS (Institute of Public Health of Serbia), 2009. *Health of Population of Serbia: Analytical Study 1997–2009.* Belgrade: Institute of Public Health of Serbia, 'Dr. Milan Jovanović Batut'.

Jones, S. G., Hilborne, L. H., Anthony, C. R., et al., 2006. *Securing Health: Lessons from Nation-Building Missions*, RAND Center for Domestic and International Health Security. Santa Monica: RAND Corporation.

Kennedy, D., 2004. *The Dark Sides of Virtue: Reassessing International Humanitarianism.* Princeton: Princeton University Press.

Kleinman, A., Das, V. and Lock, M. M., eds, 1997. *Social Suffering*. Berkeley: University of California Press.

Kunitz, S. J., 2004. The making and breaking of Yugoslavia and its impact on health. *American Journal of Public Health*, 94(11): 1894–904.

Luta, X. and Dræbel, T., 2013. Kosovo-Serbs' experiences of seeking healthcare in a post-conflict and ethnically segregated health system. *International Journal of Public Health*, 58(3): 377–383.

Marković, M., 2010. *The Right to Health.* University of Aberdeen School of Law. http://www.abdn.ac.uk/law/hhr.shtml.

McCarthy, M., 2007. Serbia rebuilds and reforms its health-care system. *Lancet*, 369: 360.

Nelson, B. D., Simić, S., Beste, L., et al., 2003. Multimodal assessment of the primary healthcare system of Serbia: A model for evaluating post conflict health systems. *Prehospital and Disaster Medicine*, 18(1): 6–13.

Petrović-Šteger, M., 2009. Anatomising Conflict: Accounting for Human Remains. In: M. McDonald and H. Lambert, eds, *Social Bodies*. Oxford: Berghahn, pp. 47–76.

Petryna, A., 2002. *Life Exposed: Biological Citizens after Chernobyl*. Princeton: Princeton University Press.

Petryna. A., 2013. The right of recovery. *Current Anthropology*, 54(S7): 67–76.

Pupavac, V., 2001. Therapeutic governance: Psycho-social intervention and trauma risk management. *Disasters*, 25(4): 358–372.

Pupavac, V., 2005. The Demoralised Subject of Global Civil Society. In G. Baker and D. Chandler, eds, *Global Civil Society: Contested Futures*. London: Routledge, pp. 45–58.

Pupavac, M. and Pupavac, V., 2012. Trauma advocacy, veteran politics and the Croatian therapeutic state. *Alternatives*, 37(2): 199–213.

Redfield, P., 2006. A less modest witness: Collective advocacy and motivated truth in a medical humanitarian movement. *American Ethnologist*, 33(1): 3–26.

Rose, N. and Novas, C., 2005. Biological Citizenship. In A. Ong and S. J. Collier, eds, *Global Assemblages: Technology, Politics, and Ethics as Anthropological Problems*. London: Blackwell, pp. 439–63.

Scheper-Hughes, N., 1992. *Death without Weeping: The Violence of Everyday Life in Brazil*. Berkeley: University of California Press.

Tapas, M., 2006. Emotions and the intergenerational embodiment of social suffering in rural Bolivia. *Medical Anthropology Quarterly*, 20(3): 399–415.

Thoms, T. O. and Ron, J., 2007. Public health, conflict and human rights: Toward a collaborative research agenda. *Conflict and Health*, 1(11), doi: 10.1186/1752-1505-1-11.

Toole, M. J., Galson, S. and Brady, W., 1993. Are war and public health compatible? *Lancet*, 341(8854): 1193–1196.

Van der Geest, S., 1984a. Anthropology and pharmaceuticals in developing countries – I. *Medical Anthropology Quarterly*, 15(3): 59–62.

Van der Geest, S., 1984b. Anthropology and pharmaceuticals in developing countries – II. *Medical Anthropology Quarterly*, 15(4): 87–90.

Vlajinac, H., Marinkovik, J., Kočev, N., et al., 2008. Years of life lost due to premature death in Serbia (excluding Kosovo and Metohia). *Journal of the Royal Institute of Public Health*, 122: 277–284.

WHO (World Health Organization), 2011. Countries: Serbia. http://www.who.int/countries/srb/en/.

Chapter 6

Doubting the Dead:
Approximations of Passing in a
Papua New Guinean Community

Anders Emil Rasmussen

Introduction: Granting Death the Benefit of the Doubt

> What, then, is it to cross the ultimate border? What is it to pass the term of one's life? Is it possible? Who has ever done it and who can testify to it? The "I enter", crossing the threshold, this "I pass" puts us on the path, if I may say, of the *aporos* or of the *aporia*: the difficult or the impracticable, here the impossible, passage, the refused, denied or prohibited passage, indeed the nonpassage, which can in fact be something else, the event of a coming or of a future advent which no longer has the form of the movement that consists in passing, traversing, or transiting. (Derrida 1993: 8)

During my most recent visit to the Mbuke Islands in Manus Province, Papua New Guinea, a group of young men and I had sailed to a small and unpopulated island where we were going to hunt sea turtles. As we had walked from the boat onto the beach one of my companions turned towards the bush that constitutes the island's interior and started talking, saying, among other things, 'We have come from Mbuke Island to catch a few sea turtles, these will be shared in the community', after which he threw a few coins and some tobacco into the bush, and we carried on without further ado. It was not at all unusual for the Mbuke men with whom I went on fishing and trading expeditions around Manus Province to make these sorts of small sacrifices or to have such brief conversations with places where they do not themselves live. One explanation they gave me was that the people who lived there before or those who died on that spot or who were buried there, might be present and might have an opinion about the presence of specific (living) others. To these presences it should be explained who we were, and why we were there, otherwise they might make it hard for us to succeed in our errand. As we proceeded down the beach I asked the young man why he had spoken into the bush, to which he answered in a somewhat indifferent tone: 'It is just custom, you know, and who knows if there are really any dead people there or not, but I did it anyway so at least if there are any, they will not be angry'.

As I argue in this chapter, many measures taken by the Mbuke in relation to those who have passed, and in dealing with localities and various kinds of containers for passing on, are, like this young man's, pragmatic acts granting the dead and the living the benefit of the doubt: just in case the spirits of the dead actually exist and can harm us, he spoke to the bush that day. I address here the apparent paradox that while many of my informants said that what happens after death cannot be known, they nevertheless do a number of things to appease the anger of the dead, to confine their movement, and to prevent aspects of persons ever to 'pass on'. Materialities of passing among the Mbuke, then, constitute 'precautionary approximations', attempts to know and act in accordance with what ultimately cannot be known. This brings me to the conclusion that doubt and uncertainty should not be understood simply as the temporary absence of knowledge or certainty, but can also be a basic assumption and knowledge proposition governing action in its own right.

The above quote from Derrida highlights the connection between passing, locality and movement. In the sense that the last anyone saw of the dead persons was when they got on the path of the *aporia,* of the passage that cannot be known, which might in fact be impassable, it is reasonable to assume that some aspects of the dead person might be stuck on the location where they entered the passage. Tracing through seemingly contradictory and indeed explorative dealings with the localities and containers of the personhood of the dead, I discuss how the dispersed, distributed and highly dangerous 'soul-stuff' of the dead causes Mbuke people to act with 'precautionary approximations', granting the dead the benefit of the doubt.

Context

Mbuke Islands constitute a small group of islands in the open sea to the far south in Manus Province, Papua New Guinea. Mbuke people belong to the ethnic group who currently identify themselves as the 'Titan' (previously simply the 'Manus', see Fortune [1935] 1969, Mead [1956] 2001) a group that was until recently part of a system of 'ecological niches' tying together several different ethnic groups in networks of barter and exchange in the southern part of Manus (Mead 1930; Schwartz 1963). Here Titans specialised in the extraction of marine resources that were bartered with other groups for garden produce, which the Titans themselves – who are more or less landless – have never themselves produced (cf. Mead 1930). The Titans, and people from southern Manus in general, are well described and well-known in anthropology through the work of authors such as Reo Fortune, who wrote about the 'ancestor cult' among Titans ([1935] 1969) to which I return below, as well as through the works of Margaret Mead ([1956] 2001) and Ted Schwartz (1962), who both wrote about cultural change, focusing in particular on the indigenous socio-religious movement, the

Paliau Movement. The Paliau Movement was inspired by the advent of WWII in Manus – in the form of the rapid construction of a vast American military base, among other things – where people in Manus were exposed to the social organisation (of army entities) and technological accomplishments (relating to war) of those who they grouped simply as 'white people'. This movement aspired for improved relations with the colonial 'masters' (as they referred to themselves as), education for locals and access to the technology and living standards of 'white people', but it also aimed at finding the true knowledge about God, which the movement's leader claimed had been kept hidden from the locals by 'white people' (Otto 1992a; 1992b). Paliau Movement's current version, known as Win Neisen, entails a combination of ancestor belief and Christianity, to which I return below.

Being poor in land, the Mbuke, like other Titans, built their houses on stilts on reefs and close to small islands, and only within the last 50 years have a growing number of houses been built on the actual islands. The current population living on – and next to – the three biggest islands of the Mbuke group of islands number around 800 to 900 people, but in addition there are approximately 600 people who identify themselves as Mbuke and live in the urban centres around the country, where many of them occupy high-end jobs due to their extraordinarily high level of education (see Rasmussen 2015a: 27–55). As I have elaborated elsewhere (ibid.) both the Paliau Movement and the gradual collapse of the system of ecological specialisations have been key factors in making education and money important parts of Mbuke peoples' lives. Almost without exception, Mbuke work migrants return to the islands when out of a job, after retirement or, finally, after death. Accompanying dead bodies back from urban centres or attending funerals are among the most usual reasons for visiting home villages, and all of the migrants I spoke to during fieldwork among urban migrants from Mbuke stated that they intended to be buried in the ancestral ground of their home villages (Rasmussen 2015a: 50–51). I have not heard of any Mbuke person who has been buried outside Mbuke Islands, and in 1999 neither had Gustafsson (1999: 78), who did fieldwork among the Mbuke in the 1980s and 90s (Gustafsson 1992; 1999). This may be due to the fact, as I return to below, that for many Mbuke people the locality of the physical and the metaphysical remains of the dead are highly intertwined. It is the dealings with and manipulation of this locality and containment of the 'stuff of the dead' that I address in this chapter.

While away, migrants provide a constant inflow of remittances and the majority of people living in the villages make their livelihoods from a combination of remittance money and the surrounding sea. Men spend much time fishing and otherwise harvesting the resources of the sea, and for this reason part of my daily participant observation entailed going fishing with bands of men. My first example of materialities of passing among the Mbuke comes from one such occasion.

Places of Passing: Knowing Where They Are Not

I was headed in a canoe with my friend Paul[1] to a reef between two uninhabited islands in Mbuke Islands. We were going to dive with spear guns for fish but had been delayed in our departure and it was afternoon already. Noting this, Paul said: 'We better go back in a few hours, because on late afternoon that place it not very good for people with your kind of skin'. Assuming that Paul was referring to my light skin tone in comparison to Mbuke people, I objected that midday is actually the worst time of day to be in the sun. 'I am not worried about the sun, I am worried that the dead people on those islands might see your different looking skin; they might get angry that you fish there'. His concern was that in a few hours the sun would start setting and the 'human shadows' (*muluan a lamat*), spirits of the dead, who might reside in that area, would become active and discover me.

One deceased person, in particular, who in fact died on that very reef, worries some Mbuke people when they travel through that area, and it was this person who Paul was especially concerned about. The reef between those particular islands is rich in a particular species of fish living in the sea grass in the shallow waters – which was why we had gone there – but under the sea one also discovers remains of houses that once stood there on poles. One of them was the house of a man called Po, whose death caused the abandoning of the group of houses built on that particular reef. Po died shortly after WWII, when he found what he thought was a discarded barrel of military supplies floating in the sea and brought it to his house. During the years immediately after the war people in Manus found many useful items drifting in the sea, things left behind by the various armies who had made their way through the province, occupying and fighting over the area (Australians, Japanese and Americans). When Po tried to dismantle the barrel with a hammer it revealed itself as a naval mine left behind by the war. The mine killed him, but not only that, the explosion scattered his remains all over his house, his neighbour's house and the nearby island. Po became a casualty of a war that had already ended, a war that concerned power relations between faraway countries. Immediately after this shocking event Po's remains were collected, wrapped in cloth and buried. His house and the neighbouring house were burned down along with everything in them in an attempt to ensure that all that was left of Po was really gone.

But Po was still there, in the area next to the beach on the shallow reefs connecting the two islands. People saw him haunt the area and no one dared go there anymore. The uneasy 'shadow' of Po haunted a large area and caused sickness and death to those who came close. Eventually it was decided to collect Po's 'soul-stuff' and try to contain it in one place. A great number of men gathered at night, sealed off their faces from possession with face decorations, and then

---

1   I have changed the names of my Mbuke informants for ethical reasons. Even if those quoted here know and have consented to the fact that I write about them, they may still prefer not to have their name quoted directly, and I have likewise avoided quotes and example where persons can be directly identified by others.

circled the area over which Po's remains had been spread, paddling in canoes, walking through the bush of the island and making noise. While beating drums and blowing horns, they gradually closed their circle, in the middle of which they had placed a clay pot floating on two rafters. With continuing noise Po was eventually 'contained' in the clay pot. The small raft was pushed in front of a canoe followed by the rest of the canoes crewed by the men, who continued their noise. Eventually the pot was set adrift and it made its way to a nearby island. According to the many versions I have been told of this local 'horror story', the move confined Po to a smaller area and made him more accommodating. In theory, the area where his house stood before should no longer be dangerous, as his ability to cause sickness and death should gradually weaken as he becomes progressively less identifiable as an entity. But Paul nevertheless felt uncertain about how Po might be able to affect and harm me while diving on the very reef where his house had stood and where he had died, uncertain whether the attempt at containing and moving Po had been successful. The paradox of this story is that in theory Po should not be there after the move, but Paul and others nevertheless grant him and those who travel there the benefit of the doubt.

The story of this tragic event reveals a tendency among some Mbuke people to associate the 'soul stuff' of the dead person with the physical matter of the person. I adopt here the term *soul-stuff* from earlier ethnographies of the Titans (Mead 1934, Fortune [1935] 1969, for example), to highlight the way in which spiritual matter is occasionally treated very much like material matter (as stuff), and the two tend to overlap and interlink, as we see also in the next section. To this day, regardless of specific religious orientation, when Mbuke people bury their dead, they will also sometimes bury with them the mat or cloth upon which the deceased lay, and quite often break up and burn the floor upon which the person died. Not only is soul-stuff associated with material stuff in the event of death, it can also *leak out* on specific locales from living persons in the event of injury. If a child falls down the stairs and breaks the skin, for example, parents will occasionally whip the steps with leaves that the child will then sleep upon the following night, so as to reabsorb from the leaves what may have spilled out. In associating the soul-stuff of the person with their physical 'stuff' after death, the skeletal remains play an important role.

Such notions were even more prevalent in pre- and early-colonial Manus. Thanks to the work of Reo Fortune, the Titans (at the time known as the Manus) were for many years well-known in anthropology for the role played among them by ancestral spirits in upholding a strict moral order, as described in Fortune's book, *Manus Religion* ([1935] 1969). At the time of Fortune's fieldwork, the spirits of the dead were most directly associated with their skeletal remains through the skulls of high-ranking men who had been leaders of extended households and who, after death, were referred to as *moenpalit* (translated by Fortune as 'Sir Ghost'). After their death, the bodies of such men were either buried and later exhumed or left in their houses to start decomposing, after which, in both cases, their heads were detached from the body and hung from the ceilings of houses or kept in some part of the house. In this way they were present to oversee the moral behaviour of those in the household, breaches of which they punished with sickness, misfortune and death, while simultaneously acting as guardian ancestral spirits of those individual households (ibid.: 5–6). Nearly all sickness and death was attributed to offended *moenpalits*, whether one's own guardian ancestral spirit or that of the offended party (Fortune [1935] 1969: 1–8). But their ability to affect the lives of the living gradually diminished with time, as they could only affect those particular persons with whom they had specific relationships before death (Gustafsson 1992: 36), and who would obviously also die eventually, and thereby diminish the number of relationships a dead person had with living persons. The dead person's agency was especially determined by their relationship with that son for whom they were the guardian spirit (cf. Fortune [1935] 1969: 13), and also, it seems, by the extent to which the son recognised the ancestor's efficacy. The *moenpalit* was considered the guardian ancestor of his successor and his 'house' until he failed in protecting the household, as revealed by some disaster befalling it (Mead 1934: 82). As Fortune noted, 'the Manus [Titans] believe in a personal guardian from death and disaster and in a moral governor ... but they quail in their belief whenever a death occurs' (1969: 8).

In these older accounts the spirits were also fairly localised and Margaret Mead noted that the ancestral spirits had no omnipresence (Mead 1934: 83) and people therefore had to call upon them, as is still the case today (cf. Rasmussen 2015a: 78ff). As we have seen above, this locality could be changed. Both in discussing the option of whether or not to convert to Christianity with Reo Fortune (missions were present in Manus also during Fortune's fieldwork) and on the occasion of deaths, informants revealed to Fortune that *moenpalits* were only powerful as long as their skulls were present. If Fortune's informants were going to convert to Christianity they would simply throw the skulls into the sea, and thereby be rid of the ancestor (Fortune [1935] 1969: 6); similarly, on the occasion of a son's death, the skull of his father would be hurled into the sea or battered to powder and thrown into the flames (ibid.: 8). After this treatment of the material remains the spirit would be reduced to a 'vague lurking danger of the middle seas, not very seriously regarded', only to gradually become a sea-slug or some other low form of sea life (ibid.: 8). There was, in this sense, no promise of eternal life in the 'ancestor cult' and eventually the guardian ancestor – previously feared for his fierceness in upholding morals – became a nameless ghost, once his own relations started dying. Finally, he was nothing but a lower form of sea life (ibid.).

Elsewhere I have discussed at length the significance of addressing the spirits of the dead with words as a way of cursing others, ultimately to affect the actions of those living others (Rasmussen 2015a: 77–99). These curses, referred to as *tandritanitani* (translated by Fortune as literally referring to 'making a ghostly influence come on top of [someone]' [1935] 1969: 78) are 'cast' onto people who fail to meet the perceived moral obligations of those who cast the curse. To this day these curses result in many different kinds difficulties such as bad luck and loss of jobs as well as, ultimately, sickness and death. In contemporary Mbuke, people are, for the most part, doubtful and uncertain about the abilities of the spirits of the dead and other classes of spirits to actually affect the living in response to these calls to them. In the case of sickness, people will try out various treatments, most often starting with 'white medicine' (medicine associated with 'white people') before consulting diviners or otherwise trying to figure out how they may have failed to live up to moral obligations. In the current use of the *tandritanitani*-curse many informants are well aware that calling upon ancestral agency to set right moral wrongs only works because people (themselves included) believe that they work: 'It is the fear that it might work that makes it work', as one informant told me in an interview (cf. Rasmussen 2015a: 89). Fortune also indicated a highly pragmatic tendency when noting that 'the Manus native [*sic*] regards belief pragmatically for its social uses' (Fortune [1935] 1969: 5), and that they 'have a social purpose for the ghosts, but they have little respect for ghosts except for this purpose' (ibid.: 6). It is also clear that Titans, both in the present and in the period described by Fortune, were full of doubt, but a doubt that was useful in itself. We might argue that even then, as now, it is the fact that 'they might be there' and 'they might be able to make me sick' that is useful in causing acts of precautionary approximation, such as compensating those who feel wronged, avoiding specific locales and speaking to spirits who may inhabit certain places.

In this section we have seen that there is no clear or simple distinction between the material remains of the dead person and that person as a metaphysical being. In that sense, certain materialities of passing contain those who have passed, and the dead's actual spiritual being might be present in the vicinity of their remains. As also noted, the presence of the dead as social agents fades with time, and this gradual process is paralleled in a series of practices of pre-death passing among the Mbuke. While we have seen here that people in Manus did much to assist and force the dead to become confined to specific locales once they had passed, it may be argued that Mbuke people do equally as much to limit the amount of 'stuff' that actually passes on with the end of a life in the first place. Much attention is given to the process of 'gradual death', which is the part of death that takes place *prior* to biological death.

Passing on Personhood: Gradual Death Prior to Death

The notion that death is not a singular moment, but rather is looked upon as a prolonged process during which the person and social relations are gradually transformed, is well-known in the ethnographic and archaeological record from around the world (see overview in this book's introduction; Lykkegård this volume; Sørensen this volume). We are familiar, for example, with mortuary practices entailing more than one burial, hence associating the gradual process of passing with aspects of what is often described in anthropology as mortuary practices or mortuary ritual (Hertz [1907] 2009; Lykkegård this volume) all of which is somehow initiated by the event of biological death (Willerslev, Christensen and Meinert 2013: 1). Hertz famously argued, drawing on material from the Dayak of Indonesia, that the processes and rituals conducted after the event of biological death were what helped people 'triumph over death' by restoring peace and order ([1907] 2009: 86). In Melanesia such gradual processes often entail various transactions and ceremonial exchanges during which social relations are reconstituted, social 'roads' are re-drawn and the person is symbolically 'decomposed' (e.g. Mosko 1983; Strathern 1992: 76; Mimica 2003) when the deceased person is 'finished' with regard to otherwise ongoing social relations (cf. Foster 1995: 97). Among the Mbuke too, passing into death and thereafter being dead may be described as a gradual transformation, a transformation of the person from being a full-fledged participant in social relations even long after death, towards an increasingly 'vague spirit of the middle waters', eventually to become a lower form of sea life.

Interestingly however, among the Mbuke the process of reconstituting social relations and the transformation or dissolution of the person starts prior to death, by the ageing person *passing on* 'parts' of themselves (abilities, rights, powers) to younger relatives (Rasmussen 2013; 2014). This aspect of gradual death indicates that it might be a mistake to reduce the study of human passing simply to actual biological death and society's subsequent attempted victory over the event, even if, as we have seen, the moment and locality of death is not unimportant. There are a number of skills and 'offices' that Mbuke people *pass on* once they find themselves ageing or anticipate their own death for any reason. In this way it may be argued that they prevent certain aspects of personhood from ever 'passing away' entirely. For example, the skill of building large seagoing outrigger canoes among the Mbuke is referred to as having an 'axe', but this is not an actual physical axe, referring rather to an exchangeable part of the canoe builder's personhood (Rasmussen 2013: Part 2). When passing this on it sometimes entails the transfer of actual tools, or alternatively chewing food and spitting it into the mouth of the receiver, but in either case the transaction entails saying 'I am giving it to you' and, most often, the statement alone constitutes the transaction (Rasmussen 2014: 66). One informant I interviewed gave an example of how the skill of building canoes is passed on from one generation to the next:

> He lines up all of his tools; "These are your tools now [the old man says to his son], I will die now", and he gives them along with that power that he has over the axe, because that axe doesn't belong to him – it was a forefather type of thing, it came, it came, and it came to him. To continue he has to give it to one of his sons, ah? (Rasmussen 2013: 89)

To continue it must be passed on. In a way the old man is correct in more than one sense to say 'I will die now' because apart from him approaching biological death, in the moment of his passing on his axe, that part of his personhood has indeed left his person. For example, one elderly canoe builder was often hanging around the places where canoes were being built during my fieldwork. He was famous for having been one of the best canoe builders on the Mbuke Islands, but when I asked him why he never helped building canoes he said: 'I have given my strength for that to my son'. In this sense, what was before contained in him had now become part of another, so this 'passing on' is in fact partial death, but it is also partial immortality. Some informants would even refer to the loosening skin of elderly people as evidence that they had begun this gradual death through distribution, emptying the container that is the body.

As Roy Wagner has noted for a different part of Papua New Guinea where a local conceptualisation of the person as someone who can be divided into parts is also present: 'People exist reproductively by being "carried" as part of another, and carry or engender others by making themselves genealogical or reproductive "factors" of these others' (Wagner: 1991: 163). Such notions of divisible personhood have been identified throughout Melanesia, and particularly in Papua New Guinea (ibid.; Mosko 2010, Strathern 1988 for example). This is a line of thought that can be traced back to the classic work of Marcell Mauss: 'Even when it [the gift] has been abandoned by the giver it still possesses something of him' (Mauss [1925] 1990: 12), and has been developed beyond the context of Oceania, for example through the work of Alfred Gell and his notion of 'the distributed person' (1998: 137ff). What is interesting in the case at hand is the very literal sense in which aspects of a person are passed on in the form of things (even if these things simply lend themselves as concepts, such as 'the axe') with the specific purpose of 'cheating death'; of ensuring that that particular aspect of personhood does not ever die. The way in which the passing on of 'axes' is practiced among the Mbuke indicates that it is envisioned as substantial parts of persons being transacted (for a detailed account see Rasmussen 2013: Part 2). However, in this context a large degree of doubt and suspicion is also present: Did the old man really pass it on? Did he have the right to do that? Is the receiver fit to hold it? Or, ultimately, did the 'axe' die with the man?

The final evidence is the actualisation of the 'axe' in the form of canoe prows in a particular shape associated with specific 'axes'. Only after having carved these is the passage of personhood from one person to the other recognised by other canoe builders. For example, when a man called Alou was a child he had received his father's axe. While he was building his first canoe, long after his father's death, a group of elderly men who sat nearby recognised 'the axe' in the shape of the canoe, and with this recognition came also the recognition that he had in fact received it, as he had claimed. According to Alou himself, one of the elderly men said, after having outlined the names of those who had built canoes looking precisely that way before Alou: 'It [the specific axe] has come to this man in this time ... all these men they are not dead, they are right there!', pointing at the canoe. No canoe builder who claims to have received his predecessor's 'axe' is ever recognised as truly a 'man with axe' (*pochimel*, literally: man-axe), before revealing this axe in the form of a canoe carved in a particular shape (Rasmussen 2013: 95–111). Even if the person can outline the genealogy of the 'axe' and his relationship with the person from whom it was obtained, it needs to be proven that the knowledge (skill) actually works. These criteria of visible proof of having received a particular skill confirms what Otto has noted about knowledge on Baluan, a neighbouring island of Mbuke: 'In general, knowledge which is not based on experience may be accepted as true if the effects of that knowledge are manifest' (Otto 1992a: 437). Even if in theory people pass on parts of themselves prior to death, and by doing so attempt to cheat death, in part, they are uncertain whether 'it' might have passed away with the dying man after all, until that aspect of personhood is rendered manifest in the form of a canoe.

Named skills (axes) appearing in the form of canoes is just one example of the incredible value Mbuke people tend to place on material evidence. My informants frequently told me that even if someone claims to be your friend or otherwise claims a particular relationship (even of kin), this cannot be believed unless tangible effects, such as gifts or acts of sharing, are evident. Relatives who do not send remittances upon request from village relatives are sometimes considered to be dead and are occasionally treated as such (by being ignored entirely) even when they visit the village (Rasmussen 2015b). Only what you have observed and personally experienced, only knowledge of which one has hard evidence, is trusted as true beyond doubt. Fortune likewise noted, with some amazement, in 1935, that Manus people had an abnormal desire for finding the truth, which he found was not very different from the scientific mode of thinking that he himself came from (Fortune [1935] 1969: xi).

Passing into Death

Alongside the potential presence of the dead in the place where they died or in their remains, and alongside the passing on of personhood prior to death, various forms of Christianity are present in Manus. Most widespread on Mbuke Islands is the religious aspects of the aforementioned social movement, Paliau Movement (see Mead [1956] 2001; Otto 1992a; 1992b; Schwartz 1962), currently known as 'Win Neisen'. Win Neisen has adopted many Christian concepts but has combined these with existing notions of ancestral presence. Ideas of an eternal afterlife, paradise, hell and the immortal soul, were all introduced by various missionaries: at first most Mbuke converted to Catholicism, (Gustafsson 1992: 102), and ideas and concepts from here have been modified in Win Neisen. These new conceptions have not, however, provided answers, but instead a series of questions, things for which they have no tangible evidence.

In contemporary Mbuke, Win Neisen's followers refer to it not as being a religion (*lotu*) but as a 'study group' (cf. Otto 1992b: 57). Thus, services in their meeting house do not include teachings and reading from the Bible but are structured around 'asking', 'informing' and 'reporting', and those who head the services are referred to as 'teachers'. All these activities revolve around a notion of continuously expanding *knowledge*[2] about the road to 'freedom', a local version of the coming of God's kingdom that entails freedom from hunger, sickness, toil, ageing and death (Otto 1992b). Because Satan entered the bodies of Adam and Eve, they lost this state of freedom, and confusion and sin have been part of all humans since (ibid.: 55). Therefore, the goal of this study group on Mbuke, as its followers on Mbuke Islands described it to me, is finding this road to the condition enjoyed by Adam and Eve prior to the fall, namely a state of freedom through *true knowledge*.

Paliau Maloat, the leader and initiator of the movement that initially carried his first name, argued that Manus people needed to create this new religion of their own, since the missions had – in conspiracy with the Australian colonial government – spoken in parables or allegories in order to keep the true knowledge from Manus people (Schwartz 1962: 257–258). To this end, Maloat told 'the long story of God' which combined stories from the Bible with local colonial history and events taking place in Manus. This story set straight some of the things 'white people' had lied about concerning the questions raised by the alleged the existence of God, the immortal soul and the afterlife (Gustafsson 1992: 107; Schwartz 1962). Maloat had received this true knowledge about Christianity directly from Jesus (Otto 1992b). According to some accounts of this exchange, collected by Schwartz, Jesus had in fact shown up in person and shown the original version of the Bible to Paliau, revealing its contents to him (Schwartz 1962: 257). A very general assumption in Win Nesien on Mbuke today is that if only everyone could be united in 'one knowledge', namely the true knowledge, rather than disagreeing about everything and coming up with his or her own specific explanations for the nature of things, then freedom would occur. Some even argue that there was, in fact, a brief period of 'freedom' in Manus after Maloat had set things straight, but that this was lost again once disagreement about the true knowledge occurred. In this sense, they explain human mortality with the absence of true human knowledge about death, and the many disagreements and doubts about it.

One might expect that the notion of an eternal soul would introduce the kind of duality between body and soul familiar from Christianity, but there seems – at least among the Mbuke members of Win Neisen – to be a continuity in associating the spiritual matter of the dead with their physical remains (as we have seen above). In situations of calling upon the spirits of the dead to participate and assist in a particular event, one will have to wait for them to walk from the cemetery, where their remains are buried (Rasmussen 2014: 70). Likewise, one elderly man who

---

2 Here the word *save* is most often used in Tok Pisin (PNG Pidgin English), the local lingua franca, which is the language often used in Win Neisen as the movement has always encompassed members from various different groups in Manus who speak different languages. In Titan language the word *pasan* is used, and is the one among several words for knowledge. I have most often heard *pasan* used in the meaning of information or factual knowledge as opposed to words like *lemwenemweneye* and *tilan*, which tend to connote things like wisdom and understanding.

was a member of Win Neisen, but who was also in the process of 'passing on' parts of himself, told me when I visited his house to say goodbye at the end of a fieldwork period, that 'next time you come around here, I will be living down there ...', pointing in the direction of the village graveyard, '... under the village'. Obviously this may have been a somewhat morbid joke, but one of the leading members of Win Neisen on Mbuke likewise claimed that the spirits of the dead actually reside under the cemetery. With the same sense of empiricism I have discussed above, he said that the notion that heaven should be 'above' makes little sense: 'Where would that be, outside the atmosphere or something?' It is, in fact, a widely shared assumption that the dead are located with their bones or are otherwise present in this world, waiting for the time of freedom to arrive. Some told me that they live in a community similar to that of the living, and that this community is enclosed by gates where gatekeepers keep track of who enters and who exits (to go visit the living).

In the early stages of the Paliau Movement the near-death experience of a man called Pondram became the basis upon which the new cemetery in the Manus village of Bunai was designed in the 1940s (Schwartz 1962: 296–297, plate 19). Pondram's experiences during his brief death included a vision of the gate to the other side. When he awoke he was temporarily speechless but constructed a model of the gate, based upon which a new gate to the village cemetery was made (ibid.: plate 19). In this case there seems also to be a fairly direct association with being buried in a specific location and entering the afterlife, since the new gate to the cemetery was constructed on the basis of the appearance of the gate to the other side as Pondram had seen it, even if it is not self-evident that those two gates should be in any way related. Again here it seems as though some Mbuke people feel they have to work to confine the dead in specific locales.

The Benefit of the Doubt: Materialities of Passing in Manus

I was sitting next to a house with a group of Mbuke people asking them about an upcoming funeral, when one of them asked me how such matters were dealt with in my own Danish family. My answer resulted in silence and frozen expressions. Having learned that all of my deceased relatives had, with my own complicity, been cremated (as is not unusual in Denmark) and after having experienced my indifference to this material fact, a woman commented, with some dismay: 'But how do you know, how *can* you know, that your ancestors will never again need their bones?!' Using the word *pasani* (know) here was no coincidence since the existence or non-existence, locality or absence, of the stuff of the dead is not, among the Mbuke, a matter of belief, but of knowing or not knowing, as should be clear from the previous sections. I had no evidence to provide this woman concerning how to be certain, for example, that no spiritual matter of my ancestors was destroyed when I had allowed for them to be burned. As Christina Toren has pointed out, when as anthropologists we characterise as *belief* what our interlocutors *know*, we misrepresent them (Toren 2007). While in Toren's case certain Fijians know that ancestors continue to live on the land that they inhabited in life (rather than believing it to be the case), Mbuke people are certain that they *possibly* do; they know that they cannot know for certain whether or not the dead reside where they did in life, whether they stay attached to their physical remains or not. They know that the destination of passing cannot fully be known, and act accordingly.

This woman's moral critique of my actions and my indifference does not simply reflect her particular beliefs concerning aspects of the dead person residing in their physical remains (since she cannot be certain that they do). Her critique was of my certainty concerning the end of passing: the fact that I had sent my dead on a particular path, a path that she felt cannot truly be known. In other words, I did not accept the cremation of my relatives because I believed that they had left their bodies anyway, but because I (claim to) know that they are completely gone. I had in no way granted my dead relatives the benefit of the doubt. Here this Mbuke woman seems to be in agreement with Elias Canetti, as discussed by Steiner ([1998] 2002), in deliberately not simply accepting death as normal and inevitable. Like religion which, according to Canetti, claims to know about the afterlife (ibid.: 16), in claiming to know the destiny of the dead we violate them; or in Canetti's words about death: 'If I accepted it, I would be a murderer'. From this perspective the atheist who also claims to know, is no better than the strongly religious person entering death confident to meet his or her maker. The passage of death puts us, as Derrida noted, on the path of the *aporia* of what might not be a passage at all (1993: 8); we can perceive that someone passed *away* but can never be certain where or what s/he passes into. At least, that would be the implication of what this woman said, and of many of the acts of precautionary approximation I have described. If the basis of knowledge is concrete observable and material evidence, which as we have seen is often the case among the Mbuke, then there can be no knowledge about death, only about passing, as noted also in the introduction of this book. Materialities and practices surrounding passing testify to a human preoccupation with approximating the limit of what can be known, in this case of trying to *confine, contain* and *explore* the matter of the dead, whether physical or metaphysical.

According to Van Gennep there is a widespread tendency in rites of passage in conjunction with death for people to have contradictory conceptions of the afterlife, and he claimed that this confusion was reflected in the rituals (1960: 146). I would argue that such incoherency is not simply 'confusion' (ibid.: 146), but constitutes a form of doubt that is useful in its own right and which does not constitute the absence of certainty or belief (cf. Pelkmans 2013), but is itself a knowledge proposition. Bloch makes a similar point in his discussion of doubt among the Zafimaniry of Madagascar. Here there is a striking similarity to the value placed on material evidence that I have discussed for Mbuke, and Bloch notes that evidence from senses is characteristic of Malagasy reasoning (2013: 49). The type of doubt that can potentially be dissolved by 'new evidence' is a type of doubt that exists within a dialogic movement from certainty towards the unknown; answers are here supported with empirical examples (ibid.: 48–49). This type of doubt may in the future be replaced by certainty when 'new empirical evidence' becomes accessible (ibid.). Bloch compares this doubt to methodological doubt in science. The other type of doubt identified by Bloch concerns things that cannot be known (ibid.: 52) and here Bloch states that even when having the same discussion twice, people agreed to completely different answers to the same questions (ibid.: 53). He attributed this to the fact that the subject matter was in doubt and will remain in doubt, and he concludes that doubt can be both a tool of gradually reaching certainty, as well as a tool for putting an end to speculation; 'this is a matter about which we cannot know', as one informant told him (ibid.: 52).

Pointing out, like others, that the anthropology of doubt is more or less non-existent, Bloch (2013: 44–45; cf. Pelkmans 2013; Bubandt 2014) argues that this is probably because of an absence of 'folk theories of doubt'. For an anthropologist it is obviously easier to deal with the sets of answers our interlocutors may provide to life's great questions, than with their questions, doubts and confusions. As I have argued elsewhere, one way of approaching social relations and the way they change is to explore the ways in which people themselves explore and change their relationships and basic assumptions through a dialectics of questions and answers (Rasmussen 2015a: 1–5). Similarly, not all actions are directed at any known goal but are rather results of preventive approximation, just in case that which might be actually is.

If 'God is Man's stolen essence' (Ludwig Fauerbach, cited in Rapport 2008: 330), and if, as Rapport argues, in anthropology 'the sociocultural is the stolen essence of the personal' (Rapport 2008: 330), then accepting and, indeed, giving direction (or meaning) to the passage into death is not simply society's victory over death, but society's victory over the dead. A victory that the woman cited above also saw as a potential violation.

Conclusion: Knowing Where They are Not

During nighttime sailing trips with Mbuke men in their large outrigger canoes, I sometimes got the unsettling sense that they did not know where we were. They rarely use navigational equipment, sometimes they were clearly just guessing, and as anyone who has tried navigating without GPS devices will know, narrowing down one's exact position is always an approximation. On one occasion, while sailing on the edge of the vast Admiralty Sea, surrounded by complete darkness, I asked the man steering our course whether he actually knew where we were: 'No, I don't. But I know where we are not'. Likewise, when dealing with the dead, my Mbuke companions did not really know where they were, how to deal with them or whether they had fully passed on or not, but dwelling in this space of doubt they found places where they knew the dead were most likely not, and in places and situations where the dead might be present, they acted in ways that granted the dead, and by inference themselves, the benefit of the doubt. Tracing through seemingly contradictory and, indeed, explorative dealings with the localities and containers of personhood, I have demonstrated how the dispersed, distributed and sometimes highly dangerous 'soul-stuff' of the dead leaves Mbuke people with no other option than to act with 'precautionary approximations'. I have argued that Mbuke peoples' dealings with the stuff of the dead reflect a form of doubt that is not simply the temporary absence of belief or certainty, but a useful knowledge proposition in its own right. For this reason the Mbuke feel they have to work to confine and contain what is potentially the stuff of the dead or of those who are in the process of dying.

References

Bloch, J., 2013. Types of shared doubt in the flow of a discussion. In M. Pelkmans, ed., *Ethnographies of Doubt*. London: IB Taurus.

Bubandt, N., 2014. *The Empty Seashell: Witchcraft and Doubt on an Indonesian Island*. Cornell: Cornell University Press.

Derrida, J., 1993. *Aporias*. Translated from French by T. Dutoit. Stanford: Stanford University Press.

Fortune, R., 1935/1969. *Manus Religion: An Ethnographic Study of the Manus Navies of the Admiralty Islands*. Lincoln: University of Nebraska Press.

Foster, R., 1995. *Social Reproduction and History in Melanesia – Mortuary Ritual, Gift Exchange, and, Custom in the Tanga Islands*. Cambridge: Cambridge University Press.

Gell, A., 1998. *Art and Agency – An Anthropological Theory.* Oxford: Clarendon Press.

Gustafsson, B., 1992. *Houses and Ancestors.* PhD. Institut for antropologi, Gøteborg Universitet.

Gustafsson, B., 1999. *Traditions and Modernities in Gender Roles – Transformations in Kinship and Marriage among the M'buke from Manus Province*. Port Moresby: National Research Institute.

Hertz, R. [1907] 2009. *Death and the Right Hand*. Aberdeen: Cohen and West.

Mauss, M. [1925] 1990. *The Gift: The Form and Reason for Exchange in Archaic Societies.* London: Routledge.

Mead, M., 1930. Melanesian middlemen. *Natural History*, 30(2): 115–130.

Mead, M., 1934. Kinship in the Admiralty Islands. *Anthropological Papers of the American Museum of Natural History*, XXXIV(II): 181–358.

Mead, M. [1956] 2001. *New Lives for Old: Cultural Transformation – Manus, 1928–1953*. New York: Perennial.

Mimica, J., 2003. The death of a strong, great, bad man: An ethnography of soul incorporation. *Oceania*, 73(4): 260–286.

Mosko, M., 1983. Composition, de-composition and social structure in Bush Mekeo culture. *Mankind*, 14: 24–33.

Mosko, M., 2010. Partible penitents: Dividual personhood and Christian practice in Melanesia and the West. *Journal of the Royal Anthropological Institute*, 16: 215–240.

Otto, T., 1992a. The Paliau Movement in Manus and the objectification of tradition. *History and Anthropology*, 5(3–4): 427–454.

Otto, T., 1992b. From Paliau Movement to Makasol: The politics of representation. *Canberra Anthropology*, 15(1): 49–68.

Pelkmans, M., 2013. Outline for an ethnography of doubt. In: M. Pelkmans, ed., *Ethnographies of Doubt*. London: IB Taurus.

Rapport, N., 2008. Gratuitousness: Notes towards an anthropology of interiority. *The Australian Journal of Anthropology*, 19(3): 330–348.

Rasmussen, A. E., 2013. *Manus Canoes: Skill, Making and Personhood in Mbuke Islands (Papua New Guinea)*. Occasional Papers, The Kon-Tiki Museum, Oslo.

Rasmussen, A. E., 2014. Infinity in a spear – things as mediations among the Mbuke (Papua New Guinea). In: D. R. Christensen and K. Sandvik, eds, *Mediating and Re-mediating Death*. Farnham: Ashgate, pp. 63–74.

Rasmussen, A. E., 2015a. *In the Absence of the Gift: New Forms of Value and Personhood in a Papua New Guinea Community*. Oxford: Berghahn.

Rasmussen, A. E., 2015b. Visible while away: Migration, personhood, and the movement of money amongst the Mbuke of Papua New Guinea. In: O. Fuglerud and L. Wainwright, eds, *Objects and Imagination: Perspectives on Materialization and Meaning*. Oxford: Berghahn, pp. 81–92.

Schwartz, T., 1962. The Paliau Movement in the Admirality Islands, 1946–54. *Anthropological Papers of the American Museum of Natural History*, 49(2): pp. 211–421.

Schwartz, T., 1963. Systems of areal integration: Some considerations based on the Admiralty Islands of Northern Melanesia. *Anthropological Forum*, 1: 56–97.

Steiner, R. [1998] 2002. Against death: The case of Elias Canetti. In: J. Malpas, and R. C. Solomon, eds, *Death and Philosophy*. London: Routledge, pp. 15–19.

Strathern, M., 1988. *The Gender of the Gift*. Berkeley: University of California Press.

Strathern, M., 1992. Parts and wholes: Refiguring relationships in a post-plural world. In: A. Kuper, ed., *Conceptualising Society*. London: Routledge. pp. 75–104.

Toren, C., 2007. 'How do we know what is true?' In: R. Astuti, J. Parry and C. Stafford, eds, *Questions of Anthropology*. Oxford: Berg.

Van Gennep, A., 1960. *The Rites of Passage*. Translated from French by M. B. Vizedom and G. L. Caffee. Chicago: University of Chicago Press.

Wagner, R., 1991. The fractal person. In: M. Godelier and M. Strathern, eds, *Great Men and Big Men: Personifications of Power in Melanesia*. Cambridge: Cambridge University Press, pp. 159–174.

Willerslev, R., Christensen, D. R. and Meinert, L., eds, 2013. Introduction. In: *Taming Time, Timing Death: Social Technologies and Ritual*. Farnham: Ashgate, pp. 1–16.

Chapter 7

Untimely Death and Spirit Mobility in a Southern African Border Zone

Per Ditlef Fredriksen

The Long Wait

What happens when a spirit lingers in the wrong place? After a tragic, untimely death the experience of loss may be augmented by a sense of spatial dislocation. The body may need to be brought to the proper place of burial or, as will be explored here, it may already be buried but the new ancestral spirit is *not yet where it should be*. The passing thus remains incomplete, and both the living and the dead linger in a state of waiting. This is a challenging 'nothingness', at once empty and filled with anticipated potential (see the introduction to this volume), where one has to deal with the danger of *non-being* in the wrong place or, even worse, in uncontained, undefined *non-place*. A violent episode on the Swaziland-South Africa border on 26 May 2011 ripped open such a spatiotemporal void, which was to be filled with hesitation and stalled emotion, persisting until the disruption was corrected. This case elucidates an array of human and nonhuman (things, materials, ancestral beings) partakers and the dynamics between them – a dynamics that cannot be detached from its temporally deeper and geographically wider backdrop.

When crossing the border on their return home from Swaziland, three South Africans, two brothers and their uncle, were shot dead by Swaziland soldiers under suspicion of cattle smuggling. The men came from a rural border area in northern KwaZulu-Natal (KZN) known as Phondwane,[1] about 25 km from the town of Pongola. The tragedy was noted by several newspapers and brought to critical attention as part of Swazi armed forces' alleged 'shoot-to-kill policy' by a media commentator at the University of Swaziland.[2] Due to increased political tension and military presence the family was unable to cross the border, normally a

---

1   The area belongs under the Ntshengase Traditional Authority. I will refer to the area as Phondwane from here on, as this is the term preferred by community members themselves, including the chief. This is also in line with official name use, as the nodal point of the community is the premises of the local school, the Phondwane Primary School.

2   See http://swazimedia.blogspot.no/2011/05/shoot-to-kill-alive-and-well.html.

simple everyday affair, to bring home the *amadlozi*, the ancestral souls or spirits,[3] of the two young men and their uncle. Having waited more than a year, and after at least one failed attempt to address the spirits from behind barbed wire on the South African side, the spirits were finally brought back on 30 June 2012.

The aim of this chapter is to come to an understanding of intimate human/ nonhuman dynamics by being sensitive to local ways of engaging with the material world, with places, spaces and spirits – and to the engagements through which people attempt to transcend the ultimate nothingness of those who, or that which, has passed. Absence may be difficult to cope with ontologically and existentially, and to communicate verbally. As pointed out by Mikkel Bille et al. (2010: 11), the archaeological perspective can help in revealing and exploring not only what people say about absence and loss, but also what they do in the presence of absence. A specific focus on bodily practices and people's engagements with material culture can potentially add insights to experiences of such voids. I will here outline an approach that actively uses comparison and contrast as a means to tease out notions of nothingness, non-being, non-place and containment. The approach emphasises human/human and human/nonhuman dynamics in this particular context as a form of 'necropolitics', and combines anthropological insights with African philosophical critique.

The discussion centres on two broad stages of the tragedy's aftermath; the transportation and the integration upon arrival, advancing from Arjun Appadurai's (1986: 5) by now classic idea about the social life of things: 'it is things-in-motion that illuminate their human and social context'. Each stage in the process of making, moving or using a thing can potentially illuminate interaction between sets of human, material and spatial partakers in new ways, thereby offering novel insights into a particular materiality of passing. Specifically, the two-stage approach seeks to identify more precisely what the materials and objects involved in the waiting period and the successful transportation of contained 'soul stuff' (see Chapter 6 this volume) to the right place can reveal about passing

---

3   I use the term 'spirit' in the following, as this is most commonly referred to by those interviewed in this study, and is also the term commonly found in anthropological literature (see e.g. White 2010 for a recent example). However, there seems to be no clear separation of the concept of 'spirit' from that of 'soul'. All persons interviewed consider themselves Christian, including those who are a healer and ritual specialist (*sangoma*) or an herbalist and witch doctor (*inyanga*). Indeed, this is so for the vast majority in the area, although there is a growing number of Muslims. Thus, although the two terms could potentially be placed differently along a mind/matter axis, the use of 'spirit' here reflects its local and everyday pragmatic meaning, with no clear conceptual boundary between 'spirit' and 'soul'. Both terms refer generically to otherworldly ancestral beings. Typically, chants and prayers address both ancestors and God. A reason for this is that there is little if any conflict involved in being a regular churchgoer and still be a medium through which ancestors communicate with the living. An example confirming this seamless merge is that Phondwane's most respected and powerful *inyanga*, a specialist in the making and use of ritual medicine, is also bishop in a Zionist church.

Figure 7.1 On the morning of 30 June 2012: A large twig has been cut off the *umLahlabantu* tree (*Ziziphus mucronata*) standing next to the homestead, normally, a bundle of collected twigs are wrapped in a small straw mat for transportation

Source: Photo by the author.

Figure 7.2 Thorns that can catch and hold on to ancestral spirits
Source: Photo by the author.

and transience. In being employed to counter the potential of non-being and non-place, certain members of the material world may thereby function as an entry into relationships between embodiment, temporality and the state of being dead.

Twigs in Motion

The centrepiece of the following discussion is the spirits' means of transport: a twig from the tree *Ziziphus mucronata*, in English known as Buffalo Thorn (Figure 7.1). The tree is a familiar botanical constituent in the surroundings of many a homestead in northern KZN, and in popular folklore its twigs are well-known spirit carriers. The thorny twigs (Figure 7.2) are said to be able to catch or attach themselves to floating spirits, thereby providing material form and substance for transportation. The Zulu name is *UmPhafa* or also *umLahlankosi* (see Hutchings et al. 1996). The latter translates as 'that which buries the chief' (Hamber 2009: 1), confirming the tree's relation to elite graves. However, while the daily language of people in the rural area is Zulu they do live in a border zone with a tightly woven societal fabric that transcends the South Africa/Swaziland border. The ancestral interconnectedness is indicated by the preference of the Swazi name *umLahlabantu*, meaning, 'that which casts away people' (Hadebe 2002: 89). As the terms indicate, twigs from *Ziziphus mucronata* are used in mortuary rituals and to carry *amadlozi* from one place to another. The twig may even be given its own seat in an overcrowded minibus taxi, often with the demand of additional payment for the extra passenger (Hamber 2009: 1).

It must be noted at the outset that references to ways of using *Ziziphus mucronata* may be found in various open online sources, such as through a simple Google search. References also occur in museum journals (e.g. Koopman 2011) and in several peer-reviewed works by scholars within ethnopharmacology and ethnobotany (e.g. Bhat and Jacobs 1995; Kunene et al. 2009 Ndawonde et al. 2007), thus providing insights into the various ways in which parts of the tree, such as its roots, bark and leaves, are utilised in everyday life in different contexts in southern Africa. Yet, mentions of *Ziziphus mucronata* and its local name variants are curiously absent in scholarly ethnography, especially in the literature on Zulu-speakers. Apart from some rather superficial efforts to link the tree's connection to the dead and their spirits with elements of Ubuntu philosophy, the ontology underpinning trees, twigs and spirits as partakers in social dynamics remains to be explored in detail.

When preparing for a spirit transportation a few twigs are cut, usually from the *umLahlabantu* tree found closest to the homestead. Relatives, most often male and elderly, travel in pairs. They go to the site of death, and one of them addresses the spirit(s). This person carries the twig/spirit for the entire journey, and will communicate exclusively with it. In particular, he gives warnings before crossing water, a potential peril well-known to readers of 'classic' ethnographic accounts of Zulu (and, linguistically more broadly, Nguni) customs and local practice, seeking to calm his dead companion. The travel companion will take care of practicalities like asking for directions, organising bus or taxi travel and talking to fellow passengers. As we shall see, the careful and anxious silence while the journey is underway stands in striking contrast to the loud and festive successful arrival at home, a celebration meant for living and dead alike.

I will return in more detail to the unfolding of events on the arrival of the spirits of the three men back home, as these are a primary analytical focus. The exploratory path chosen here is to view the incident against the spatiotemporal background captured in previous comparative efforts to come to terms with rural engagements with clay and soil in south-eastern Africa (Fredriksen 2007, 2011, 2012). As it happens, I had been working closely with members of the family of the three killed men since 2007, including the paternal grandmother of the two brothers (she was also their uncle's paternal aunt). I was therefore allowed to join and observe the spirit transportation.

When tragedy struck in May 2011 I had slightly shifted attention to the various dynamics surfacing in the wake of the introduction of electricity in October 2010. Following the very same people in their domestic spaces, the aim was to add new layers of information about engagements with the material world. In addition, the scope was broadened to include all ritual specialists, both *sangoma* and *inyanga* (see discussion below), in the area. A core reason for this interest was that some community members spoke against the use of electricity in certain household spaces, on the grounds that loud sounds and flickering, flashing lights disturbed the ancestors. This was a reference to the potential harm caused by discontented spirits. While in general understood as powers of good, the spirits are also dangerous. To ignore them is to expose oneself to the danger of sickness and misfortune.

The Rural Home and Post-Apartheid 'Necropolitics'

The study's focus was now centred on the ways in which sensory experiences of the living formed part of continuous engagements with the *amadlozi*, and how such experiential qualities were ascribed by the living to the dead members of society. This shift was inspired by Jean-Pierre Warnier's (e.g. 2001; 2007; 2009) 'praxeological' ethnographic approach. Warnier's work qualifies multi-layered analysis of human bodies' constant involvement with the material world, thus providing context-sensitive ways to understand how human bodies' sensory-motoricity is implemented through materiality, and vice versa. In addition, by exploring further the originally Foucaldian notion of 'governmentality', Warnier's approach has a significant political dimension, thus enabling intimate human/ nonhuman engagements to be framed within local and regional power dynamics.

Hylton White's (2010; 2011) stirring analyses of northern KZN rural homes provided important insights into this combination of material intimacy and politics. White places rural Zulu households within a sociospatial 'necroculture':

the installation of deceased family members in the main house of the homestead (see discussion below) is viewed against a temporal background extending back to precolonial times; a dynamics of marriage exchange involving cattle wealth and a primary focus on the homestead's reproductive capacity. This organisation (see e.g. Guy 1979; 1987; 2005; Kuper 1980; 1982; Hall 1984; Huffman 2007) was shattered during the decades around the turn of the twentieth century, and replaced by a colonial-capitalist articulation of the rural household as the home of fathers who were migrant workers, thereby characterising it by the oscillating absence/presence of male family heads (White 2010: 508; 2011: 109; see also Hunter 2008). In this manner, the urban/rural separation was not only aligned with the work/home split but the separation was also perpetuated as an enduring geographical dualism. This dualism corresponded to distinctions made within colonial and apartheid discourse, between European modern urbanity and rural African tradition and kinship. Therefore, to many Zulu-speakers today, the city is still a place of 'whiteness' while the rural area is 'where the homes are' (see White 2010: 508–511). Consequently, the home in rural areas like Phondwane became a space where acts of memory and longing by families of migrants kept their presence alive.

The post-apartheid era has been characterised by a rise in mass unemployment (Barchiesi 2008), and White (2010: 513–514) observes that the place of the dead in the rural home continues to be a two-sided matter where dynamics of renewed estrangement and paradox have emerged. While ancestral spirits are still sources of aid and comfort, avoidance of rupture in relations with them continues to be important to the lives and livelihoods of the living. On the one hand the dead are desired to be close, for example in economic projects to improve domestic living conditions. On the other hand, however, to ancestral spirits such new schemes represent estranging or alienating desires that undermine their spaces, especially the *umsamo* or back part of the Great House (*indlunkulu*) of a homestead. This estrangement is often described by elderly members of the community in terms of unfamiliar and sharp sounds, bright and flickering lights, new (and non-smoky) smells associated with cooking, and novel tastes from (processed) foods. In other words, in this setting the introduction of gas stoves and electricity entailed the encounter of nonhumans (ancestors and mass-produced household utensils using electricity), spiralling into a novel, largely unforeseen dynamics, in some ways paralleling examples from eastern Africa (e.g. Winther 2005). Broadly speaking, as noted by White (2010: 511–516), this new, post-apartheid version of ancestral ambivalence means that the dead no longer embody the duality of the collective cultural past and hoped-for personal future. Instead, they have become sources of a foreign kind of power-relations characterised by anxiety and continuously unsettled compromise.

The unfolding of events discussed here, the aftermath of the three men's tragic deaths on 26 May 2011, should be seen against this background. The present post-apartheid status can be described as a form of 'necropolitics', in which the rural household is the arena for always-ongoing human/ancestral engagement and negotiation. The ways that the family in Phondwane dealt with the long-drawn-out wait for the spirits to return home were grounded in a spatiotemporal framework where the crucial point is for spirits to move from a state of relative *absence* in undefined, insecure non-space to a *presence* in secure, defined space. Rural families are more or less continuously seeking to solve the all-too-familiar problem of absent, oscillating male household members and the issue of their return as living fathers or sons or, alternatively, as ancestral beings who will be engaged in continued communication. The following account of the transport/ arrival of the three spirits thus depicts the experience of anxiety for dis-connection between spirit and home, and the efforts of bringing spirits from non-being in non-place to a place of socially mediated perpetual containment. As such, this Zulu case, perhaps in particular the concern with use of twigs for transport and containment of 'soul-stuff' and constant flip-side relationship between the living and ancestors, elucidates interesting parallels to Jeanette Lykkegaard's Siberian Chuckshi example (see Chapter 9 this volume).

Before proceeding to discuss in more detail the transport and return of the spirits, however, a few initial clarifications of key terms is necessary, as they relate to the intimacy between ancestors and certain dwelled-in household spaces.

Material Attention in Dwelled-in Spaces

The long wait should end when the three *amadlozi* were brought to the *umsamo* in the Great House or the *indlunkulu*, the focal point for communication with deceased homestead members. This very same space was vital to my previous analysis, now appearing in a new light. Communication with *amadlozi*, however, is not only verbal but also gestural, epitomised in a perpetual wariness towards potential deviation from respectful behaviour, or *hlonipha*. The expression translates to the English term 'to respect' and is found commonly used among both Nguni- and Sotho-speakers. *Hlonipha* (or *hlonepha* in Sotho) involves both action and speech as forms of respect (e.g. Kunene 1958; Finlayson 1984; R. Herbert 1990). According to Armstrong et al. (2008: 515), *hlonipha* as the basis for appropriate behaviour is still significant, especially in rural areas, and serves to protect the integrity of patrilineal descent – of what classic cultural anthropologists have referred to as the homestead head's agnatic cluster. As is traditionally common among Zulu-speakers, people in northern KZN may still today practice fierce exogamy; a man cannot marry a woman from any of the clans of his four grandparents (see Armstrong et al. 2008). A characteristic trait for Nguni-speakers involves the ideology of pollution. While pollution ideas among Shona- and Tswana-speakers, for example, were expressed through the concept of heat, among Nguni-speakers the classificatory ambiguity and threat to social order represented by pollution was more often expressed through concepts of dirt and inner darkness. Contamination was believed to render people vulnerable to bad luck and sickness, especially in terms of the productive and reproductive success of family and homestead. In relation to this, as we shall return to, previous anthropologists and ethnographers have drawn attention to the ambiguity of the 'outsider wife'. Since exogamy made the wife a stranger to her husband's ancestors or *amadlozi*, she has been particularly susceptible to suspicion and accusation about pollution.

Drawing on ethnographic[4] and ethnoarchaeological[5] insights, my initial analysis of clay and soil (Fredriksen 2011; 2012) focused on how household spaces in Phondwane were embedded in *hlonipha* problem solving strategies by women making pottery. The movement of clay in the production of pottery from the excavation, via transport home, storage, production and use as potting and building material provided a means to sequence, isolate and illuminate various aspects of intimate human/material/ancestral engagements in household space. Interestingly, in contrast to comparative examples from other regions in southern Africa (see also Fredriksen 2007), communication with ancestor spirits never took place at the clay source, always in the *umsamo* inside the Great House of the homestead. Indeed, very few explicit links between earth materials and the spirit world were found. The most important social dynamics relating to clay seemed to be the relationships between the various members of the homestead and their respective ancestral links; between wife and husband, between wife and mother-in-law, and between the different wives in a polygynous household.

At first glance the list of pollution ideas confirms Eugenia Herbert's articulation of potting as located 'within the nexus of sexual, menstrual and pregnancy taboos' (E. Herbert 1993: 215). However, when comparing the data on material and spiritual associations to clay from Phondwane with those from two other studies I conducted, among Shona-speakers in Manica in Mozambique and Tswana-speakers in the Tswapong Hills in Botswana, an interesting distinction emerged. In particular, the ambiguity of clay as somewhere between earth and water proved significant. In Manica and the Tswapong Hills the issues that had to do with pollution and ancestors' roles in matters of pottery making and house construction were solved at the sites where materials were collected. This form of problem solving at the source was combined with conceptualizations of clay as being closer to water than to earth, and thus linked to aquatic animals and beings.[6] In Phondwane, on the other hand, the defining character of the pollution ideas

---

4   The works of Raum (1973), Berglund (1976) Ngubane (1977) and Hammond-Tooke (1962, 1981) are significant here.

5   The study by Mack, Maggs and Oswald (1991) pays particular attention to homestead spatiality, and works by Jolles (2005), Fowler (2006), Huffman (2007) and Armstrong, Whitelaw and Reusch (2008) concern various aspects of Zulu ceramics.

6   In Manica it was in the form of hippos, crocodiles, snakes and the infamous *nzuzu*, the mermaid living in pools who lures men into the deep. Similarly, among the Tswana-speaking Kgatla, for example, Isaac Schapera (1971: 92–93) has noted the links in seasonal taboos between digging pot clay, making pots and building houses and the killing of aquatic animals such as lizards, iguanas and crocodiles.

associated with clay was that they found their place within the wider *hlonipha* system of avoidances. Problem solving that involved ancestors and earth materials for potting and building took place at the *umsamo* inside the Great Hut, and clay seemed more closely related to earth than to water.

This stimulated my analytical emphasis on the implications of this particular contrast between endogamous Sotho/Tswana and exogamous Nguni for social interaction in household space, resulting in a relative contrast in *material attention*. In known Sotho/Tswana examples there is a dual attention to problem solving in relation to pollution that links female bodily heat with drought, thereby construing it as a danger to agricultural fertility and crops. The primary concern of the notion of pollution is with the work of the female body within agricultural cycles. This focus on the fertility of cultivated soil was contrasted with my observations from Phondwane, which found support in, for example, ethnographer Robert Herbert's (1990) comparative analysis of Sotho *hlonepha* and Nguni *hlonipha* practices. Here a defining characteristic for the social dynamics in relation to pollution ideas seemed to be the degree to which the member's ancestral links were seen to represent a threat to the rest of the household. Thus, there was an important difference in the perception of the dangers involved when working with clay between the Nguni and the Sotho/Tswana cases: whereas female bodily heat and the associated perils of drought are prominent among Tswana-speakers, the most important source of danger to clay in the Nguni world is found in the personhood of the wife coming from outside and, above all, her ancestral links that are brought into the household.

An implication of this marked attention to how human/material/ancestral dynamics are shaped by the relative movements of female 'outsider' bodies, which is also indicated by ethnographer O.M.F. Raum's (1973: 147–148) observations, is that the built environment in rural northern KZN, in relative comparison to other rural areas in southern Africa, is fluid and in constant movement. When relatively less attention is paid to the polluting dangers of clay and earthworks, houses and homesteads can more easily be built, moved and rebuilt (see Fredriksen 2012: 92). It is interesting to note here that the Great Hut with its *umsamo* can be torn down and relocated without much difficulty, and this may be observed frequently in Phondwane. The *amadlozi* residing in the old house is simply moved to the *umsamo* in the new house by following a similar procedure as described in detail below – by using one simple twig to move all *amadlozi* to the new location before tearing down the old building.

Significantly, this relative 'detachment' means that problem solving – the communication by which the living consult ancestors on various matters that relate to homestead and family – is not situated at the various places where these matters actually happen and are played out. Rather, the issues are brought to the *umsamo* where ancestral presence and powers are most strongly felt – to the space where people should act and speak in a respectful manner under the watchful eyes, ears and noses of the dead. This is the space for keeping, regaining or obtaining situational control when facing 'strangers'. And, as we have seen, while there is a long tradition for focusing such attention on the outsider female body it seems that the presence of nonhuman 'strangers' has been an increasing concern for quite a while already.

Thus, to sum up in brief, in Phondwane the conceptualization of earth materials is that they are relatively transient and easy-to-move, clearly indicating more attention to people and their bodily presence than to the materials of the built environment. This attention seems also to extend to ancestors: sounds and smells are important sensuous components in the ritual communication with otherworldly beings.

The Dead Can See, Hear, Smell and Taste

The potential problem solving involving the bodily presence of an outsider wife in the household adds a further dimension to the oscillating absence/presence dynamics for male homestead heads, as discussed by White. The spirits' preoccupation with a living outsider necessitates a perspective on the sensuous perception of the *amadlozi*, a perspective that not only takes into account *lived* bodily experience but also seeks to grasp *otherworldly experience* of this world, people's understanding of how the *amadlozi* perceive the living.

This recognition of the capacity of the dead for attention to particular aspects of the material world threw new light on my previous analysis of earth/soil. Although hinted at, I had not grasped the contextually specific material attention now identified as a two-way communication, not grasped it as channelling a *passing* by materially perceived, sensuous means. As we shall see, what really matters in this particular materiality of passing is attention to the bodily presence of the living and the sensuous presence of ancestors – and whether this presence of living and dead alike is imbued in *silence* or in *noise*. In the rural homestead attention is divided into the silent, slow serenity and cooling shade of the ancestral *umsamo* inside the Great House on the one hand and the outside everyday life on the other, the latter exposed to noise, sunlight, rain and constantly moving people. Commonly, therefore, *amadlozi* are startled by flickering electrical light bulbs or flat screen TVs, and ringing cell phones and blaring radios or stereos annoy them. However, *amadlozi* are positively attracted by ceremonial chanting and singing, and by the sharp sour smell of fermenting beer, by the smoky smells of burning charcoal and cooking meat. During ceremonies involving animal sacrifice, for example, White (2011: 111–112) notes that the bellowing of the animals after having received the deadly cut is a sound by which gathered spirits accept the sacrifice. Silent death, on the other hand, means misfortune and that the living/dead mediation is cut short.

When viewing the moving of ancestor spirits in this light, the silence/noise contrast seems highly relevant. In other words, a layer of sensuous experience should be added to the material world of dwelled-in spaces. In addition, as the contrast between transport and arrival will make clear, there is a duality to silence that is at work: outside the *umsamo* there is non-defined space in singularity, in loneliness, and a void to be filled with malcontent dis-connectedness; once inside the *umsamo* the silence around the ancestors is one of content, peaceful connectedness.

Silent Journey, Noisy Arrival

The spirits of the three men were brought home to their homestead's *umsamo* on 30 June 2012. A previous effort, about two months after the incident, had failed due to the presence of military and border police. The same two men, the father of the two youngest men and his elder brother, who accompanied the twigs this second time, had called the spirits from behind barbed wire on the South African side, a few hundred metres from the site. Upon arrival at home the men had decided the twig did not contain the spirits. Despite several efforts I have not managed to establish precisely *how* they knew that the ancestors were not present in the *umsamo* on arrival, thus still lingering at the place of death. The reason as to *why* the first attempt was unsuccessful was, however, clearly articulated by the two men. As the twig carrier simply put it, 'I don't think they liked me shouting at them that way. It's not *hlonipha* [respectful]'.

This second time we were able to approach the site by walking slowly in a respectful manner, speaking in low voices or whispering quietly, carrying the twigs we had cut that same morning, off the *umLahlabantu* tree that stands some 50 metres from the family homestead. The eldest, soon to be the twig carrier, sat down and lit a small bundle of *imphepho*.[7] He laid the *umLahlabantu* twig on the ground while addressing the three deceased men by their full family names. He told them in a low, soothing voice that they had been away for too long, and that they were sorely missed. He then asked them to come with him to the homestead. The rest of us kept a respectful distance, kneeling or sitting down. The small ceremony was over in a few minutes. On our return journey back home the twig carrier spoke only to the twig/spirits, and he only did so on three occasions, using the same reassuring voice: when entering the car, when about to cross a river bridge on the main road (as explained above, water is considered a dangerous medium) and on arrival when leaving the car.

In my opinion, the transport and, perhaps in particular, the previous failed attempt, both attest to the need for the spirit to be contained. Simultaneously, the efforts indicate the perceived dangers of non-containment in the wrong place as a form of non-being. Interestingly, the contained situatedness sought is not the re-alignment of spirit and body in the grave. While the bodies of the three men are buried next to the homestead, their spirits had to be brought to another location, to the *umsamo*.

---

7   *Imphepho* or *Helichyrum odoratissimum* is a well-known medicinal plant, and is also widely used in various rituals. For example, when lit its smoke is inhaled by *sangomas* to induce a state of trance.

On arrival at home the silence was definitively broken. The twig was brought to the *umsamo* in the Great House and a new bundle of *imphepho* was lit. Then it was laid down carefully on the floor on a straw mat, and lay there for the rest of the day. On this occasion the three spirits were addressed again by the twig carrier, but now in a more firm voice and clearly indicating that he also addressed the other spirits already there. The rest of that Saturday was a day of feasting. A goat was presented to the ancestors in the *umsamo* and then sacrificed. There was drinking of sour beer and eating of roasted goat, chicken and cattle meat, and continuous singing and chanting. The twig carrier and his companion, the father of two of the three men, deemed the arrival a success. The reason, I was told, was that the smell of beer and meat was right, and the ancestor spirits had seen and heard everything that happened.

That night, after all the guests had left, the twig was lifted up and stuck into the straw roof, joining the row of ancestral twigs. Importantly, each and every twig refers to one particular occasion in which one or more family member passed away (Figure 7.3). This also goes for situations where the body is buried away from home, often in the case of migrant workers, in cities like Johannesburg or Durban. Consequently, there are often a number of twigs in an *umsamo* (I have on several occasions counted five or six, sometimes more). They are at different stages of decay, depending on the time that has passed since death.

The stage of decay, the physical dwindling of the twig, is seen as parallel to their relative position in the spirit world. In this manner, material decay becomes memory work. The slow drying, dwindling and decomposition of the twig's leaves, eventually leading to the leaves falling on the *umsamo* floor, is a form of resistance by the life gradually deteriorating; the visual appearance of the twig becomes a way of measuring the new ancestor's distance to this world. As the most recent arrivals in the otherworldly are the ones to address and to bring news and current matters to their elders on the other side, the level of decay of twigs not only indicates who died most recently, but also whom to address among the collective of ancestors. To me, this is a visually striking example of how temporality becomes available to the senses, of how particular sensuous and material qualities constitute frameworks for reflecting on our understanding of the temporality of death and decay.

Moreover, as sensuous perception, especially specific elements of sound/ vision, plays an important part in this particular memory work, our case shows how the senses focus on a certain material attention for those who expect to become ancestors someday. The materiality of passing may thus be seen as the fusion of past, present and future, which would otherwise not be perceived in material form.

It should be emphasised that the use of *umLahlabantu* twigs for spirit mobility is a small but significant, even omnipresent, aspect of 'necropolitics' in this part of northern KZN. Twigs are constantly involved in ongoing memory work and healing, and of course found in far less dramatic situations than the tragic deaths discussed here. For example, a frequently recurring issue in Phondwane is discussions of how to handle ancestral spirits who communicate their discontent about the homestead and the *umsamo* they have been placed in. Usually the

Figure 7.3   The silence of decaying *umLahlabantu* twigs in the *umsamo*
Note: The stage of decay indicates the relative time that has passed since death. This is a way of measuring the ancestor's distance to the world of the living, and thereby whom to address among recent arrivals in the ancestral world. The twigs go quietly about their work of dwindling commemoration, continuously tying past family members to the world of the living.
Source: Photo by the author.

message, conveyed by a *sangoma*, is that the ancestor wants to move to the homestead of another living relative. In this manner, living family members who have their own projects, economical or otherwise, to pursue, may actively involve the discontent of the dead.

'Necropolitics' as an Expanded Notion of Material Causation

The efforts to close the yearlong open void that appeared between the death of the three men and the return of their spirits illustrate the material roles of *umLahlabantu* twigs as containers. In order to regain containment and spatial connectedness, a form of problem solving took place. I have argued that this is intertwined with a particular material attention in lived-in spaces, an attention that often involves the engagement of ritual specialists with particular skills and is directed towards specific people, ancestors and objects. Once integrated in the homestead, the decaying objects of commemoration are not only tied to certain ancestors, thus making them accessible to human experience, but their very state of decay also articulates the spirits' dwindling grip on the everyday reality of the living. The more dried up the twig is, the more blurred and farther away the spirit is from the world of the living.

As we do not see time itself, only movements or changes that find their form in decay and transition (see introduction to this volume), I find the form of attention to the material world identified here to be illuminated in the two stages of transportation and arrival and the different roles assigned to the two men accompanying the spirits home on that Saturday in June 2012 to reflect a juxtaposition of silence and noise. The very materiality of the twig offers containment, and the carrier of the twig/spirit has a silent presence which is similar to the presence expected when the materialised spirit is in place at the *umsamo*. This is the feeling of home, the sound of the *umsamo*, the quiet familiar voice of the person normally addressing the ancestral spirit. The living thus seeks to create an atmosphere of communication the spirit can recognise. The travel companion, on the other hand, is not in touch with the spirit but acts as a shield against the outside, noisy world, by absorbing the communication of everyday life, the sounds of the practical dealings of the everyday. Once successfully integrated in the family's *umsamo*, however, the silence is broken by familiar sounds meant to please and attract the otherworldly beings.

Some of the key dynamics at work in this particular case seem to closely resemble the Tanzanian example recently discussed by Stacey Langwick (2011) as an 'ontological politics' of healing, thus clearly indicating that the term politics should not mean the give-and-take of an exclusive human club. This epistemic point is made by Bruno Latour (2004) in his critical employment of the term 'cosmo-politics'. The presence of *cosmos* in cosmo-politics resists the tendency of politics to be a human affair only. Cosmos must embrace everything, including nonhumans (things, ancestral beings). And the presence of the term *politics* limits the number of relevant entities that should be taken into account.

The use of the term 'necropolitics', a form of dynamics that includes both humans and nonhumans, focuses attention on intentionality as an aspect belonging to both sides of the divide, to those who have already passed and those who will do so sometime in the future. Some form of ill will among certain ancestral beings causes the void, and it is therefore seen as a deliberate act to keep the spirits floating, being separated from the bodies and *not* grounded in the *umsamo,* as they should be.

To me, this evokes the treatise on nature, agency and causation by Nigerian philosopher Ifeanyi Menkiti (2004). Menkiti identifies certain significant epistemic differences between his African examples and post-Cartesian ways of knowing the material world. For the former he employs what he terms 'an expanded notion of material causation'. The implication is that humans and nonhumans share the ability for action, belonging on the same undivided plane of material causation. Viewing 'necropolitics' in general, and spirit mobility in particular, as a version of Menkiti's expanded notion of material causation may serve as inspiration to future engagements with the meeting between differing knowledges of the material world. I will briefly point out two interesting directions for future inquiry.

Firstly, practices relating to spirit mobility refer to powers in the past and the present at the same time. They articulate in interesting ways with burial practices, as discussed in detail by Axel-Ivar Berglund (1976) among others, and with practices of commemoration. More specifically, a case where spirits are brought to another location than the body or the burial ground may offer novel insights into the roles of materials, things and spaces that are involved in continuous engagements with members of society who are no longer living, and thereby also novel insights into how various nonhumans can be embedded in power dynamics. Here the notions of absence and presence should not be pursued as contrary or opposed phenomena but as entangled, as noted by Tim Flohr Sørensen: The role of absent/present may be reversed; the absent one is not necessarily the deceased (Sørensen 2010: 128). In Phondwane the oscillating lives of migrant (male) workers cause long periods of absence from home, while the *amadlozi* are always present in the *umsamo* at home. Thus, future studies should take into account the dead's relative proximity and influence on the everyday lives and various projects of the living.

Secondly, spirit mobility relates to heritage as linked to identities rooted in cultural systems. Existing scholarly ethnography is often written from a structuralist perspective, which may be one reason why it is hard to find reference to the practices involving *umLahlabantu* twigs. In combination with a particular form of backwards gaze on Zulu heritage that focus on common links that tie practices together, the result is often a past heritage where inconsistencies can be brushed away. More often than not there is a search for system and coherence in the past, and not the breaches, glitches or problems of the present.

Concluding Remarks

To enter a rural area like Phondwane could be seen as entering a world of contrasts or even dichotomies, and thereby a potentially inviting world for researchers with a structuralist bent. However, to view the dynamics between being in clearly defined domestic *umsamo* space and non-being in undefined non-place as a version of a nature/culture divide, for example, may be to misconstrue a form of containment with an inside (where people, domestic animals and the built, organised environment belong) and an outside (peopled with 'other' beings) (see Warnier 2006). Importantly, these insides/outsides should be viewed as always changing, always adjusted to a certain specific situation. In other words, they are not the products of ready-made templates but are lived-in through everyday engagement with the surrounding environment.

By actively using comparison and contrast, by seeing successful passing to the otherworldly against its contextually perceived negative counterpart, without resorting to any simplified form of binarism, we may be able to see more clearly just what makes the ancestor spirits vulnerable, and people's perception and communication of what precisely it is they find *lacking*. And, conversely, by juxtaposing in order to identify, we may learn more about perception of 'bad' in order to understand more of what is considered 'good'. In other words, we may learn more about existence via fear of non-existence, containment via fear of non-containment, about place via fear of non-place, and about passing between forms of existence via fear of non-passing or standstill. In this manner, a focus on perception of the dead and the material forms given to that which has vanished enables the identification of places for two-way communication between living and dead. That is, not only where people address the ancestors, but the specific spaces where ancestors 'talk back', either by their material presence or by communicating their needs, wishes and desires.

Perhaps a reason for the apparent ethnographic lack of mention of at least some of the constituents of this materiality of passing is their *silence*. On the move the thorny twigs are temporary and rather inconspicuous containers and once in place in the *umsamo*, the quiet centre in a constantly moving world of necropolitics, the twigs do their work of decaying commemoration and dwindling memory quietly. The various objects of tradition that has attracted the attention of past ethnographers and Zulu traditionalists are, in contrast, not particularly inconspicuous, nor are they shrouded in silence. The ancestral spear and the Zulu beer vessels of various functions, shapes and names are objects of conflict or ceremony, associated with the smoky smells and chanting sounds of ritual. In this setting it is easy to overlook the silent, decaying twigs, as I also did at first. And if you do take notice they are not necessarily easy to talk about. They may relate to stories that are too painful to tell.

Acknowledgements

This chapter is dedicated to the memory of Juliet Armstrong. Juliet introduced me to the families in Phondwane in 2007 and was a good friend and constant source of support until her untimely passing in August 2012. I am also thankful to her husband Mike Hart for continued support and friendship. I thank Gavin Whitelaw for encouraging and helpful case discussions. Innocent Thobile Dladla has been a steady companion in the field for years, and the results would probably have been very different without his deep knowledge of local politics and language. Last but not least, I thank the family of the three deceased men in Phondwane for generously allowing Innocent and myself into their lives in such difficult times. The views expressed in this chapter are, of course, my own, and I am solely responsible for any errors or oversights.

References

Appadurai, A., 1986. Introduction: Commodities and the politics of value. In: A. Appadurai, ed., *The Social Life of Things: Commodities in Cultural Perspective*. Cambridge: Cambridge University Press, pp. 3–63.

Armstrong, J., Whitelaw, G. and Reusch, D., 2008. Pots that talk, *izinkambaezik-hulumayo. Southern African Humanities*, 20: 513–548.

Barchiesi, F., 2008. Wage labour, precarious employment, and social inclusion in the making of South Africa's postapartheid transition. *African Studies Review*, 51(2): 119–142.

Berglund, A.-I., 1976. *Zulu Thought-Patterns and Symbolism*. Bloomington and Indianapolis: Indiana University Press.

Bhat, R. B. and Jacobs, T. V., 1995. Traditional herbal medicine in Transkei. *Journal of Ethnopharmacology*, 48, 7–12.

Bille, M., Hastrup, F. and Sørensen, T.F., 2010. Introduction: An Anthropology of absence. In: M. Bille, F. Hastrup and T.F. Sørensen, eds, *An Anthropology of Absence: Materializations of Transcendence and Loss*. New York: Springer, pp. 3–22.

Finlayson, R., 1984. The changing nature of *Isihlonipho Sabafazi*. *African Studies*, 43(2): 137–146.

Fowler, K.D., 2006. Classification and collapse: The ethnohistory of Zulu ceramic use. *Southern African Humanities*, 18(2): 93–117.

Fredriksen, P.D., 2007. Approaching intimacy: Interpretations of changes in Moloko household space. *South African Archaeological Bulletin*, 62(186): 126–139.

Fredriksen, P.D., 2011. When knowledges meet: Engagements with clay and soil in southern Africa. *Journal of Social Archaeology*, 11(3): 283–310.

Fredriksen, P.D., 2012. *Material Knowledges, Thermodynamic Spaces and the Moloko Sequence of the Late Iron Age (AD 1300–1840) in Southern Africa*. Cambridge Monographs in African Archaeology 80. British Archaeological Reports, International series 2387. Cambridge: Archaeopress.

Guy, J., 1979. *The Destruction of the Zulu Kingdom: The Civil War in Zululand, 1897–1884*. London: Longman.

Guy, J., 1987. Analysing pre-capitalist societies in Southern Africa. *Journal of Southern African Studies*, 14(1): 18–37.

Guy, J., 2005. *The Maphumulo Uprising: Law, War and Ritual in the Zulu Rebellion*. Scottsville: University of KwaZulu-Natal Press.

Hall, M., 1984. The myth of the Zulu homestead: Archaeology and ethnography. *Africa*, 54(1): 65–79.

Hamber, B., 2009. Looking back, moving forward. In: B. Hamber, ed., *Transforming Societies after Political Violence*. New York: Springer, pp. 1–9.

Hammond-Tooke, W.D., 1962. *Bhaca Society*. Cape Town: Oxford University Press.

Hammond-Tooke, W.D., 1981. *Boundaries and Belief: The Structure of a Sotho Worldview*. Johannesburg: Witwatersrand University Press.

Herbert, E.W., 1993. *Iron, Gender and Power: Rituals of Transformation in African Societies*. Bloomington and Indianapolis: Indiana University Press.

Herbert, R.K., 1990. *Hlonipha* and the ambiguous woman. *Anthropos*, 85: 455–473.

Huffman, T.N., 2007. *Handbook to the Iron Age: The Archaeology of Pre-Colonial Farming Societies in Southern Africa*. Scottsville: University of KwaZulu-Natal Press.

Hunter, M., 2008. IsiZulu-speaking men and changing households: From providers within marriage to providers outside marriage. In: B. Carton, J. Laband and

J. Sithole, eds, *Zulu Identities: Being Zulu, Past and Present*. Scottsville: University of KwaZulu-Natal Press, pp. 566–572.

Jolles, F., 2005. The origins of the twentieth century Zulu beer vessel styles. *Southern African Humanities*, 17, 101–151.

Koopman, A., 2011. Lightning Birds and Thunder Trees. *Natalia*, 41, 40–60.

Kunene, D. P., 1958. Notes on *Hlonepha* among the Southern Sotho. *African Studies*, 17(3): 159–182.

Kunene, N., Wilson, R. A. C. and Myeni, N. P., 2009. The use of trees, shrubs and herbs in livestock production by communal farmers in northern KwaZulu-Natal, South Africa. *African Journal of Range and Forage Science*, 20(3): 271–274.

Kuper, A., 1980. Symbolic dimensions of the Southern Bantu homestead. *Africa*, 50(1): 8–23.

Kuper, A., 1982. *Wives for Cattle: Bridewealth and Marriage in Southern Africa*. London: Routledge & Kegan Paul.

Langwick, S. A., 2011. *Bodies, Politics, and African Healing: The Matter of Maladies in Tanzania*. Bloomington: Indiana University Press.

Latour, B., 2004. Whose cosmos, which cosmopolitics? Comments on the peace terms of Ulrich Beck. *Common Knowledge*, 10(3): 450–462.

Mack, K., Maggs T. M. and Oswald, D., 1991. Homesteads in two rural Zulu communities: An ethnoarchaeological investigation. *Natal Museum Journal of Humanities*, 3, 79–129.

Menkiti, I. A., 2004. Physical and metaphysical understanding: Nature, agency, and causation in African traditional thought. In: L. M. Brown, ed., *African Philosophy: New and Traditional Perspectives*. Oxford: Oxford University Press, pp. 84–106.

Ndawonde, B. G., Zobolo, A. M., Dlamini, E. T. and Siebert, S. J., 2007. A survey of plants sold by traders at Zululand muthi markets, with a view to selecting popular plant species for propagation in communal gardens. *African Journal of Range and Forage Science*, 24(2): 103–107.

Ngubane, H., 1977. *Body and Mind in Zulu Medicine*. London and New York: Academic Press.

Raum, O. F., 1973. *The Social Functions of Avoidances and Taboos among the Zulu*. Monographien zur Völkerkunde 4, Hamburgischen Museum für Völkerkunde. Berlin and New York: Walter de Gruyter.

Schapera, I., 1971. *Rainmaking Rites of Tswana Tribes*. Leiden: African Study Centre.

Sørensen, T. F., 2010. A saturated void: Anticipating and preparing presence in contemporary Danish cemetery culture. In: M. Bille, F. Hastrup and T. F. Sørensen, eds, *An Anthropology of Absence: Materializations of Transcendence and Loss*. New York: Springer, pp. 115–130.

Warnier, J.-P. 2001. A praxeological approach to subjectivation in a material world. *Journal of Material Culture*, 6(1): 5–24.

Warnier, J.-P., 2006. Inside and outside, surface and containers. In: C. Tilley, W. Keane, S. Kuechler, M. et al., eds., *Handbook of Material Culture*. London: Sage, pp. 186–195.

Warnier, J.-P., 2007. *The Pot-King: The Body and Technologies of Power*. Leiden: Brill.

Warnier, J-P., 2009. Technology as efficacious action on objects ... and subjects. *Journal of Material Culture*, 14(4): 459–470.

White, H., 2010. Outside the dwelling of culture: Estrangement and difference in postcolonial Zululand. *Anthropological Quarterly*, 83(3): 497–518.

White, H., 2011. Beastly whiteness: Animal kinds and the social imagination in South Africa. *Anthropology Southern Africa*, 34(3 and 4): 104–113.

Winther, T., 2005. *Current Styles: Introducing Electricity in a Zanzibari Village*. PhD. Department of Social Anthropology, University of Oslo.

Chapter 8

Post-Mortem Photography and Two Visual Representations

Susan Matland

Introduction

In this chapter it is argued that post-mortem, or *lit de parade*, photographs provide an indeterminate state between the living and the dead, with the deceased captured as being and not being within the photograph. For some, the act of photographing the dead can be seen as blurring the lines between the dead and living, while for others this blurring may allow the bereaved to maintain and create new bonds and relationships with the deceased. Thus a dynamic process is created, with the post-mortem photographs acting as a tool to help the living to come to terms with death, while at the same time keeping the dead alive.

Historically, this usage of post-mortem photographs, as a visual tie and social process in relocating the dead, is seen since the birth of photography (Hallam, Hockey and Howarth 1999; Linkman 2006, 2011). Technological changes within photography, as well as the manner in which post-mortem photographs are taken, accepted and used, reflect changing attitudes towards death and the relationship between the living and the dead (ibid.).

Over time post-mortem photographs have evolved from being primarily a personal undertaking to being acceptable as an expression of art. Photographer Sally Mann is one who has chosen to photograph dead bodies. However, Mann's interest is in the remains of a body after a period of decomposition, and not in her relationship to the deceased. This manner of photographing the dead differs greatly from other post-mortem photographs, where remembrance and maintaining the social identity of the deceased are major reasons for taking the image.

By examining the implications and usages of these two different types of post-mortem photography in Western societies, this chapter will explore how these images represent different aspects of temporal passing. It discusses how they are used to convey the passing of the dead in a proper manner, from one state to another; additionally they allow for a presence of the person within a liminal stage, while evoking a continuing relationship with the deceased. They also, as seen in the photographs of Sally Mann, invoke a supra-human temporal passage that is available to the senses through the focus on the decaying body.

Post-Mortem Photographs

Post-mortem photographs are photographic representations of the dead. They include photographs taken by hospitals for medical reasons, by journalists and the media, war photographs, and those taken by artists who photograph human remains as a form of art. And they are taken by family members as a lasting memory of loved ones. Post-mortem photographs visually illustrate how bodies are represented, seen and experienced. At the same time, through the observer's involvement with these photographs, these bodies become social and changeable through experiences and time, with some conforming to the prevalent social values while others do not (Henning 2006). And while post-mortem photographs can be interpreted as documentary images of an event that has taken place at a given time and place, providing a certainty of death, they also 'are equally dedicated to the evocation of the invisible – relationships, emotions, memories' (Batchen 2004: 96).

Furthermore, the post-mortem photograph often creates an indeterminate state between the living and the dead, interrupting the passing on, with the deceased captured as 'being at the same time here and not here', while making 'permanent and unchanging the very moment of transience and incipient decay' (Bruce 2005: 32). And '[t]hrough its anachrony, its bringing back, or returning, of the material traces of the past to the present, the postmortem photograph interrupts the trajectory from birth, through life, to death and finally burial, undermining its most fundamental certainties' (ibid.), thus allowing a continuation of the deceased's social life and identity (Fernandez 2011).

Geoffrey Batchen (2004: 97) argues that post-mortem photographs 'affirm the close proximity of life and death, and attempt, against common sense, to use one to deny the finality of the other'. Hence it can be argued that these photographs have been taken in an attempt to allow one to deny, as well as accept, the finality of death. And because of these interactions, post-mortem photographs become one of the tools used in the development and adjustment of relationships with the dead (ibid.).

Post-Mortem Photographs of the Late Nineteenth and Early Twentieth Centuries

Historically, the trajectory of post-mortem photographs is seen in Western societies since the emergence of photography, with the photographic medium progressing from the daguerreotype of the mid 1800s (images fixed onto a copper plate coated with silver), to glass plates, the Brownie camera, through the Polaroid era and compact cameras, and into the digital era. In step with these technological changes, the photographic techniques and styles in which the deceased are photographed, as well as the role of the photographer, have also changed; changes in attitudes towards religion and death also play a part in the ready acceptance and manner of taking such photographs.

Prior to the development of photography, those wishing a memento mori of a deceased loved one would often engage an artist to paint a likeness of the deceased. This changed with the appearance of the daguerreotype photographic technique in 1839. Paintings continued to be commissioned, but a number of painters began using this new media to capture 'the likeness of the dead' (Fink 1990; Linkman 2011; Ruby 1995). At the same time, photography 'appropriated many of the practices and ideas connected with the art of painting' (Linkman 2011: 10). And as the number of daguerreotypists (photographers) increased during the 1840s, a greater number of individuals gained the financial possibility of having 'a likeness' of a deceased loved one taken (Fink 1990; Linkman 2006).

It was not until the invention of the collodion process in 1841 that photographers were able to produce a number of print copies from one negative (daguerreotype images could only be reproduced by re-photographing them) (Gernsheim 1965; Gustavson 2012). The further development of the wet collodion plates in 1852 and dry collodion plates in 1871 enabled a quicker and easier developing process for the photographers (Gustavson 2012). Parallel to these developments was the invention of the photographic carte-de-visite or cabinet card, which were photographs mounted upon a thick cardboard that was usually framed (Linkman 2011; Snickare 2002). The size and sturdiness of the cabinet card ensured that the photographs were handy enough to be given to relatives and others as a memento mori (ibid.).

The practice of photographing the dead as if they were sleeping was a common theme throughout the latter half of the nineteenth century and into the twentieth century (Henning 2006; Hilliker 2006; Linkman 2011; Ruby 1995). Photographers advertised their skills and abilities to create a likeness of the deceased that portrayed them as alive (Linkman 2006, 2011; Ruby 1995). By photographing the dead as if they were sleeping one allowed the illusion that the deceased were actually alive, while also accepting the fact that death had visited. This was especially the case with regard to children (Kildegaard 1985). Metaphorically, the illusion of sleep was seen as an event from which one would eventually awake. Children were often regarded as being pure and innocent, and because of this they had no need to dread death, as they would be readily accepted into God's realm (Linkman 2011). This approach, of alluding to death so that it was not so harsh, allowed one, for a short time, to deny that one's loved one had died, while at the same time allowing one an inner peace in the knowledge that they would not awaken in this world, but in a better place (ibid.). In this manner the materiality of a loved one's passing is both encumbered and acknowledged. These photographs also served as a visual reminder for society that the deceased had a good death – surrounded by family members and sustained by their religion. Here the photographs conveyed a spiritual aspect in the anticipation of resurrection of a life. And in the case of deceased children, post-mortem photographs would often be the only photograph of the child the family would possess (Hannavy 1997; Ruby 1995).

During this period photographing the recently deceased was a normal occurrence; the dead were photographed as sleeping, sitting, in a coffin, and often with family members gathered around. Photographs were placed in specifically produced photograph albums, framed and displayed openly on walls and mantels, and were sent to relatives and friends, many who could not attend the funeral (Henning 2006; Hilliker 2006; Linkman 2006, 2011).

These photographs were taken either in the home, at a photographer's studio or at a funeral parlour (Linkman 2011; Ruby 1995). Initially professional photographers were called in to homes to photograph the recently deceased (Ruby 1995). Later, with the development of affordable cameras, families were enabled to take their own post-mortem photographs, thus eliminating the need or want of a professional photographer (Hilliker 2006; Linkman 2011) although the usage of professional photographers continued.

It was primarily through the development of the first roll-film camera by Eastman Kodak in 1888 that a move from the professional photographer to the private realm occurred (Gustavson 2012). But it was the relatively inexpensive Brownie cameras, costing one US dollar and first introduced in 1900, that revolutionised photography for the common person. Within the first six months of production over 100,000 examples were sold in Europe and the United States (Coe 1978). And with the Brownie cameras came an increased usage of the snapshot, which was one of the contributors to the decline in popularity of the cabinet card by the late 1920s (Ruby 1995).

Figure 8.1   Laura Johanne Skjelstad, 1886–1905, Skjelle farm, Skogn, Levanger, Nord-Trondelag, Norway

Source: Photograph by Sverre Bjerkan. © Levanger Museum, Norway. LEM.0011905K.0039.

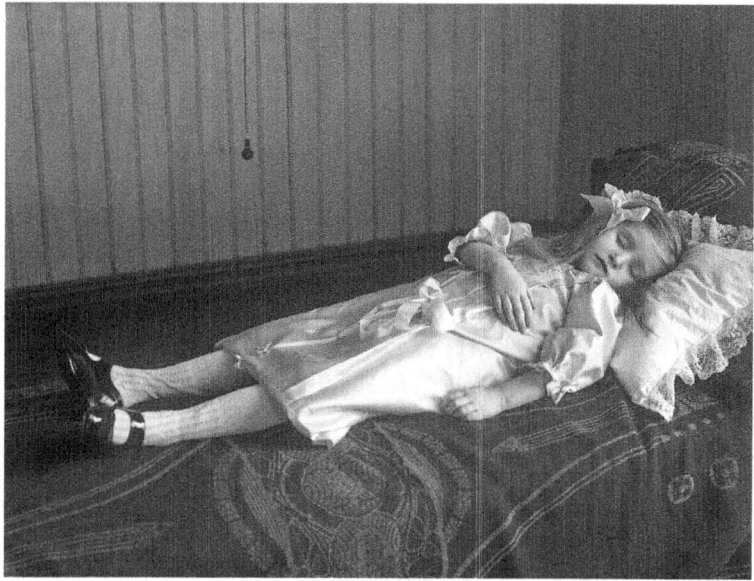

Figure 8.2   Young girl who died of Tuberculosis in 1911, Steinkjær, Nord-Trondelag, Norway
Source: Photograph by Sverre Bjerkan. © Levanger Museum. LEM0011911K.0005.

Changing Attitudes

Parallel with this change to families taking their own post-mortem photographs, death gradually became increasingly professionalised, institutionalised, medicalised and managed. And through this medicalisation, death and dying have, for the most part, been removed from the home to hospitals, institutions or hospices (Haddars 2011; Howarth 2000; Mellor and Shilling 1993; Seale 1998; Walter 1994). Earlier, with family members most often dying at home, the family was the main caregiver of the dying, and also responsible for preparing the corpse for burial. However, with a move from the home to institutions, families gradually distanced themselves from activities surrounding dying and death. Professional caretakers have now become primarily responsible for the dying, as well as for the handling and disposal of the corpse (Hilliker 2006; Walter 1994). Thus one can argue that, through the privatisation, professionalisation and institutionalisation of death, people have gradually become removed from dealing with death (Mellor and Shilling 1993; Seale 1998), and in particular the dead body. A result of this is that death becomes a distant and often an unfamiliar occurrence for many.

In *Constructing Death: The Sociology of Dying and Bereavement*, Clive Seale differentiates between the 'psychological denial of death and the sociological denial of death' (Seale 1998: 3). He sees the 'social organization for death in late modernity [as] remarkably active, realistic and death accepting' (ibid.). Likewise, Tony Walter (1994) in *The Revival of Death* has addressed the increased interest in death and dying that has emerged in the Western world. For more than three decades we have seen a steady growth of what Walter calls a revivalism and a revivalist discourse concerning end-of-life care and death. This movement can be seen as a reaction against what has been criticised as the overly routinized, medicalised and technological treatment of death and dying within modern healthcare (Chambliss 1996; Moller 1990, 2000). Equally, current research on death and dying in a Norwegian palliative medicine unit shows that family members are taking a central role in the process of dying (Haddars 2011) and are not standing by as passive observers.

This shift in how society manages death, from being more open and familiar to institutionalised and hidden, and once again visible, is also reflected in the changing attitudes towards the displaying of post-mortem photographs. As mentioned above, these photographs were previously shown and exhibited within the family. Later they were moved from the public sphere and became more private; they were no longer openly displayed, although the practice of taking them continued (Hilliker 2006; Linkman 2011; Ruby 1995). As Laurel Hilliker (2006) notes, the main reason for this privatisation of the photographs seemed to be a general consensus that these are private and personal, along with the fear that the reason for taking them could be misinterpreted.

Despite a general consensus that images of dead bodies should be contained within the private realm, post-mortem photographs are still being taken. Polaroid photographs may be taken by funeral home directors upon request by family members (Ruby 1995) or grieving family members may use mobile telephones to take post-mortem photographs at a hospital (Burch 2009). Also, immigrant families are still sending post-mortem photographs to those 'back home' (Hilliker 2006; Linkman 2011; Ruby 1995). Furthermore, since the late 1970s Western hospitals have actively been taking photographs of stillborn children and children who die shortly after birth for their families, to help them cope with the loss of their child (Hochberg 2003; Linkman 2011; Michelson et al. 2003; Reddin 1987; Ruby 1995). All these kinds of photographs present opportunities in which new stories can be created, encouraging a continuation of history in the social life of the deceased. In reminiscences about earlier post-mortem photographs of children, these photographs become a visible proof that the child did exist (Reddin 1987).

Even though the showing of post-mortem photographs in the public sphere is still unusual, it is becoming increasingly common for certain groups of people. Some families are now actively sharing their stories and photographs of their stillborn children through the development of memorial sites found on the internet and through sharing with friends and families through Facebook and other social media. This usage of social media, combined with the accessibility of mobile telephones, provides a broader arena in which individuals are able to participate in recording activities surrounding death and dying. A photograph often 'provide[s] a means of reclaiming the deceased from their position as a patient, re-humanizing them and reasserting their individuality' (Ennis 2011: 138). Helen Ennis (2011) argues that the digital era allows for a greater circulation of post-mortem photographs, while the technology allows individuals a spontaneous approach to photographing the dying and dead; at the same time a level of control over when the photograph is taken is ensured.

Sally Mann

While the taking of post-mortem photographs by private persons is still being practised, and often remains personal, it has become, in some arenas, respectable, as well as acceptable, to take post-mortem photographs as an expression of art.

However, post-mortem photographs taken as memento mori differ greatly from post-mortem photographs created as art work. Likewise, artistic photographs differ greatly between artists. Photographer Andres Serrano has taken photographs of bodies at morgues, and photographer Joel-Peter Witkin uses body parts from morgues. Serrano's work is stark and chillingly realistic in a medical documentation manner, while photographer Joel-Peter Witkin incorporates corpses, or body parts, in a jigsaw manner in his photographs that seems to be created with the intent to shock.

Sally Mann is also one of those who have endeavoured to photograph dead bodies. However, Mann's post-mortem photographs from the Body Farm (Mann 2003) differ from these other photographers' work both in the photographic technique – that can be inferred as an intentional blurring of the image in a manner so as to allude to death and decay of the flesh – and in the initial reason for creating them.

It is difficult to separate the person Sally Mann from her work. Her personality is apparent in her work, and as she herself has said, 'unless you photograph what you love, you're not going to make good art' (Mann cited in Aletti 2006: 41). Her loves are her family and the landscape that surrounds their Virginian farm. She was especially close to her father, a doctor who considered death, including his own impending death, as a basic fact of life (Mann 2003).

Mann credits her father as partially responsible for her interest in what happens at the end of a life. And it is because of his influence, along with her affection for the land, that she started taking photographs that engaged the subject of death and remains (Ravenal 2010). This resulted in a project that would take almost five years to complete and encompassed many aspects of death. This journey resulted in a documentary film by Steven Cantor, a book and a photographic exhibition, all called *What Remains* (HBO Documentary Films 2005). Mann stated that the main reason for the book, and the activities surrounding it, was a curiosity about what happens when bodies decay (ibid.).

Mann's inquiry into what was remaining of a body, be it human or animal, after a period of decomposition, began with the death of her greyhound, Eva (Jones 2003; Ravenal 2010). Confronted with Eva's death, Mann began to wonder what was happening: 'she [Eva] was so there and so not there. I was trying to figure out what it was all about, what happens after death' (Mann cited in Jones 2003: 56). Mann 'just wanted to see how something that beloved could turn into the earth ... It was a way to come to grips with the finality of death' (ibid.). Thus, after a period of decomposition, Mann exhumed the skeletal remains of Eva from the earth, laid them out, and photographed them.

Richard Gottlieb describes Sally Mann's photographs from her book *What Remains* as a means by which she is processing her loss and grief through her 'desire to know what happens to us and our loved ones after we die; she wants desperately to study these phenomena in order to undo death itself' (Gottlieb 2007: 1235). Through her exploration into what had become of her greyhound, Gottlieb argues that, by fixing Eva's image onto film, Mann is working through her loss, while wishing for a restoration and rebirth of Eva, a desire to 'reclaim those she has lost' (ibid.: 1236).

Body Farm

This interest in decomposed remains, and in due course their disappearance into the earth, eventually led Sally Mann to the University of Tennessee Forensic Anthropology Center, commonly known as the Body Farm, to photograph human remains in different stages of decomposition (Bellafante 2007). The Body Farm is a forensic laboratory where scientists study the manner in which a body decomposes under different conditions in order to aid the police in determining cause and time of death at crime scenes.

Mann's photographing of unidentified corpses at the Body Farm (figures 8.3 and 8.4) differs greatly from post-mortem photographs taken by family members of their deceased loved ones, in which remembrance as well as personal and social identity are central for the taking of the photograph. It is a different kind of relation, where the deceased is unknown and the initial reason for taking the photographs is primarily that of documenting, through an artistic eye, death and decay.

Mary Ann Perkins (2008: 44), in her discussion of Mann's post-mortem photographs, argues that, since these are images of unknown corpses, with no known history or identity, 'only one role remains for the viewer: to become a dispassionate observer of death. Much as Mann was when she visited the forensic site'. However, one can equally argue that few can gaze at these images without involving themselves, for better or worse. Nor was Mann unaffected by them.

At first, Mann's attraction to photographing these remains could be described as being purely scientific: photographing corpses in different stages of decay. Therefore she viewed these corpses as no longer containing an identity, since a corpse consists of just flesh and bones. Nonetheless, she found it difficult to photograph them (HBO Documentary Films 2005):

Figure 8.3   *Untitled 61*, 2000
Source: © Sally Mann. Courtesy Gagosian Gallery.

> It was not the smell or even the sometimes horrible sights but it was the human-
> ness that remained in spite of death ... they still had stories to tell and I wanted
> to hear them ... I wanted to ask the dead bodies, "How the hell did you get here?
> How did you lose your leg? Why did you have that terrible tattoo put on your
> shoulder? Do you really think that hair colour suits you?" In spite of being stone
> cold dead, there still was the presence of their lives and that was what made it
> difficult. (HBO Documentary Films 2005: 12)

A main difference between the post-mortem photographs taken by or for private
family members and those Sally Mann has taken is that the private person knew the
deceased and, because of this, the social identity of the deceased was maintained.
Sally Mann did not have such knowledge, nor was she asked to photograph
corpses at the Body Farm for family members or for anyone else. She was taking
photographs of them for herself: for personal as well as artistic reasons. And
although these bodies were not intimate to Mann, in the sense that she personally
knew them, they were distinctive on another level. Mann herself expressed interest
in the person these corpses were, and, in the process of photographing the corpses
she engaged them in a dialogue through which they were incorporated within her

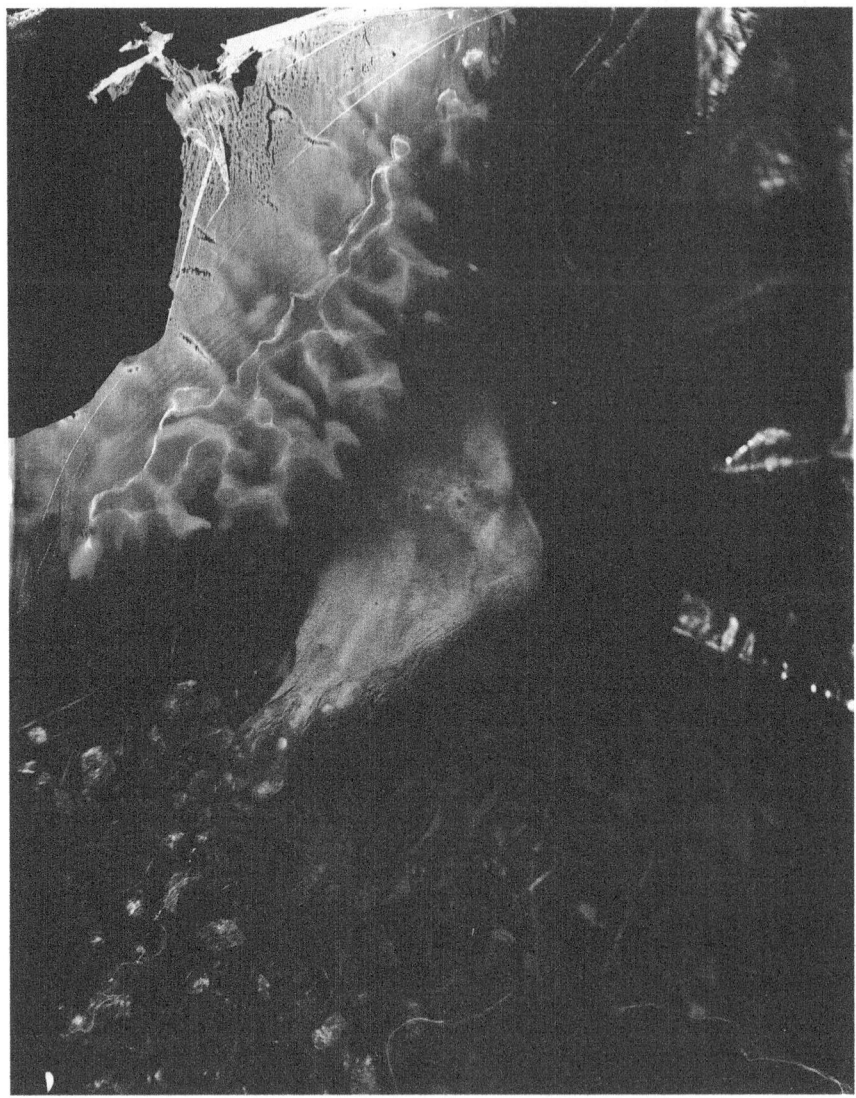

Figure 8.4   *Untitled 69*, 2000
Source: © Sally Mann. Courtesy Gagosian Gallery.

social space. This dialogue resulted in embodying them with a social identity, not their original social identity, but a new one formed through Mann's dialogue with them.

While Mann took these photographs because of her personal need to explore and know more about humanity, through the process of decay, they became public:

viewed in a book, a film and an exhibition that has evoked varied responses. Through her photographs Mann recreates 'the presence' of the deceased while bringing them into the public sphere. It is through the public and the personal sphere that these corpses reacquired both a personal identity and a social identity.

Reactions

As mentioned earlier, the practice of taking and showing post-mortem photographs changed as familiarity with the viewing of dead bodies became less common, because of changing cultural norms and attitudes towards death (Henning 2006; Hilliker 2006; Linkman 2011; Ruby 1995). Alongside this distancing, the reactions to post-mortem photographs also changed, from being considered culturally acceptable to being sometimes viewed as morbid and troubling (Henning 2006; Hilliker 2006; Linkman 2011; Ruby 1995).

And although the practice of showing post-mortem photographs is increasing, there are some who still find them disturbing. If one takes into account that Sally Mann herself found it difficult to photograph bodies of strangers, something that strengthens her personal approach to photographing them, then one should not be surprised that others experienced the exhibition *What Remains*, as being extremely difficult to view.

Sarah Boxer, a journalist for the *New York Times*, in her review of *What Remains*, felt that the photographs were 'morbid' and 'disgusting', stating that Mann was 'violat[ing] ... the privacy and the decency of the dead' (Boxer 2004: 1). Furthermore, she felt that Sally Mann was 'assisting the decomposition' of these corpses (ibid.).

However, not everyone shared this view. Arts critic Eleanor Heartney felt, '[t]he individuality of the bodies has been erased by decomposition and the abstraction of the photographic process' (Heartney 2005: 52), and '[a]t times the figures are barely recognizable as human remains' (ibid.). Likewise, she saw the photographs as peaceful, where '[b]loated bodies are softly sculptural' (ibid.). This softness, or blurring, was achieved through Mann's photographic technique known as wet-plate collodion process, developed in 1851 (Boxer 2004; Heartney 2005), the same process that was used to produce those earlier *lit de parade* photographs. The process involves pouring silver nitrate over the glass plate, providing the photographer with only minutes in which to expose and develop the plate, requiring a portable lab to use in the field (Boxer 2004; Heartney 2005; Ravenal 2010).

What is interesting is that Heartney, by viewing these photographs, felt that the individuality of the person was no longer present. One of the reasons for her not feeling offence at viewing these photographs was that the visual representation of a body had been blurred and allowed a distancing through the manner in which Mann photographed and developed the prints. Nevertheless, Boxer did not see these photographs as having softness, but instead she felt that they 'often look burned, torn or spotted ...' and that it was difficult to know 'where the violence of death itself ends and where the violence in the picture making begins' (Boxer 2004: 1).

One could argue that Mann purposely used the wet-plate collodion process on these images just to achieve the effect that so disturbed Boxer. Arguably the visual effect was created on purpose, as it is a technique that Mann has utilised throughout her career. However, these photographs were not made with the intent to shock, but to actively engage the viewer, as well as the bodies, in a fundamentally different manner from the photographs of artists such as Witkin. Mann herself says that her reasons for taking these photographs at the Body Farm were to make 'people more comfortable with death … To make people think about death, therefore, thereby, live life more fully' (Nieman 2004: 20). Through these photographs she aims to encourage a more open relation to death, thereby producing a greater sense of living and presence. Additionally, because of the photographic process she utilises one can also envision that these photographs are part of a process of decay; they are an acknowledgement that, with the passing of time, the material evidence that these photographs were taken, or that the subject matter existed, will disappear.

Criticism towards the taking and displaying of post-mortem photographs is quick to surface, often by those who view this type of photograph as disrespectful. Attitudes similar to Boxer's can also be seen with regard to the post-mortem photographs taken by private family members, some of whom are now not inclined to display them for public viewing. This may be because of a fear that the reason they were taken will be misinterpreted and that the person who has taken the photograph would be seen as having, in some manner, violated the deceased and as being morbid (Hilliker 2006). Similarly, artists such as Sally Mann are often unable to avoid criticism since, if their images are too realistic they are 'accused of being morbid, voyeuristic and sick' (Heartney 2005: 55); alternatively, with photographs 'perceived as being too beautiful, [the photographers] … are said to romanticize death …' (ibid.).

Roland Barthes maintained that one's horror at viewing photographs of the dead was connected to the idea that photographs depict real things and that 'we tend to conflate the real and the live' (Henning 2006: 245). Consequently, a photograph of a corpse would be perceived as acknowledging the corpse as being alive at the time of photographing in that 'it is the living image of a dead thing' (Barthes 1984: 78, cited in Henning 2006:189). Enabling the dead to inhabit the present is, for some, an unsettling thought.

Similarly, Mary O'Neill (2011) argues that some initial reactions and discomfort to post-mortem photographs arise through the discord of seeing images that remind one of one's own imperative death: thus we may feel uncomfortable. O'Neill (2011: 300) also maintains, 'images of the dead are acceptable as long as they do not cause pain to the living, as in a video game or a fiction, or are seen as other and distant'. Interaction with images of the dead on this level is therefore safe and does not demand participation, which is seen as personal.

Photographs have the power to evoke strong emotional reactions, and the image that the photograph reflects is never in itself passive, static or 'a neutral representation' (Clarke 1997: 28). The context, as well as the setting in which these images are encountered (in an exhibition, through a website or privately), along with the viewers' conception of their place within society and their social norms, will have a profound bearing on how one engages with these images (Hilliker 2006; Wells 2003). Thus the photograph becomes what one reads into it, and because of this people's reactions to post-mortem photographs vary. Therefore, Boxer's reaction to Sally Mann's photographs is, alongside her outlook as a critic, dictated by her social preconceptions and norms. Boxer's and other similar reactions can be interpreted as a distancing from acknowledgement of death, an acknowledgement that family members of the late nineteenth and early twentieth centuries could more readily accept, just because of its familiarity; and although Heartney's view can be argued to be socially based, it differs from Boxer's in that her reaction does not contain a horror of death. While Heartney felt that the personal identity of these corpses was no longer present, for Boxer, based upon her reactions, the identity remained.

Awareness of Time, Passing and Identity

If one looks at Western post-mortem photographs of the early nineteenth and twentieth centuries, one is drawn to the care that has been taken to present the dead as potentially alive or sleeping, blurring the passage from life to death. At the same time these photographs convey to society that the deceased had a good death, in which their journey to eternal life was secured. The photographs convey the materiality of passing from one state to another by using intangible means. They are often visually pleasant, while simultaneously observing the integrity of the deceased. They shift between distance and nearness, living and dead, and they also provide a concrete memento for continuing bonds with the deceased.

This awareness of the deceased's identity is also present in the photographs currently being taken by families. Be those photographs of stillborn children, or Mann's own photograph of her deceased father, as he lay on the family divan, they all reflect the underlying reasons for capturing the final moments of death and have been taken with the love and respect that one has come to associate with these photographs. And as do others, Mann has also chosen to display the post-mortem photograph of her father in the public area of her home (Linkman 2011).

By contrast, Sally Mann's post-mortem photographs from the Body Farm do not initiate similar reactions or ideals. In her images of a corpse in an advanced state of decay, there is no hope that it will wake up. Moreover, an initial viewing of these photographs does not invite a possibility of a dialogue, or continuing bond, between the dead and the living as *lit de parade* photographs do. Nor does one believe that these corpses, or the persons they were, are in a state of passing – other than biologically. Primarily Mann's photographs convey finality, in which the social involvement with the person, now a corpse, is finished. The only thing remaining is simply a biological fact, a natural consequence of death – that is, decomposition. With these photographs one can speculate that Mann is exploring an aspect of supra-human temporal passing: the examination of what is left and what may be passed on, in a biological sense, after death occurs. This type of post-mortem photograph differs from those in which remembrance and continuing bonds are central motives behind the reasons for taking them.

However, as I have argued above, because of Mann's introduction of these corpses into the public arena through the photographs, eventually they will engage one in dialogue. One can speculate that the temporal passing projected in Mann's photographs through the acceptance of decay is continued and reversed – a regeneration of life occurs as the dead obtain new identities through dialogue with the observer. These photographs are transgressing the boundaries between the dead and living, offering something to us that an ordinary 'social' person could not provide.

Final Remarks: Identity, Passing, Continuing Bonds

In the wake of late-modern trends to celebrate the social identity and biography of the deceased, there is an increasing individualised secular practice and improvisation connected to relocating or incorporating the dead within the world of the living (Seale 1998; Hallam, Hockey and Howarth 1999; Davies 2005; Heessels, Poots and Venbrux 2012).

Benjamin R. Smith and Richard Vokes (2008) claim that photographs have the ability to convey a presence while at the same time showing an absence, allowing the dead to inhabit the present – being here and not. It is this presence–absence that defines the spatial timeline between the living and the dead and allows the dead to move freely between the two realms. Therefore, through the act of taking post-mortem photographs one can bring the past forward and the present into the past (Unruh 1983; Masterton, Hansson and Höglund 2010); in this manner the dead are kept 'alive', passing effortlessly from the realm of the dead and back to the living. Post-mortem photographs embody the deceased with a 'visible lifelike presence that allows it to unthreateningly inhabit the space of the living for a prolonged space of time' (Fernandez 2011: 346). Simultaneously these *lit de parade* photographs remove the presence, or reality, of the deceased as a corpse (Fernandez 2011).

Masterton, Hansson and Höglund (2010: 341) maintain that personal identity is grounded in storytelling and that we understand and create ourselves through stories, both stories you tell and those told by others. These stories or narratives are continuous and interlinked – collectively dependent upon each other, even beyond death (Mellor and Shilling 1993; Masterton, Hansson and Höglund 2010). And since a person's identity is tied up in narratives, there is no defined start or end to a person's identity; 'the narrative of a person continues to represent that person's life, even if the person is no longer alive' (Masterton, Hansson and Höglund 2010: 344). These dialogues, or narratives, are important, since through the retelling of stories the living are preserving and developing the dead person's self (Unruh 1983: 340), and, in the process, are forming new relationships with the dead, in order to maintain their own identity and biographies (O'Neill 2011).

Sally Mann's post-mortem photographs do not initially induce a desire for a relationship with the dead. This is because they are too realistic. They convey a certainty of death that is based in a biological process showing the ravages of time and nature, a finality that brings home our own recognisable end. And although one can discuss the apparent aspects of Sally Mann's photographs that convey a transcending state between the living and the dead different from *lit de parade* photographs, her photographs are primarily a stark reminder of the passage of time and death. However, because she has engaged the corpses at the Body Farm in a dialogue, through the process of photographing and displaying them in a social context, Sally Mann has thereby embedded them with an identity, a personhood, which enables them to develop narratives with the living.

One can conclude that it is through narratives that the post-mortem photographs have an active role in how some families and individuals view life and death. Because these photographs are taken in a temporary state, capturing and blurring the transition between the living and the dead, they allow for the creation of narratives, new identities and memories that are in a state of constant flux, changing–developing. Therefore, post-mortem photographs have often been used as lasting mementos – helping the living come to terms with death, while assisting with the passing of the deceased from the realm of the living to that of the dead. At the same time they accommodate the continuation, development and re-establishment of a relationship with the dead (Riches and Dawson 1998; Goss and Klass 2005; Hilliker 2006). These continuing bonds, and how they are undertaken, are means of 'rejection of the spatial and temporal boundaries between life and death' (Howarth 2000: 133). Thus the passing from one realm to another is interrupted, or sometimes folded back upon itself, representing an interim between the here and now that allows the dead to re-inhabit the realm of the living.

Post-mortem photographs evoke an array of emotions, from hostility and disgust, to longing and love, and they are often regarded as a piece of art. But individuals' ideas and visions of death, as well as their relationships with the dead, are constantly being altered as their conceptions of themselves, and their place within time and society, change. Accordingly the mechanisms for relocation of the dead are ever changing, allowing one to speculate whether the materiality of the passing of a corpse is final. But no matter how one feels about post-mortem photographs in general, and specifically the post-mortem photographs of Sally Mann, these photographs draw our empathic view, allowing us to acknowledge and ponder the finality of death.

References

Aletti, V., 2006. What Remains: Life, Love and Death through the Lens of Sally Mann. *Modern Painters*, June, 40–43.

Barthes, R., 1984. *Camera Lucida*. London: Fontana.

Batchen, G., 2004. *Forget Me Not. Photography & Remembrance*. New York: Princeton Architectural Press.

Bellafante, G., 2007. Sally Mann Portrait in Which She's the Star. *The New York Times* [online], at http://www.nytimes.com/2007/01/31/arts/television/31sall.html.

Boxer, S., 2004. Slogging Through the Valley of the Shutter of Death. *The New York Times* [online], at http://nytimes.com/2004/07/23/arts/design/23BOXE.html.

Bruce, S., 2005. Sympathy for the Dead: (G)hosts, Hostilities and Mediums in Alejandro Amenábar's *The Others* and Post-mortem Photography. *Discourse: Journal for Theoretical Studies in Media and Culture*, 27(2): 21–40.

Burch, P., 2009. Mobile Phones in Hospital. Resurgence in Memorial Postmortem Photography? *BMJ*, 338: b1063.

Chambliss, D. F., 1996. *Beyond Caring: Hospitals, Nurses, and the Social Organization of Ethics*. Chicago: University of Chicago Press.

Clarke, G., 1997. *The Photograph*. Oxford: Oxford University Press.

Coe, B., 1978. *CAMERAS: From Daguerreotypes to Instant Pictures*. New York: Crown Publishers.

Davies, D. J., 2005. *A Brief History of Death*. Oxford: Blackwell Publishing.

Ennis, H., 2011. Death and Digital Photography. *Cultural Studies Review*, 17(1): 125–145.

Fernandez, I., 2011. The Lives of Corpses: Narratives of the Image in American Memorial Photography. *Mortality*, 16(4): 343–364.

Fink, D., 1990. Funerary, Posthumous, Post-mortem Daguerreotypes. *The Daguerreian Annual*: 55–65.

Gernsheim, H. 1965. *A Concise History of Photography*. London: Thames & Hudson.

Goss, R. E. and Klass, D., 2005. *Dead but Not Lost: Grief Narratives in Religious Traditions*. Walnut Creek: AltaMira Press.

Gottlieb, R. M., 2007. The Reassembly of the Body from Parts: Psychoanalytic Reflections on Death, Resurrection, and Cannibalism. *Journal of American Psychoanalytic Association*, 55(4): 1217–1251.

Gustavson, T., 2012. *Camera: A History of Photography from Daguerreotype to Digital*. New York: Sterling.

Haddars, H., 2011. Negotiating Leave-taking Events in the Palliative Medicine Unit. *Qualitative Health Research*, 21(2): 223–232.

Hallam, E., Hockey, J. and Howarth, G., 1999. *Beyond the Body: Death and Social Identity*. London: Routledge.

Hannavy, J., 1997. *Victorian Photographers at Work: A History in Camera*. Princes Risborough: Shire Publications.

HBO Documentary Films, 2005. *What Remains: A Film About the Life and Work of Sally Mann*, Preliminary Press Notes [online], at http://scholar.google.com/

scholar?q=HBO+Documentary+Films+Presents+WHAT+REMAINS&hl=no
&lr=&btnG=S%C3%B8k.

Heartney, E., 2005. The Forensic Eye. *Art in America*, 93(1): 50–55.

Heessels, S. M., Poots, F. and Venbrux, E., 2012. In Touch with the Deceased: Animate Objects and Human Ashes. *Material Religion*, 8(4): 466–488.

Henning, M., 2006. The Subject as Object: Photography and the Human Body. In: L. Wells, ed., *Photography: A Critical Introduction*. Third Edition. London: Routledge, pp. 159–192.

Hilliker, L., 2006. Letting Go While Holding On: Post-mortem Photography as an Aid in the Grieving Process. *Illness, Crisis & Loss*, 14(3): 245–269.

Hochberg, T., 2003. Touching Souls: Healing with Bereavement Photography. *The Forum*, 29(2): 6.

Howarth, G., 2000. Dismantling the Boundaries between Life and Death. *Mortality*, 5(2): 127–138.

Jones, M., 2003. Love, Death, Light. *Newsweek*, 8 September, 54–6.

Kildegaard, B., 1985. Unlimited Memory: Photography and the Differentiation of Familiar Intimacy. *Ethnologia Scandinavica. A Journal for Nordic Ethnology*, 71–89.

Linkman, A., 2006. Taken from Life: Post-mortem Portraiture in Britain, 1860–1910. *History of Photography*, 30(4): 309–347.

Linkman, A., 2011. *Photography and Death*. London: Reaktion Books.

Mann, S., 2003. *What Remains*. New York: Bulfinch Press.

Masterton, M., Hansson, M. G. and Höglund, A. T., 2010. In Search of the Missing Subject: Narrative Identity and Posthumous Wronging. *Studies in History and Philosophy of Biological and Biomedical Sciences*, 41(4): 340–346.

Mellor, P. and Shilling, C., 1993. Modernity, Self-identity and the Sequestration of Death. *Sociology*, 27(3): 411–431.

Michelson, K., Blehart, K., Hochberg, T. et al., 2013. Bereavement Photography for Children: Program Development and Health Care Professionals' Response. *Death Studies*, 37(6): 513–528.

Moller, D. W., 1990. *On Death Without Dignity: The Human Impact of Technological Dying*. Amityville: Baywood.

Moller, D. W., 2000. *Life's End: Technocratic Dying in an Age of Spiritual Yearning*. Amityville: Baywood.

Nieman, C., 2004. Mann's World: On the Farm with Controversial Photographer Sally Mann. *Style Weekly*, 21 April, 18–27.

O'Neill, M., 2011. Speaking to the Dead: Images of the Dead in Contemporary Art. *Health*, 15(3): 299–312.

Perkins, M. A., 2008. *Death and Memory in the Photography of Sally Mann*. MA thesis, Master of Arts in Humanities, California State University Dominguez Hills.

Ravenal, J., 2010. *Sally Mann: The Flesh and the Spirit*. Richmond/New York: Aperture/Virginia Museum of Fine Arts.

Reddin, S. K., 1987. The Photography of Stillborn Children and Neonatal Deaths. *Journal of Audiovisual Media in Medicine*, 10(2): 49–51.

Riches, G. and Dawson, P., 1998. Lost Children, Living Memories: The Role of Photographs in Processes of Grief and Adjustment Among Bereaved Parent. *Death Studies*, 22(2): 121–140.

Ruby, J., 1995. *Secure the Shadow: Death and Photography in America*. Cambridge, MA: MIT Press.

Seale, C., 1998. *Constructing Death: The Sociology of Dying and Bereavement*. Cambridge: Cambridge University Press.

Smith, B. R. and Vokes, R., 2008. Introduction: Haunting Images. *Visual Anthropology*, 21(4): 283–291.

Snickare, E. Å., 2002. *Døden, kroppen och moderniteten*. Stockholm: Carlsson Bokförlag.

Unruh, D. R., 1983. Death and Personal History: Strategies of Identity Preservation. *Social Problems*, 30(3): 340–351.

Walter, T., 1994. *The Revival of Death*. London: Routledge.

PART III:
Transience:
Passing On, Passing Through

Chapter 9

The Third Burial: Passing between Worlds and Points of Transformation among the Siberian Chukchi

Jeanette Lykkegård

Birth and death; the two seemingly opposite extremes that appear to frame our existence are also possibly the most incomprehensible. As Françoise Dastur (2012) remarks, they are the two all-important events of our lives that we will never experience for ourselves. How we confront death thus becomes a question of how we confront the death of *others*.

In this chapter I explore the ways in which the Chukchi inhabitants of Achaivayam in the Northern Kamchatka confront death. The Chukchi is a group of indigenous people numbering about 15,000 who live in the north-eastern part of the Russian Far East, mainly in Chukotka and the northern part of the Kamchatka peninsula (Schweitzer 1999: 137). I conducted multiple fieldworks, amounting to one year in total, in Kamchatka in the period from 2011 to 2014, mainly in and around the village of Achaivayam. It is a village of around 400 inhabitants consisting of primarily Chukchi, but Even[1] people and a handful of Russians and Ukrainians also live there. The inhabitants differentiate themselves according to ethnicity; even when intermixed through marriage, they will note which ethnic group they consider themselves as belonging to. The sense of belonging to Russia – that is being of Russian nationality – is generally speaking non-existent.

For most Chukchi of Achaivayam,[2] the understanding of birth, life and death rests on the cycle of life as observed and experienced in nature. The sun is seen as the ultimate life source or life (*Unatgirgin**[3]) itself and its circular movement as well as its death and resurrection appear to be an inspiration for daily life and

---

1 The Even is another indigenous group of people of Siberia, numbering around 19,000.

2 Mention of the Chukchi further in this chapter refers mainly to the Chukchi of Achaivayam, unless it is with reference to earlier ethnography.

3 Words marked by an asterisk (*), when first mentioned, are in the local language, which is a mix of Koryak and Chukchi. The largest indigenous population of the northern Kamchatka is the Koryak, which bear many similarities to the Chukchi, both in culture and language. When the Chukchi immigrated they adopted part of the Koryak dialect (see also Jochelsen 1908; Plattet 2005; King 2011).

rituals. In earlier times, when a woman got pregnant she had to get up every day at sunrise and circle around her tent in the direction of the movement of the sun in order to ensure a good birth (Bogoras 1904–9: 509). This daily ritual is no longer performed, but circles and circular movements still appear often: during the spring ritual *Kilvey*,[4] and the 'thanksgiving ritual',[5] the participants circle around the tent in the direction of the sun; during the ritualised reindeer slaughter, the reindeer is, after its death, circulated in the direction of the sun; the original skin tents, *Yarangas* are round and are said to be a constellation of the universe; the fireplace is round and is considered the most important life source after the sun; many of the amulets sewn onto the traditional clothing for protection are circular too. Reminders of the circularity of life and the understanding that life endlessly feeds on life are everywhere. Once, when a reindeer herder revealed the secret of good health and longevity to me, I was told that 'the circular movement of life is sometimes almost imperceptible, like the breath'. If you pay attention to the cycles of inhalation and exhalation of your breath his words will prove to be true. It is difficult to pinpoint the exact moment of change; it is almost a dimensionless point that you pass through. Where does it come from? Where does it go? When does it begin? When does it end? This is very much like the infinite cycle of life: birth – life – death – birth – life – death – birth …

In Achaivayam, belief in reincarnation is pervasive[6] and death is generally understood as a transformation rather than a definite end. When you die in this world the goal is to be reborn as an ancestor, and when ancestors die, they are considered as being spontaneously reborn here (see also Willerslev 2009; 2013). The circle thus becomes birth, human life, death, birth, ancestor life, death, birth, human life, and so on, but this circle can be broken at any point, whether in life, in death, in birth or maybe especially in between two of those states, namely death and birth.

In this chapter I examine the passage between death and birth and aim to understand how this passing is enabled and thus maintains the entire life-giving circulation of souls. I especially engage with people's involvement with their material surroundings in rituals that are performed to make this passage possible. The exploration takes its point of departure in the ritual *Pominki*, which is generally referred to as a commemorative ritual. Through my analysis I will show how this

---

4   This ritual is meant to ensure that many and healthy reindeer calves are born and survive, in order for the herd to grow and thus food and clothing to be plentiful.

5   Also called 'closed Yaranga', referring to the performance that has to take place in a traditional closed tent, in response to a dream, often if something good or bad has happened to the person arranging it.

6   There are some among the younger generation who have their doubts about this belief. Influenced by schooling and television they find themselves caught between different worldviews. I have, for example, experienced women who joke about the traditional beliefs, but nevertheless agree to name their children according to tradition, that is, after the ancestors who were re-born in their child.

ritual ought to rather be seen as part of a mortuary ritual, engaging with the proper ways of passing between the world of the living and that of the dead. Only through this ritual can the spirits of those who died during the past year finally embark on their journey to the world of the ancestors and the actual *passing* begin. This is partly facilitated – as we shall come to see – through yet another circle, namely an encirclement of the world of the ancestors, which allows it a temporary presence in the world of the living.

Encountering the So-Called *Pominki*

On 3 October 2011, I woke up to the sound of Babushka[7] Nadiesta[8] filling the wood stove. The tent soon became warm after the frosty night and I started to feel the excitement of the event of the day; *Pominki*. I had been told that this is one of the most important rituals of the year. It seemed as if everyone woke up at this instant and the quiet camp became lively at once, as breakfast was prepared at the bonfires. The sky was blue and the temperature mild. The snow had not yet fallen and the tundra appeared warm and welcoming, bathed in the brown, yellow and orange colours of autumn. Approximately 75 people had gathered at this riverside the night before, and were now waiting for the private reindeer herd.[9] Suddenly one of the men shouted: 'They are here'. That seemed to be the code for 'go' and everyone grabbed their belongings and started to walk eastwards. Not far from the campsite we halted and the ritual was immediately initiated. The men began to dig a grave while some of the women took on the task of making a fire and building a frame for the big pots. Other women began the creation of the lasso-rings. First they caught a willow twig with the lasso, and then opened the lasso noose, thus creating a circular space in which the twig was placed in an upright position, as if planted anew in the ground. Seven such rings were made. Along with each twig were placed three river stones taken from this side of the river. The stones were characterised by their smooth surface. As soon as every circle contained twigs and stones I was hurried into placing my offerings, consisting of biscuits, tea, tobacco, *yukala** (dried fish), sweets and bread, and everyone else did the same.

As people shuffled up around the lasso-rings I observed their doings and followed suit. It all seemed very rushed and, in a way, unceremonious. When everyone had made their gift-offerings, the first reindeer for sacrifice had already been caught. It was a young calf from the same year. It was explained to me that a young boy had died and for that reason a young reindeer was sacrificed for

---

7 Babushka is the Russian word for grandmother. All elderly women of Achaivayam and in Russia generally, are referred to as Babushka, whether related or not.

8 All the names used are aliases.

9 During the time of the Soviet Union most of the reindeer were taken from the people and turned into state-owned herds (*Sovkhoz*) but the people of Achaivayam managed to keep a small private herd (*Chasnaya*) (see also Plattet 2010).

Figure 9.1   At Tentyk, October 2011
Note: The lasso-ring with the food and the 'deceased' in the form of three stones, and the 'souls of all living people and reindeer' in the form of a willow twig.
Source: Photo by author.

him. I looked at the calf fighting for his life and at the same time emerged into an empathetic feeling for the father who fought with the calf to make him surrender.[10] It all seemed very violent and the situation culminated when the calf finally stood in the correct position and the father stabbed it in the heart, causing blood to squirt out onto his face.

I looked around and saw what seemed like chaos. There were people everywhere. Some were selecting and catching reindeer. Some were struggling with captured reindeer. Others were skinning, dismembering and deboning the carcasses in various places. Others again were boiling meat and some were spreading the skins to dry in the sun. All the blood, the stomachs, the intestines, the hooves, the ears, the mouths and the tails were placed in the grave, which caused people to walk between carcasses and grave with bowls of blood or in pairs carrying a heavy stomach. Everything that went into the grave was meant to ensure that the reindeer would live on to enter a healthy life 'on the other side'

---

10   Although there is an initial fight between the herder and the reindeer, the reindeer cannot be sacrificed until he stands calmly with the head lowered and the front legs in a forward position, thus signalling that he willingly lets himself be sacrificed.

**Figure 9.2   The participants have tea next to the lasso-rings, this one
containing the delicate bone-marrow**

Source: Photo by author.

with the deceased. A little blood from each reindeer was smeared onto the stones
in their respective owner's circle.

After getting a grip on the procedures I took part in the practice; first in
emptying the blood from the reindeer bodies and placing the blood in the grave,
later in deboning. The importance of ending up with completely meatless bones
was pointed out to me repeatedly. Some bones were broken to extract the marrow.
In those instances the fragmented bones would also be thrown into the grave. The
marrow along with the brain, the kidneys, the eyes and sinew were placed on ritual
dishes as the main delicacies. Other meats were cooked and some of them cut into
small pieces and others again into bigger lumps, which were likewise placed on

**Figure 9.3   Reindeer meat is placed in the lasso-ring as a sacrifice for
              the ancestors**

Source: Photo by author.

the ritual dishes. Everyone gathered and placed small pieces of meat in the lasso-
rings. Standing almost on top of each other the participants all seemed to wish to
place the meat at once. As soon as the small pieces of meat had been placed I was
told to sit down and eat: 'Now they [the ancestors] have eaten, so we can eat'. It
was a feast.

The men gathered and placed all the antlers with the top of the skull, as well
as what the Chukchi consider the essential bones of the reindeer – the femurs,
the jawbones[11] and the first cervical bone – in a row. The antlers and bones were
intertwined and the arrangement was then covered with stones to hold all parts in
place. They were placed in such a manner that these certain and very specific bones
and antlers looked like a row of reindeer. In fact I was told that they were reindeer.

---

11 It is not unusual among various groups of peoples in the world to connect certain
bones of human and animals to an essence. In example, the lower jawbone of an animal
alone is believed by many Indigenous Mesoamericans to be connected to the animal's
spiritual essence (Foster 1945).

Figure 9.4   The sacrificed reindeer are reconstructed from their essential anatomical parts

Source: Photo by author.

The whole arrangement was facing north. Oblivious as I was at the time, I asked how these reindeer were to take the deceased with them and got the following answer: 'Well, how can I explain it? You know Santa Claus right?' I nodded. 'It's like that. His reindeer also take him everywhere, right?'

This was the end of it. The bone-free meat left over was distributed in such a manner that no one carried home anything from his or her own private reindeer. Everything in the lasso rings stayed there except for the twigs. The twigs were brought home. The explanation for this varies. Some say it is to ensure that the deceased will come back, others that it is the family soul, which must carry on here on earth. At home, the family members either burn the twig in their family fire or they tie it around the neck of their family idol, the *Gihr-Gihr**, where it becomes a lasso. The grave was covered and we all went back to the campsite where drumming and singing took place. In the afternoon a rainbow decorated the sky and as darkness fell on the evening a dark red sunset mixed with a snowstorm over the mountains completed the dramatic and beautiful day.

Pominki is Not Pominki – it is Tentyk

As I mentioned earlier, I was introduced to this ritual as *Pominki*. I did not understand why I had never read about this ritual before; after all, I was told it is one of the most important rituals among the Chukchi. *Pominki* is the Russian word for commemoration. When looking for old records of Chukchi commemorative praxis I found that according to Bogoras (1904–9) and Sverdrup (1939), a kind of yearly commemorative practice did take place for each deceased person, when the Chukchi still lived purely as reindeer nomads. It took place every year after a person's death, when the herd would pass the place where the funeral had been conducted. The family would visit and bring antlers to the 'burial' site, which they had stored away from their reindeer slaughters (Bogoras 1904–9: 534), but these were nothing like *Pominki*. Today when any Chukchi pass the sacred hill close to Achaivayam on which the cremation takes place, they will likewise make offerings, not in the form of antlers but rather tobacco, bread or sweets. Bogoras and Sverdrup furthermore mention that in relation to certain ceremonies the ancestors were likewise honoured by offerings. This is still true today, but although I searched in the old records I never managed to find any mention of a commemorative ritual remotely similar to *Pominki*, which I found rather intriguing, to say the least! Had I discovered an ancient ritual that had been overlooked by classic ethnographers?

As everyone speaks Russian to me when I am in Achaivayam, the word *Pominki* was always used, but during my search for information about it, I learned that the Russian word *Pominki* (commemoration) does not encompass the meaning of the Chukchi word for this ritual, which is *Tentyk**.[12] *Tentyk* was translated to me as the Russian word *nastupit*, which has several meanings including 'to proceed' or 'to step on'. One person translated *Tentyk* with both *nastupit* and *ubrat*. *Ubrat* means 'to clean' or 'to remove'. I searched for information about *Tentyk* in The Chukchee (1904–9) – the masterpiece by Bogoras – as it is an extraordinarily detailed monograph. Yet again: nothing!

Gaining knowledge about the Chukchi word *Tentyk* nevertheless led me in a new direction, towards an understanding of the ritual. I asked about the confusing use of the word *Pominki* to describe *Tentyk* and I was told: 'The Russians saw what we did, and they thought it was a commemoration and they called it that – but this is wrong'. The two terms carry very different meanings. 'We don't have such a thing as commemoration (*Pominki*). What we do is that we send the reindeer along with them [the deceased]; we send them to "the other side". It is not a commemoration – it is *Tentyk*. It is like they have all left, we send them to the other

---

12   *Tentyk* is also sometimes called *tantergyn** or *tantegiain**, which stem from the same root and have the same meaning. Many Chukchi of Achaivayam do not speak their own language, and therefore refer to *Tentyk* with the Russian word *Pominki*, without thinking more deeply about the meaning of the word.

side and everyone moves on.' *Tentyk* is thus not a mere remembering of the dead or the ancestors, rather it is a necessary arrangement for life to proceed, as I was told: 'It is for *everyone* to move on'. From the explanations, *Tentyk* sounded more like some kind of mortuary ritual and I turned my attention to classic anthropological literature on mortuary rituals.

Death as a Process

Robert Hertz's work on 'death as a process' became directive in my exploration of *Tentyk*. Hertz drew mainly on materials from Indonesia, in particular from the island of Borneo. Common to the societies he discussed in his work titled *Death and the Right Hand* is the idea that death is not seen as instantaneous. Death as such becomes a temporal transformative state in the same way as the Chukchi of Achaivayam perceive it. Furthermore, Hertz stated that death leads to ideas and practices which concern three aspects; the body, the soul and the bereaved (Hertz [1960] 2004: 29). Hertz described how in Borneo, people conceive of a period where the person is neither alive nor dead, which he called the 'intermediary period'. This intermediary period starts with what Hertz called the 'first burial', which removes the flesh and the identity of the deceased and ends with the 'second burial', which deals with the bones and gives way to a new identity for the deceased among the ancestors (Hertz [1960] 2004). During the intermediary period, the soul is still somewhat attached to the body and remains on earth, often unhappy, and dangerous for the living, who enter a period of mourning and taboos (Hertz [1960] 2004: 197). 'The "second burial" ending this period is marked by a great feast during which the remains of the deceased are recovered, ritually processed and moved to a new location' (Huntington and Metcalf 1979: 13).

The categorisation of the double burial practices by Hertz led me to think that there was a connection between the 'second burial' and *Tentyk*. I was told that when a person is cremated, 'he leaves, but he cannot leave. He has to wait for his reindeer, only at *Tentyk* he leaves'. We here get the sense that *Tentyk* is a part of the Chukchi mortuary rituals, since this ritual and great feast seem to mark the end of the intermediary period between what Hertz described as the 'first burial' and the 'second burial'. It is worth noting the resemblance of the purpose of 'the 'second burial' to the meaning of the word *Tentyk*: 'to proceed' or 'to remove'.

Van Gennep (1960) addressed rituals that accompany the transitional stages in life – birth, puberty, marriage and death as 'rite de passage' – and saw them as serving an important psychological and sociological function by ensuring the orderly progression between categories. According to Victor Turner, who was extensively inspired by van Gennep, rites of passage are found in all societies, but tend to reach their maximal expression in small-scale *cyclical* societies, where change is closely connected to biological and meteorological rhythms and recurrences rather than with technological innovations (Turner 1987: 4) – a description that fits very well with the Chukchi society I know. Van Gennep divides the rites of passage into three stages. The first stage comprises symbolic behaviour signifying detachment or separation of the individual or group from an earlier fixed point in the structure or from cultural conditions (*first burial* for Hertz). The second stage denotes an ambiguous transitional or liminal position (*intermediary period* in Hertz's terminology). The third stage is consummation of the rite of passage through reincorporation or aggregation (*second burial*).

Van Gennep expected rites of separation to be the most prominent component in funeral ceremonies in contrast to rites of transition and rites of incorporation. His studies, however, revealed that the rites of separation are few in number and very simple, while the transition rites in funeral ceremonies are so dominating and complex that sometimes they ought to be granted a sort of autonomy (van Gennep, 1960: 146). Van Gennep noted that in some cases the transitional period of the living is a counterpart to the transitional period of the deceased (ibid.: 147). This appears to be true among the Chukchi. It was described to me how the transition of the deceased and his incorporation into the world of the ancestors is a precondition for a safe and normalised life among the living. The transitional period in Achaivayam is described as a dangerous period, where passageways between the different worlds of different beings are open. I was told that *Tentyk* is the ritual that enables the passage from the liminal period into stability, for both the deceased and the bereaved: for the deceased in that they leave the world of the living in order to enter and be reborn among the ancestors, and for the community, because they pass from a period of uncertainty into a period of relative safety, since the deceased have left and thus have been removed from this sphere and into their proper environment. But why does the passing only take place at *Tentyk* and not at the mortuary rituals following immediately after the person's death?

Following Hertz's definition of *double burials*, in the case of the Chukchi mortuary rituals cremation becomes the 'first burial', where the body is destroyed and the flesh separated from the bones. In Achaivayam, as in Hertz's example of ancient Indian rituals, the remains of the cremated body as well as the ashes must be collected (Hertz [1960] 2004: 42). Now this is done the day after the cremation and constitutes the 'second burial'. Following Hertz, the 'second burial' should enable the deceased to take their place among the ancestors. But as mentioned, the deceased do not leave. The question is why? I decided to take first things first, and start with the mortuary rituals and compare the materials described in old records to the contemporary mortuary rituals.

First Burial

On the day of the cremation[13] the deceased is dressed in a death suit,[14] which guides him/her towards 'the other side' in various ways; for instance, the left boot is put on the right hand and vice versa, and the same applies to the mittens. This is based on the cosmological conceptions of the Chukchi in which the different worlds are placed on top of each other as each other's mirroring world (see also Bogoras 1904–9; Willerslev 2013). The deceased is likewise equipped with a walking stick, bells, a cup, a knife, fire tools and resin as well as personal amulets attained in life.[15] Furthermore, he is wrapped with a lasso, which contains the spirit until cremation takes place.

The deceased is then taken to a cremation site situated at the edge of the village at the sacred hill, Shamanka (Russian for shamaness), also called *Appapo** (grandfather) in the local language. Patrick Plattet, who has carried out extensive fieldwork in Achaivayam, was told that it is from this spot that the human dead and the sacrificed reindeer are ritually dispatched to the other side (Plattet 2010: 107). However, this is not entirely consistent with what I was repeatedly told, namely that 'he leaves, but he cannot leave', indicating that the deceased may well have been dispatched but still somehow gets stuck and is, in fact, unable to reach the other side from this site.[16]

The pyre is built up like a sleigh and the construction starts with the runners in the form of two wooden beams. Then a reindeer in the form of a substitute called *zjozjat**[17] is sacrificed. It is cut into two, lengthwise, and each half is placed under the runner to make it run smoothly. In between the runners at the north end three river stones are placed. Thereafter the rest of the pyre is built.

---

13   The cremation as well as the preparations for it take place through detailed ritual behaviour but I include here only what is interesting in relation to understanding *Tentyk*.

14   The death suit is preferably almost finished early in life, and always made from the individual's own personal reindeer. If the suit has not been made in advance, the women who keep the deceased company just after his death sew it.

15   All the objects are chosen to aid the deceased on his strenuous journey. The resin, for example, will function as chewing gum when the deceased arrives among the ancestors, as everyone will ask him how their relatives are and at some point the deceased will not have the energy to answer more questions and he will chew on the resin.

16   The Chukchi rituals and cosmological beliefs vary a little between each family as they were originally formed in smaller family communities or clans; but in spite of variations, they are nevertheless very similar to each other. Plattet may have been told other variations, but everyone I spoke to agreed that the deceased cannot leave this world until after *Tentyk*, as he is waiting for his reindeer. Plattet, in the cited work, does mention *Tentyk*, he recognises its connection to the mortuary ritual, but he still refers to it as a commemorative ritual and thus has a different understanding of the ritual as well as the direction of the bone-altar (for comparison or further information see Plattet 2010: 107–112).

17   This is the third stomach of a reindeer, stuffed with fat; a common sacrificial 'stand-in' for a live reindeer.

The body is placed on the pyre with the head facing north, in the direction of the Polar Star. The polar star is referred to in the local language as 'the Immobile Star' (Iluk-eŋer*) or 'The Nail Star' (əlqer-eŋer*) (Siimets 2006: 147) and is seen as the home of the creator as well as the centre of the universe (Bogoras 1925: 212). According to Chukchi mythology, the hole in the sky through which you pass into the other world is placed just beneath the Polar Star (Siimets 2006: 147) and the directional placement of the body functions, like the death suit, as guidance for the deceased.

At the time of Bogoras' and Sverdrup's presence among the Chukchi the deceased would be either exposed in the open or cremated, but in both cases they would, if possible, be placed on a sleigh and always, as said, with the head pointing north, towards the Polar Star. The body was enclosed by stones (sometimes just three stones placed around the head) and the two poles that had supported the sleigh on the way to the site of cremation or disposal were placed next to the body on either side, supporting the enclosure (Bogoras 1904–9; Sverdrup 1939. Instead of a *zjozjat,* a live reindeer was sacrificed.[18] The reindeer was tied to the sleigh and killed slowly in such a manner that is looked like it was running and thus pulling the deceased. When dead, the reindeer was placed within the enclosure of the deceased and skinned. The meat was cut off in thin slices, the bones of the legs were broken and the antlers chopped off.

When comparing the old way of doing the 'first burial' with the contemporary, we see that the main difference is the lack of a live reindeer to sacrifice. The *zjozjat* is treated in just the same way as the ordinary reindeer, though, and I was always told that the is, in fact, the reindeer in that moment. Shapeshifting or changing bodies is often described in animist countries, and Eduardo Viveiros de Castro describes the animist perception of the body as something made, rather than something given (1998: 480). The reindeer externalised as a *zjozjat* has different qualities in comparison with the reindeer externalised as a reindeer. It is much like donning a certain bodily quality but maintaining the inner character or spirit (ibid.: 482). Keeping in mind that the inner being of both reindeer and *zjozjat* are essentially the same, the 'first burial' seems to live up to its prescriptions and there is no apparent reason for the deceased not to leave the body. The deceased is thus now something else, not spiritually but in body, and with the bodily change comes the change of world. The deceased no longer belongs to the world of the living and not yet to the world of the ancestor, he is by all means 'betwixt and between' (Turner 1987).

Second Burial

In Achaivayam, the participants in the 'first burial' return to the cremation site the following morning. They enter carefully and start by throwing a stone at the burnt out fire to scare away *Ke'let**, a term used for all malevolent beings.

---

18   One or several will be sacrificed according to the wealth of the deceased.

While approaching the fireplace, a lasso is thrown at the ashes, thus catching the spirit of the deceased. Afterwards the bones and ashes are collected, including the three stones, and it is all encircled by a lasso-ring very similar to the *Tentyk*. The participants place offerings of tobacco, bread, tea and sweets inside the lasso-ring and take their place around it. This is described as 'having a last tea with the deceased'.

Turning to Bogoras's descriptions, I found that the first part of the 'second burial' is so alike the contemporary 'second burial', that describing it would be a mere repetition. But the contemporary ritual ends here, whereas Bogoras description shows that originally the ritual had more to it. What follows in the description from Bogoras's is non-existent in the contemporary 'second burial', but it is much similar to *Tentyk*;

> Then the slaughtering begins … The legs of the reindeer are broken and the marrow is extracted. The heads are cooked in large kettles, and the feast begins, during which the corpse receives its share of all the courses. The antlers are hewn off, as usual, with the tops of the crown, and are burned for a few seconds in the fire to make them secure against harm by wild beasts, which the odour of the smoke will frighten away. After that, the antlers are arranged in a line extending from the head of the corpse toward the direction of midnight. The antlers of each set are pointed upward, and their bases are pressed firmly into the ground, and made fast with stones or logs. The heap of antlers is called "antlers' store" (tl'nmai). (Bogoras 1904–9: 530–531)

In comparing the contemporary 'second burial' to the old practice it becomes apparent that the sacrifices of the reindeer and the composition of the antlers are missing in the contemporary 'second burial'. At the same time it becomes clear that *Tentyk* is constructed precisely to finalise the 'second burial' in the manner of the old 'second burial', turning it into what I will call a 'third burial', to stay with the terminology of Hertz. When asked directly, the eldest women in Achaivayam confirmed this. When I finally understood that the 'second burial' originally included reindeer sacrifices, I also understood the significant reconstruction of the mortuary rituals since the time of Bogoras' description is related to historical changes, which have led to a division between the reindeer and the inhabitants of Achaivayam.

Changes that Caused a Third Burial

The Chukchi are known for their resistance towards Russianization. As Bogoras wrote:

> The first thing brought by the Russians was a request for tribute and war … They (the Chukchee) successfully repelled the first and held their ground in the second;

and when the war at last ceased, they preserved intact all their national vigor ...
The Russianization of the Chukchee has made no progress at all during the two
centuries of Russian intercourse with the Chukchee. The Chukchee kept their
language, all their ways of living, and their religion ... (Bogoras 1904–9: 732)

It was only after 1930 that changes took place. At this time, Russian control
expanded as part of Stalinism. The village of Achaivayam developed in 1934
but, as with Chukotka and the rest of the northern Kamchatka, the greatest
transformation took place from the 1950s to the 1970s, when infrastructure in the
form of helicopter routes was established. During this period, Chukchi herders
were forcibly collectivized (Kerttula 2000) and the nomadic herders slowly moved
into settlements as their herds were converted into state farms (sovkhoz) and the
herders operated within a Soviet system where nomadic herding became a job
rather than a lifestyle. The children were sent to boarding schools and the cultural
ceremonies and the Chukchi language abandoned. In spite of this, the Chukchi
never converted to Orthodox Christianity, unlike many of the neighbouring groups
of indigenous people who did.

After the fall of the Soviet Union, the non-indigenous population of Achaivayam
fell drastically and the helicopters did not arrive. The shops accordingly failed
to supply many of the food products the inhabitants had grown accustomed to.
The only way to survive, I was told, was 'po staramu' which is Russian for 'the
old way'.

Reindeer herding, fishing, hunting and gathering once more became the
only trustworthy means of survival in Achaivayam. The helicopter routes have
been reopened and the food situation and economy is once again better, but the
population stresses the importance of their traditional way of life as the foundation
for survival. Nevertheless, the Chukchi are no longer full-time nomads, but have
kept to the soviet system. The herders are part-time nomads and many villagers
only see the reindeer when they are brought from their pastures and into the village
for ceremonial occasions and ritual slaughtering. This has caused a physical
distance between the people and the herd, which made the accomplishment of the
'second burial' impossible – and thus arose *Tentyk.*

An elderly woman explained that '*Tentyk* takes place when the reindeer are
no longer shedding and the skins are good for making clothes'. Searching once
again for an explanation in the detailed monograph by Bogoras I found that
Tentyk appear to take place at the time of what he described as the second of
the opening rituals of the cycle of 'genuine sacrifices'[19] – the ritual of 'making
skins for wearing' (*têêtawñl'Irgin*) (Bogoras 1904–9: 372). The cycle refers to the
fact that the Chukchi sacrificial rituals form a yearly cycle in accordance with the
seasons and the subject matter related to that season. The placement seems logical;
whereas the autumn rituals mark the transition from summer to winter, the 'dead
period', the spring is the time of *Kilvej*, the celebration of the birth of the reindeer

---

19   Their essential feature is the slaughtering of reindeer for sacrifice.

calves. As the world of the ancestors mirrors this world, autumn among the living is spring among the ancestors (ibid.; Willerslev 2013). Autumn is the time for slaughtering, whereas in spring, in the period following *Kilvej*, it is forbidden to slaughter reindeer. *Tentyk* then becomes the *Kilvej* of the ancestors, and the fall slaughtering among the living a point of transition both in the world of the living and the world of the ancestors, and the circulation of life goes on.

One important question still persists, though. If the liminary period is characterised by danger, why could the Chukchi not have used substitutes for the 'second burial' just as they did during the 'first burial'?

Inadequate Substitutes

The sacrifice of a reindeer in the material form of a *zjozjat* is evidently not sufficient in the 'second burial', but why? If the *zjozjat is* the reindeer, how can it then not be a sufficient reindeer? How is it that two material forms are the same and yet not the same?

To fully understand the need for the *Tentyk,* it is necessary to understand the logic of sacrificial substitutes among the Chukchi, which Rane Willerslev has engaged with in his writings. He explains that each substitute is regarded as taking the place of a real reindeer and is, therefore, stabbed with a knife to represent actual slaughter. However, all these substitutes are not considered to be equal but are organised in a hierarchical order: the grading moves from the most complex and rare, to the simpler and more common (Willerslev 2013: 6).

He continues, and this is important: 'the troubling fact, however, is that the value hierarchy of substitutes is shadowed by its contrary so that in a certain sense the lowest is also considered the highest' (ibid.). In other words, the lowest and the highest are each other's flipsides in much the same way as the living and the ancestors are each other's flipsides, or shadows. They are thus immanent in each other but, each being the reverse of the other; nevertheless have different powers and qualities. So the question is: What qualities does the *zjozjat* lack in comparison to the reindeer?

Let me take you back to *Tentyk*. During *Tentyk* the three stones representing the face of the deceased are smeared with blood from his sacrificed reindeer. This was explained to me in this way: 'you see, the three stones, they are him [the deceased], that is why we smear them with the blood, because it is him'. Smearing blood in Chukchi sacrificial rituals always has to do with a form of 'bringing together'. For this reason, smearing blood was originally also an essential part of the marriage ceremony (Bogoras 1904–9: 361). Painting with the blood of the sacrifice is symbolical of the membership of all members of the family (ibid.). In other words, smearing the stones with the blood of the reindeer resembles the connection between reindeer and the deceased – they are as a family. The blood smearing becomes a manifestation of the close bond and interdependence between the man and his reindeer. I venture to say that the sacrifice of a private reindeer could not be substituted by the *zjozjat* partly because it lacks the individuality of a privately owned, earmarked reindeer. As I was told, the 'deceased is waiting for *his* reindeer' – a *zjozjat* cannot be anyone's as it is anonymous. Lacking the quality of identification, the *zjozjat* is not suitable in this situation, as the deceased needs to carry forward and continue his personal herd in the world of the ancestors.

Another important quality lacked by the *zjozjat* is the bones. Often bones are associated with life instead of death, as they are the seat of the vital principle. The key role of bones in mortuary rituals is therefore widespread, especially among people in northern Eurasia as well as parts of Asia, as bones can be reanimated and therefore are essential to rebirth (Henninger 1987: 284). The 'second burial' as defined by Hertz conforms to this idea exactly in that it deals with the bones and gives way to a new identity for the deceased among his ancestors. The bones become the facilitator of the continuation of the life of the deceased. In some South American tribes the bones are pulverised and swallowed with water. They hope that by doing this, the deceased will resurrect inside themselves (Hertz [1960] 2004: 72). Among the Chukchi it is not possible for life to continue if not in the circular movement between this world and the world of the ancestors, and as the worlds are mirroring each other de-fleshing the bones in this world means re-fleshing in the world of the ancestors.

Thus shape shifting and substitution is accepted, and a reindeer *can* take the body of a *zjozjat*. What differentiates the two are the certain qualities carried by their bodily manifestation. In ensuring rebirth and a good, continuous life of the deceased among the ancestors, the individuality and revitalising qualities of the bones are simply irreplaceable.

Conclusion

I have argued that *Tentyk* – which was initially presented to me as the commemorative ritual, *Pominki* – is in fact a mortuary ritual which I have called a 'third burial'. *Tentyk* finalises the contemporary 'second burial' in a manner that lives up the 'second burial' the Chukchi carried out during the time of Bogoras's research a century ago.

The materials used during *Tentyk* are no longer just materials; they are actors, guides, enclosures, boundaries and souls. The lasso ring forms a circle, which is explained as a physical manifestation of the world of the ancestors. A circle appears to be timeless – in that it has no beginning and no end – but simultaneously is time enclosing space (Cooper 1978). Inside the circle you have ancestor time, which is the reverse of our time. The lasso-ring is, however, not just a circle, it is also a circumference. Enclosing beings, objects or figures within a circumference has a double meaning (Cirlot 1962). Seen from the inside it implies a limitation and a definition – following the Chukchi description, a territory. The outside is then protected. The circumference is a defence from what is enclosed (ibid.) – in this case the ancestors. Without limitations, the ancestor's presence in this earthly world would be equal to chaos. As the physical body of the deceased is non-existent at the time of *Tentyk*, the deceased is introduced into the territory of the ancestors in the form of three smooth stones. Sometimes stones are seen to have life giving potency – or people can be turned into sacred stones (ibid.). In *Tentyk* the stones become the deceased, now with regenerative power that should ensure a good birth for him/her among the ancestors.[20]

Shape shifting is often described in animist countries, and Eduardo Vivieros de Castro describes the animist perception of the body as something made, rather than something given (1998: 480). It is much like donning a certain bodily quality but maintaining the inner character or spirit (ibid.: 482). As we have seen in the case of *Tentyk*, while shape shifting and substitution is accepted, a certain shape or body is needed. The reindeer as a *zjozjat* has different qualities in comparison with the reindeer as a reindeer. The *zjozjat* is simply inadequate for *Tentyk*; unable to enable the passing of a deceased from this world to the next. The *zjozjat*, I argue, lacks the quality of identification and the regenerative qualities inherent in bones – both of which the reindeer accommodate.

This adds to one of the biggest questions in sacrificial studies, namely that of substitutes. The hierarchical system of substitutes among the Chukchi – which Plattet (2005) and Willerslev (2013) discuss – is not purely a matter of complex value hierarchy of substitutes shadowed by their contraries. We can now add to the complexity the understanding that each substitute has its very own quality that may not be replaced by any other form. But if the reindeer sacrificed at *Tentyk* cannot be substituted is it then still a substitute? Willerslev, among others, argues that 'it is the substitution that defines sacrifice as sacrifice and which distinguishes it from other related forms of death' (Willerslev 2013: 6). He refers to reindeer as the prototypical substitute in the Siberian North, which stands in for the person or persons who are making the sacrifice (ibid.). Comparing the Chukchi to the Nuer as described by Evans-Prichard, Willerslev argues that when the Chukchi sacrifice their reindeer, they also give a part of themselves (ibid.). In the case of *Tentyk*, the reindeer is closely connected to the deceased, but cannot be a substitute for the deceased, as he/she is already dead. I suggest that the deceased and his/her reindeer are a sacrificial pair. When the Chukchi make reindeer sacrifices – whether to the sun, the ancestors, the ocean or someone else – they often accompany that sacrifice with another sacrifice, be it another reindeer or a reindeer in another form (e.g. *zjozjat* or stone). They explain that this is to give the first sacrifice a partner to accompany them on the journey to and during life in the next world. Sometimes the sacrificial partner is referred to as a love partner, necessary for reproduction.

---

20   At childbirth a Chukchi's first challenge is finding a name. The use of a stone in a pendant is still a common tool in Achaivayam to foretell which ancestor(s) came back in a new-born baby, thus enabling a good life for him/her here on Earth. This praxis was used in almost the same way around a hundred years back, only then the stone would be allowed to strike a drum, and the sound would be interpreted as a name, which was given to the child (Bogoras 1904–9; Sverdrup 1939: 136).

In the case of *Tentyk*, the reindeer would then be the accompanying sacrifice to the deceased.[21] Both the deceased and the reindeer sacrificed at *Tentyk* then become substitutes for the living, as a promise that they will follow later, but hopefully not too soon.

The Chukchi worlds with its different beings are simultaneously different entities and at the same time equal to their unity. They are interdependent and must endlessly inter-exchange life in a way that enables the continuation of all the different manifestations of life. The mortuary rituals create and maintain death as something temporal and transformative. The Chukchi thus confront death through ritual acts by which they sustain life through death in an endless cycle of repetition, always the same, always different.

References

Bogoras, W., 1904–9. *The Chukchee*. Jesup North Pacific Expedition 7. Leiden: E. J. Brill.

Bogoras, W., 1925. Ideas of Space and Time in the Conception of Primitive Religion. *American Anthropologist*. New Series, 27(2): 205–66.

Cirlot, J. E., 1962. *A Dictionary of Symbols*. New York: Philosophical Library.

Cooper, J. C., 1978. *An Illustrated Encyclopaedia of Traditional Symbols*. London: Thames & Hudson Ltd.

Dastur, F., 2012. *How Are We to Confront Death? An Introduction to Philosophy*. New York: Fordham University Press.

Foster, G., 1945. Sierra Popoluca Folklore and Beliefs. *Archaeology and Ethnology*, 42(2): 177–250.

Hertz, R. [1960] 2004. *Death and the Right Hand*. London and New York: Routledge.

Henninger, J., 1987. Bones. In: M. Eliade, ed., *The Encyclopedia of Religion*, vol. 2. New York: Macmillan and Free Press.

Huntington, R. and Metcalf, P., 1979. *Celebrations of Death: The Anthropology of Mortuary Ritual*. Cambridge: Cambridge University Press.

Jochelsen, W., 1908. *The Koryak*. Memoirs of the American Museum of Natural History, vol. 10, parts 1–2. The Jesup North Pacific Expedition. Leiden: E. J. Brill.

Kerttula, A. M., 2000. *Antler on the Sea: The Yup'ik and Chukchi of the Russian Far East*. Ithaca and London: Cornell University Press.

King, A.D., 2011. *Living with Koryak Traditions: Playing with Culture in Siberia*. Lincoln and London: University of Nebraska Press.

Plattet, P., 2005. *Le double jeu de la chance: Imitation et substitution dans les rituels chamaniques contemporains de deux population rurales du Nord-*

---

21 For more details on how the deceased is to be understood as a sacrifice, see Lykkegård and Willerslev (in process).

Kamchatka – les chasseurs maritimes de lesnaija et les éleveurs de rennes d'Achaïvaiam. PhD. Neuchatel: Université de Neuchatel.

Plattet, P., 2010. Landscapes in Motion: Opening Pathways in Kamchatkan Hunting and Herding Rituals. In: Peter Jordan, ed., *Landscape and Culture in Northern Euroasia*. Walnut Creek: Left Coast Press, pp. 97–116.

Schweitzer, P. P., 1999. The Chukchi and Siberian Yupik of the Chukchi Peninsula, Russia. In: R. B. Lee and R. Daly, eds, *The Cambridge Encyclopedia of Hunters and Gatherers*. Cambridge: Cambridge University Press, pp. 137–141.

Siimets, Ü., 2006. The Sun, the Moon and the Firmament in Chukchi Mythology and on the Relations of Celestial Bodies and Sacrifices. In: *Electronic Journal of Folklore* (Estonian Folklore), 32: 129–156.

Sverdrup, H., 1939. *Among the Tundra People*. San Diego: University of California

Turner, V., 1987. Betwixt and Between: The Liminal Period in Rites de Passage. In: L. C. Mahdi, S. Foster and M. Little, eds, *Betwixt & Between: Patterns of Masculine and Feminine Initiation*. Portland: Open Court Publishing Company, pp. 46–55.

Van Gennep, A., 1960. *Rite de Passage*. London: The University of Chicago Press.

Viveiros de Castro, E., 1998. Cosmological Deixis and Amerindian Perspectivism. *Journal of the Royal Anthropological Institute*, 4(3): 469–488.

Willerslev, R., 2007. *Soul Hunters*. Berkeley: University of California Press.

Willerslev, R., 2009. The optimal sacrifice: A study of voluntary death among the Siberian Chukchi. *American Ethnologist*, 36(4): 693–704.

Willerslev, R., 2013. God on trial: Human sacrifice, trickery, and faith. *HAU: Journal of Ethnographic Theory*, 3(1): 140–154.

Chapter 10

Ambiguous Mobility in the Viking Age Ship Burial from Oseberg

Jan Bill

Introduction

The idea that the soul of a newly dead person is embarking on a voyage to reach another place to dwell in the afterlife is widespread in time and space (see e.g. Assmann 2005: 209–210, 389–391, 398–402; Johnson and McGee 1998: 266–269, 272–275). Skaldic poetry, supported by iconographic evidence from Gotlandic picture stones and bracteates, suggest that in Late Iron and Viking Age too, Scandinavian ideas of such posthumous voyages existed, be it to the nether world *Hel* (only later turned into the appalling *Hell*) or to the banquet halls of the gods in their heavenly world, *Asgard* (Andrén 1993: 41; Davidson 1943: 65–83; Pesch 2002: 67, 70). These ideas existed alongside other, probably older ones, which envisaged an afterlife in the grave or inside holy mountains together with the ancestors (Davidson 1943: 87–96; Steinsland and Meulengracht Sørensen 1994: 89–91).

The archaeological record provides us with plenty of finds from graves that can be interpreted as materialisations of such beliefs, in the shape of, for instance, food, drinks and games that can be enjoyed in the afterlife, or horses and riding gear, sledges or boats that could be used for a post-mortem journey. These objects, whatever their function, are deposited by the burying community and can be understood as an investment into the burial ritual to ensure its success. As such, they are *materialities of passing*, objects that help the passing to take place. We may note, however, that passings may not exclusively consider/relate to the deceased person, but perhaps as much those who stay back, and that the deposited objects may also serve to reconcile them with their loss and the new situation that arises as a result of it. It has been pointed out that a burial may also mark the passing – such as of property, position or offices – from the deceased to the heirs, and that this is something that has to be negotiated by the burying community (Oestigaard and Goldhahn 2006: 31–32). Objects in graves may thus also be reflections of this type of passing, most markedly perhaps in founders' graves, where the burial becomes a manifestation for posterity of a new order, and the passing is a passing over from one person to another (on founders' graves, see Pearsson 1999: 17).

The aim of this chapter is to discuss one aspect of the rituals of passing, that of expectations of the dead going on a posthumous travel, that is possibly reflected in the burial of a high-ranking woman in AD 834 at Oseberg in present day Eastern Norway (Bonde and Christensen 1993; Brøgger, Shetelig and Holmboe 1917). This particular burial is ideal for this purpose, since its grave inventory is extraordinarily rich and well-preserved, and contains a whole series of transport devices. At the same time it belongs to a group of burials, for which the present author has recently argued that its main transport device, the ship, which contains almost everything else accompanying the deceased, owes its presence in the grave to its role as signifier of the royal line of the deceased (Bill 2015). It is, however, a

**Figure 10.1   The location of the Oseberg burial in the Slagen Valley,
                 Vestfold, Eastern Norway**
Source: Photo from Google Earth and Digital Globe/Image Landsat.

premise for the present text that objects in graves may well be engaged on different symbolic levels at the same time. So, the ship in the Oseberg grave may well have been placed there in the first place to promote a specific ideology, but once it was there, it also has to be dealt with as a transport device, and thus becomes entangled with ideas and representations of posthumous mobility.

The chapter will consist of three short parts. First, a brief presentation of the Oseberg find will be given, with emphasis on a reconstruction of the burial ritual. In the second part, material indicators of mobility and immobility in the find will be identified and discussed, and in the third part these indications will be deliberated in the perspective of the ship burial ritual itself possibly also having a more unique, ideological function as propagator of royal birth right.

The Oseberg Find

The Oseberg ship burial was excavated by Gabriel Gustafson in 1904, and has been dated by dendrochronology to the precise year AD 834 (Bonde and Christensen 1993). It was situated next to the farm, Oseberg, in the centre of the Slagen valley, to the north of present day Tønsberg, which is located in Vestfold on the western side of the Oslo Fjord. The burial, which was built on a subsoil of marine clays, was covered with a 40 m wide and more than 6 m high mound of stone, clay and turf, and consisted of a 21.5 m long ship with a tent-shaped, timber-built and 5.6 m long burial chamber erected immediately aft of amidships. Early on, the weight of the mound pressed the ship and the burial chamber down below the groundwater table, creating superb preservation conditions for the constructions and the mainly organic grave goods. A plundering of the burial, carried out in the second half of the tenth century, caused extensive disturbance inside the burial chamber, but very little elsewhere (Bill and Daly 2012). During the excavation, which lasted several months, scale drawings and photos were used to document the very complicated find situation created by the wealth of artefacts, the distortions caused by the weight of the mound and the disturbances due to the break-in. On the basis of this documentation it has been possible to describe the burial ritual in some detail.

The ship had originally been pulled up from the shore more than a kilometre away, brought to the site of the burial and placed in a shallow trench with its stem pointing to the south, towards the water. Corpses of horses and a cow were placed in the trench at the stem and covered with stones transported to the site from a rock outcrop 200 m away. A particularly large stone was placed in front of the stem and the ship was moored to it with a thick rope. After the construction of the burial chamber, objects related to food production (kitchen utensils, a quern, some furniture and a slaughtered cow) were placed in the stern of the ship, and necessary ship equipment, such as oars, anchor and rigging, was brought on board. Large amounts of stone were then transported to the ship and piled over the aft of the vessel, high enough to cover the gable and spill onto the lower parts of the roof of the grave chamber.

Probably in a procession consisting of no less than five vehicles – one wagon and four sledges – the body of the deceased noblewoman was next brought to the site of the grave ship (Bill forthcoming). The body was carried into the burial chamber where it was placed in a decorated bed, surrounded with personal belongings, as well as food, drink, furniture, textiles and textile tools and a number of other objects, including some that may have been removed by the grave robbers. The body of another woman was also placed in the burial chamber, and it was closed by nailing massive oak planks over its open gable. Subsequently, the fore of the vessel was filled up with the disassembled wagon and the sledges, as well

**Figure 10.2　The stem of the Oseberg ship during excavation in 1904,
　　　　　　　with its intact mooring to a large stone originating from
　　　　　　　a 200 m distant source**

Source: Photo from Museum of Cultural History, University of Oslo, reproduced with permission.

as with furniture and equipment that had not found space in the burial chamber. In addition, the bodies of 10 horses and several dogs were deposited in the foreship. Large quantities of stone, again transported to the burial site, were deposited over and among the grave goods. Finally the entire ship was covered with a large mound, constructed of turf cut from the surrounding area.

Indicators of Mobility and Immobility in the Oseberg Burial

A surprisingly large part of the Oseberg grave may, directly or indirectly, have implications for the issue of post mortem mobility.

The ship is the most obvious means of transportation that is present. It is without doubt a real ship that we are facing in the burial; dendrochronological investigations have documented that it was built about 14 years before the burial took place, and that the construction took place in western Norway, very far from its resting place in the Oseberg mound. Further, several repairs have been identified in the vessel, documenting that it had indeed been sailing. There are, however, some peculiarities to note. It is not, even by early ninth century standards, a very seaworthy vessel and, uniquely for Viking ships, most of its deck planking has been nailed to the beams, prohibiting access to most of the limited storage space on board. This, together with the lavish decorations of the stem and stern has led to suggestions of the ship being purely a ceremonial vessel; but in the light of the ship's attested journey from western to eastern Norway it is, probably, more correct to see it as a royal barge for shorter, coastal voyages, than as a purely ritualistic tool.

The dendrochronological investigation has also demonstrated that a final overhauling of the vessel was carried out shortly before or at the occasion of the burial. Certainly, the ship's gear was made complete for the ceremony: 30 new oars were made, along with a new yardarm. Also, an anchor was placed in the ship, and a mast set up, which was integrated in the construction of the burial chamber. Rigging details like a parrel and large amounts of rope and rope fittings were present, and probably also a sail, all placed in the burial chamber (Ingstad 2006: 234–235). Moreover, the rudder was in place, and even a bailer and a gangway was to be found in the ship, in addition to water containers and tents to be used for camping on the shore.

So, there is no doubt that significant efforts were put into making the vessel ship-shape for departure prior to the burial. Still, there are some noticeable shortcomings in this effort. The iron anchor, measuring only 1.06 m in length and weighing only 9.8 kg, is very small for a vessel this size, and is probably not what you would have used on a real voyage. The yardarm – definitely too long with its 12 m length – was not completed before being placed in the ship, and nor were nine of the 30 oars. In general the oars were, albeit new, poorly adapted to the ship; the blades of most of them are too wide to make proper use of the oar holes in the ship's sides. Although it obviously was important for the burying community to ensure that everything necessary for a sea voyage was present in the grave, it was completeness, rather than any practical functionality, that they aimed for. This is well in line with the fact that in order to construct the burial chamber, several of the beams as well as parts of the mast support were cut away – an act that would, in real life, render the ship close to useless. The timbers were, however, not removed from the boat, but laid down in the bottom of the burial chamber.

The thought that the ship really was supposed to set off on a posthumous journey with its passengers is further elucidated by the mooring rock at the stem and the way some of the oars had been placed in the ship. While most oars were stowed on deck, fore and aft, or on the roof of the burial chamber, four had been placed in rowing positions in oar holes: three were fixed in a short sequence on the starboard side in the fore, the fourth alone in the port side aft, too close to the burial chamber to allow for actual rowing (Schetelig 1917: 317–318). What could the hidden meaning be in this peculiar pattern? First we may notice that with four oars positioned in this manner the ship could not move forwards since the propulsive power would be concentrated in one quarter of the ship only, and the restricting power – the oar that could not be rowed, but only held in the water – in the opposite quarter. The result would be a ship that slowly turned clockwise around a point to its port side aft. If, however, we understand the positioned oars as part of the same symbolic representation as the mooring of the ship to the big stone, an interpretable pattern appears. The ship is lying ready for departure, but is still connected to the imaginary coast, that is, the rock, with a mooring. Oars have been prepared for backing it out from the shore and turning it around to set a course away from the shore, towards its destination.

Reading the arrangement of the grave in this way gives interesting indications of beliefs in another world, which were present in the society burying the Oseberg women. In the real world, the Oseberg ship is carefully positioned with the stem pointing straight south, towards the sea. If, however, the rock at its stem is to be understood as a coast, then the vessel is floating on and preparing for a crossing of an imaginary sea stretching in the opposite direction, to the north, where its destination would be. The orientation of the ship with the stem pointing south is not unique for the Oseberg grave; it can also be found in the other Norwegian ship graves. So the stem is pointing south in the ship graves from Gokstad, Tune and Storhaug, south-southwest in the ship grave from Grønhaug, and west-southwest in the ship grave from Borre (Müller-Wille 1970: 161–164, 168). The indication is that there existed a widespread idea in Norse mythology that the world where the dead were going was placed in a northerly direction. This is in concordance with the writings in *Gylfaginning* of the thirteenth century Icelandic author Snorre Sturlasson, but has been considered an idea of his own, since it cannot be attested by any of the presumed older Scaldic sources (Davidson 1943).

The sledges and *the wagon* found in the foreship are obviously also devices for (signalling) transport. All of them were equipped with superstructures, wagon- and sledge-bodies, making them suitable for personnel transport. The wagon and three of the sledges were highly decorated, while the fourth sledge was of a much

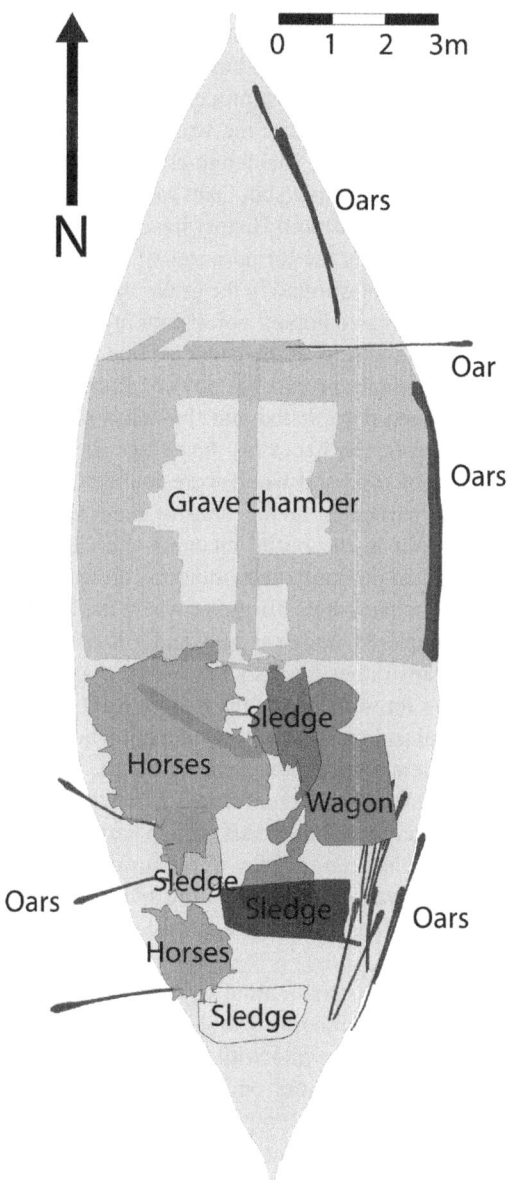

Figure 10.3   The location of selected finds in the Oseberg burial

Note: The plan is constructed on the basis of archival and published accounts and plans from the excavation. The position of the oars on the burial chamber roof is known from textual sources only.

Source: Graphics by the author based on archival materials from the Museum of Cultural History.

more mundane nature. Repairs can be found on all the fine vehicles, showing that they were not new items produced for the burial, but objects with a long history of use. Inspired by the images of wagons in processions on textiles from the Oseberg burial, it has often been suggested that the wagon was only for ceremonial use (Ingstad 1995: 144; Steinsland and Meulengracht Sørensen 1994: 85). Although the opposite has been claimed (Schovsbo, Dahl Møller and Tauber 1987: 33–34), experiments at the Museum of Cultural History have shown that there is nothing in its construction that prohibits its use for purposes of ordinary transport.

The wagon- and sledge-poles found in the grave show that each of the vehicles was designed to be pulled by two horses, corresponding to the 10 horses that were found in the fore of the grave ship. It thus appears that care was taken to provide the deceased with the necessary propulsive power for the sledges and the wagon, even if the horses had been decapitated and the heads placed in separate heaps. Strangely enough, however, the necessary harnesses for the horses seem to be missing. Simple tethers of rope and wood were found with the horses, showing that they had not been harnessed at the time of their killing. In the disturbed layers left by the break-in in the burial chamber the excavators found several metal ornaments which had probably been mounted on leather straps, but none of them are necessarily from harnesses. The layer where the break-in took place also contained an almost complete wooden saddle, and it is conceivable that the metal ornaments should perhaps rather be associated with that than with the vehicles and horses placed in the foreship. It should also be mentioned that five so-called 'rattles', devices of metal and rope of unknown function but usually found together with horses in burials, were found in the Oseberg burial. Their find contexts were, however, very special, since most of them were found with their rope parts passing through the mouths of carved animal heads, which had apparently been used in a burial procession (Bill forthcoming). They were thus not used as part of harnesses when the sledges and the wagon drove up to the site of the burial, and it may be questioned whether the sledges and the wagon were actually pulled by horses at all on this occasion?

It thus seems that there exists a qualitative difference in the perception of the ship and the land vehicles in the funeral. The ship was being equipped and prepared for the burial as if for a voyage, while with the wagon and the sledges, a central piece of equipment, the harness, was omitted. Hence the intention of mobility which is so clearly expressed in the preparation of the ship is, in the case of the wagon and the sledges, replaced by a prohibitive omission: Without harnesses there is no mobility. It seems clear that these land vehicles were not placed in the grave in order to allow the dead woman to travel over land with the same ease and comfort as the ship provided for a sea-journey. Perhaps they only joined the burial as a display of wealth? Or, perhaps more likely, they had outlived their usefulness in the funeral ritual by bringing the deceased and her personal belongings to the site of the burial, and now simply had to be disposed of.

A prohibitive exclusion similar to that for the land vehicles may also be noted in the case of the saddle. Here the harness may have been present, but since all the

10 horses in the foreship belong to the land vehicles, the riding horse is missing. Another four horses are indeed found outside the fore of the ship, but since they are not in the boat, they were obviously not intended to join it on the voyage.

The stones that weigh down the Oseberg burial are the final element to be considered as an indicator of mobility or immobility in the grave. The stones were, as mentioned, brought to the burial from a nearby rock outcrop. About 125 m^3 of stones, weighing some 180 tons, had been transported 200 m over quite swampy grounds to form the first filling over and around the fore and the aft of the ship (Brøgger 1917: 184, 187). Why?

To put stones over the feet or over other parts of the deceased is a practice which does occur in some Viking Age burials, and it is often interpreted as an act meant to restrict the mobility of the deceased (Gardela 2013). However, it seems unlikely that this should be the explanation in the case of the Oseberg ship grave, since the stone packing only covers small parts of the burial chamber – and certainly not the central, highest part, where the bed of the women was placed. They were thus not kept in place by the stone packing, although it has to be admitted that the stones definitely served to block the gables of the chamber, which is the closest one comes to an entrance to the chamber.

Another interpretation of the stone packing might be to understand it as part of the preparation for the posthumous voyage. Instead of adding the ballast first – which in a ship of this size would amount to a few tons of stone, mainly placed in the area of the grave chamber – it was added as the last thing, and to such an extent that it certainly would sink the vessel and everything on it. This might look like a way to immobilise the ship and everything on it, but in the world of the afterlife it would perhaps have another meaning. A couple of Skaldic poems of supposed tenth century date, from the MS *Codex Regius* (Wimmer and Finnur 1891), inform us that *Hel*, the Germanic realm of death, is subterranean. In *Völuspa* (stanza 35) it is said that the cock from the halls of Hel will crow down below the earth, and *Grímnismál* (stanza 31) places *Hel* below one of the roots of *Yggdrasil*, the tree of life. In the context of a voyage to an underground place, the loading of the vessel with large amounts of stone may thus be seen as a help, rather than a restriction.

The Ambiguous Mobility in the Oseberg Find

What does the Oseberg find tell us about beliefs about afterlife voyages in the community that buried the Oseberg women, and how does it illuminate their concept of time and passing? The analysis above has, I believe, clearly demonstrated that afterlife mobility was certainly an issue – in some sense the deceased was indeed thought to be able to depart from the present world, in order to arrive at another place. Also, she was apparently able to bring a lot of objects with her. This mobility was, however, conditional, and could to some extent be controlled through the burial ritual. The ship was prepared for a journey, and everything was made ready for departure, before its passengers were brought on board. A sea voyage was made possible and perhaps even attractive through the luxury amassed in the grave chamber; the ship was intended to be used. Land travelling was certainly not intended, and explicitly barred by the community through omitting key elements of the necessary gear. The dead woman was thus not given the freedom of choice in this matter, demonstrating the importance of her reaching the envisioned destination via a particular route – and perhaps also of preventing her from escaping the ship and remaining in the world of the living.

It is thus clear that the ship plays a central role in the burial ritual, as the only permitted vehicle for a seemingly – at least for the community – very important journey. This is peculiar, since it is a female burial. Indeed, female boat burials are not unusual, but they are few, and Oseberg is the only one in a ship; ships and boats tend to be much more of a male *signum*, while wagons – which were also present in the grave – belong to the female sphere (Andrén 1993: 43–46). Why this enhanced role for the ship in the Oseberg burial?

The reason may be found in the above-mentioned ideological function of the ship in the burial (Bill 2015). Seeing the Oseberg burial as being inspired by an early version of the *Scyldinge*-myth known from *Beowulf*, it becomes essential that the woman actually make her journey to the afterlife in a ship, in order to emulate the burial of her mythical, royal ancestor. In the first part of the Beowulf poem it is told how king Scyld came to the Danes as a small boy, lying on a shield on a drifting boat, and how he later, after having been a successful king for the Danes, is buried by being put on a ship with rich burial gifts and pushed out in the sea currents which takes him away (Cotton MS Vitellius A XV: 132v-133r). It seem plausible that there was not much of a choice in the case of the Oseberg woman – the role that she played in the passing of royal authority from one generation to the next also dictated her mode of transportation in death.

There are some other interesting aspects of the burial to be considered too. Several authors have pointed to the mooring of the ship to the stone as a means to ensure that it stayed in the burial mound, as a permanent home for the dead (Ingstad 1995: 147; Solli 2002: 229). If, however, we are ready to accept that the oars have been placed in the oar holes with the purpose of manoeuvring the ship, it is clear that other actions could also be taken, including letting the mooring go, and the idea of a mooring for eternity has to be discarded. The mooring, however, provides us with another important piece of information. The fact that it was still intact at the time of excavation in 1904 makes it possible for us to define very precisely the situation in which the community was taking leave of its dead member. Everything had been brought on board and all necessary rituals for the departure had been concluded, but the ship had not yet been untied and begun its journey. We cannot know, but this may have left a certain degree of sovereignty to the buried woman: She could perhaps not decide where or how to go, but could possibly decide when. The lack of indication of an instant departure makes it possible – but certainly not sure – that the dead went through a phase as 'mound dweller' before finally leaving her community. A single material aspect of the burial rite may be of importance in this context.

When the mound was erected over the ship, the mast would have been standing several metres proud of it. The ship had thus not disappeared though it was covered with the burial mound – its presence would still be highly visible, and probably so for some years after the burial. Over time rot would of course make the mast fall, at what time the ship would finally disappear – perhaps a symbolic departure. However, the Vikings were familiar with the temporality and decay of the flesh, as so clearly demonstrated in the Ibn Fadlan citation below, and had probably no difficulties in realising what was actually happening inside a burial mound. From that perspective, I find it more likely that their belief included the notion of some immaterial aspect of things and persons, a 'soul', which was what travelled between here and the otherworld. In a sense that puts a certain twist on the materiality of passing – because things, when included in a ritual of passing, become immaterial and only in that state can fulfil their purpose. The real Oseberg ship was to rot in the mound, but because it was placed there, it could bring the Oseberg woman to her posthumous dwelling place. There is a very 'down to earth' flair to this way of looking at passing, which is probably why it was acceptable to cheat a little with some of the ship's equipment. Since only an immaterial essence of the physical objects were travelling, and not the objects themselves, it was not important that they would work, in reality.

Does this mean that the decay processes in the grave were considered part of the process of passing by the burying community? This is obviously difficult to answer on the basis of the grave itself. We know from a slightly later and geographically remote source that in some Scandinavian communities this was clearly the case. When, around AD 921, the Islamic diplomat Ibn Fadlan was present at the ship cremation burial of a Rus chieftain in the area of the Volga Bulgars, he was told by a Rus that he and his like were stupid 'because you take the one who is most loved by people and honoured among you and throw him into the earth. And the earth, and worms and maggots eat him. But we, we burn him in a moment and he enters Paradise at once' (Ibn Fadlan §92, translated by Tina Sass in Christensen et al. 1995: 137). Indeed, among the Rus – who were people of Scandinavian descent who had settled in Russia – there were also communities that practiced inhumation burials, and it has been suggested that the scorn was rather directed towards them (Warmind 1995: 133). However, the same dichotomy between cremation and inhumation burial is also found in Scandinavia in the Viking Age, and it might be suggested that it does address the issue of passing most definitely. In this respect the Oseberg mound may be a useful case study.

Burial mounds are in general placed at elevated, exposed locations, but this only true to a limited degree for the Oseberg mound, and also for its neighbouring ship grave to the south, the Gokstad mound from around AD 900. Both these mounds are placed low in valleys, near streams, and in fairly damp conditions.

This has also secured their survival, because water and clay formed an airtight sealing which significantly limited the decay of organic matter inside the mounds. Could it be that this was not done by chance, but a deliberate choice by the burying communities, in order to ensure that the objects and the dead in the two mounds would continue to exist as long as possible? In Skaldic prose there are several references to afterlife in the burial mounds, and although it dates to a period later than the Viking Age it would be surprising if this literature should not have roots in real tradition. So, all three versions of *Landnámabók* relate the story about Asmundur Atlason, who is being buried with a slave in a ship. Asmundur is not pleased with the company, and complains by singing so loudly that people passing the mound hear him, and consequently the mound is opened and the thrall removed (see e.g. Sturla Þórðarson, *Sturlubók*, 27 as cited by Müller-Wille 1970: 136). By chance we have documentation that in the case of the Oseberg and Gokstad mounds, physical content was indeed expected still to exist at some point between AD 953 and AD 975, 120 years or more after the burial of the Oseberg women, when both mounds were broken into in a coordinated action; this included the excavation of a more than 20 m long, 5–6 m deep and several metres wide, open trench in each mound, the opening and plundering of both grave chambers, removal of parts of the skeletons, and destruction of vital parts of the two ships (Bill and Daly 2012). The act, which falls in a period in which king Harald Bluetooth is regaining Danish control over Eastern Norway, seem to serve to deprive the burials of their power to legitimate other rulers in the area and is as such a testimony of some sort of belief in a continued existence in the mound.

It thus appears that many concepts of passing come together in the Oseberg burial. Efforts are made to ensure that the dead woman can embark on a posthumous voyage to a remote otherworld. At the same time the burial seems constructed with an eye to preservation and was, more than a century after its completion, still expected to possess power through its preserved, and thus destructible, content. Moreover, in all likelihood the mast of the ship was left protruding out of the mound, demonstrating both the continued presence of the ship in spite of any departure for the otherworld and, through its inevitable and visible decay, the temporality of this world. As such, the materiality of the Oseberg burial makes claims in widely different directions: on eternity through the preservation; on temporality through the observable decay; on presence through the visibility; and on absence and the otherworld through the narrative of the voyage expressed so clearly in its composition. Is this chaos of contradictory messages a problem? I don't think so. In contemporary Western society the rituals and behaviour surrounding death are also layered and contradictory, composed as they are of traditions, economic rationalism, changing ethics and our wish to create memories that we can live with. I think that this is true throughout society; it should not surprise us if it was also true for the rituals of passing that unfolded on the occasion of a death, where much more was at stake for community than at any burial any of us will ever attend.

References

Andrén, A., 1993. Doors to other worlds: Scandinavian death rituals in Gotlandic perspective. *Journal of European Archaeology*, 1, 33–55.

Assmann, J., 2005. *Death and Salvation in Ancient Egypt*. Ithaca: Cornell University Press.

Bill, J., 2015. Vikingetidens monumentale skibsgrave. In: A. Pedersen and S.M Sindbæk, eds, *Et fælles hav – Skagerrak og Kattegat i vikingetiden*. Copenhagen: Nationalmuseet, pp. 152–167.

Bill, J., forthcoming. Protecting against the dead? On the possible use of apotropaic magic in the Oseberg burial. *Cambridge Archaeological Journal*, 25(1).

Bill, J. and Daly, A., 2012. The plundering of the ship graves from Oseberg and Gokstad: An example of power politics? *Antiquity*, 86(333): 808–824.

Bonde, N. and Christensen, A.E., 1993. Dendrochronological dating of the Viking Age ship burials at Oseberg, Gokstad and Tune, Norway. *Antiquity*, 67(256): 575–583.

Brøgger, W. C., 1917. Oseberghaugens historie. In: A. W. Brøgger, H. Falk and H. Schetelig, eds, *Osebergfundet*. Kristiania: Den Norske Stat.

Brøgger, A. W., Schetelig, H. and Holmboe, J., 1917. *Osebergfunnet*. Kristiania: Den Norske Stat, pp. 167–197.

Christensen, A. E., Ingstad, A. S., Crumlin-Pedersen, O. and Thye, B. M., 1995. *The Ship as Symbol in Prehistoric and Medieval Scandinavia*. Copenhagen, National Museum of Denmark, Department of Archaeology and Early History.

Cotton MS Vitellius A XV. Available at: http://www.bl.uk/manuscripts/FullDisplay. aspx?ref=cotton_ms_vitellius_a_xv.

Davidson, H. R. E., 1943. *The Road to Hell: A Study of the Conception of the Dead in Old Norse Literature*. London: Cambridge University Press.

Gardela, L., 2013. The Dangerous Dead? Rethinking Viking-Age Deviant Burials. In: L. Slupecki and R. Simek, eds, *Conversions: Looking for Ideological Change in the Early Middle Ages*. Vienna: Fassbaender, pp. 99–136.

Ingstad, A. S., 1995. The Interpretation of the Oseberg-find. In: O. Crumlin-Pedersen and B. M. Thye, eds, *The Ship as Symbol in Prehistoric and Medieval Scandinavia*. Copenhagen: Danish National Museum, pp. 139–148.

Ingstad, A. S., 2006. Brukstekstilene. In: A. E. Christensen and M. Nockert, eds, *Tekstilene*. Kulturhistorisk Museum, Universitetet i Oslo, pp. 185–276.

Johnson, C. J. and McGee, M. G., 1998. *How Different Religions View Death & Afterlife*. Philadelphia, PA: Charles Press.

Müller-Wille, M., 1970. *Bestattung im Boot. Studien zu einer nord-europäischen Grabsitte*. Neumünster: Karl Wachholtz Verlag.

Oestigaard, T. and Goldhahn, J., 2006. From the Dead to the Living: Death as Transactions and Re-negotiations. *Norwegian Archaeological Review*, 39(1): 27–48.

Pearsson, M. P., 1999. *The Archaeology of Death and Burial*. Stroud: Sutton.

Pesch, A., 2002. Frauen und Brakteaten – eine Skizze. In: W. Heizmann, R. Simek and L. Motz, eds, *Mythological Women: Studies in Memory of Lotte Motz (1922–1997)*. Wien: Fassbaender, pp. 33–80.

Schetelig, H., 1917. Skibet. In: A.W. Brøgger, H. Falk and H. Schetelig, eds, *Osebergfundet*. Kristiania: Den Norske Stat, pp. 283–366.

Schovsbo, P.O., Dahl Møller, J. and Tauber, H., 1987. *Oldtidens vogne i Norden: arkæologiske undersøgelser af mose- og jordfundne vogndele af træ fra neolitikum til ældre middelalder*. Odense: Bangsbomuseet.

Solli, B., 2002. *Seid. Myter, sjamanisme og kjønn i vikingenes tid*. Oslo: Pax forlag.

Steinsland, G. and Meulengracht Sørensen, P., 1994. *Menneske og makter i vikingenes verden*. Oslo: Universitetsforlaget/Bokklubben kunnskap og kultur.

Warmind, M. L., 1995. Ibn Fadlan in the Context of his Age. In: O. Crumlin-Pedersen and B.M. Thye, eds, *The Ship as Symbol in Prehistoric and Medieval Scandinavia*. Copenhagen: The National Museum, pp. 131–138.

Wimmer, L. F. A. and Finnur, J., 1891. *Håndskriftet Nr. 2365 4to gl. kgl. samling på det store Kgl. bibliothek i København: (Codex regius af den ældre Edda) i fototypisk og diplomatisk gengivelse*. København: S. L. Møllers bogtrykkeri.

Chapter 11

Assembling the 'Spark of Life'

Peter Bjerregaard and Rane Willerslev

Introduction

A persistent critique of the museum as an institution has concerned the museum's apparent lack of life. The argument goes that, with its focus on storing and displaying objects, the museum brings life to death by freezing the intentionality and flow of life into categories and harsh material objectivity (Ames 1992; Boon 1991; Duncan 1995). Andrea Witcomb (2003) has used Theodor Adorno's notion of the museum as a mausoleum to describe the ways in which the museum 'encloses objects, separating them from the life forces which gave them their original social and political meanings' (Witcomb 2003: 104).

However, Adorno's idea of the mausoleum was more subtle than a simple critique of the objectifying effects of the museum. In his essay on Valery and Proust (Adorno [1967] 1983), Adorno speaks of two different positions on the relation between the museum and death. On one side Valery sees the museum as an institution that destroys art by displacing works from their intended location and placing them in the midst of a cacophony of dis-connected works. In this way the museum kills the object by displacing it from the life it was intended for. On the other side, Proust was much more open to the popular taste of the museum. In Proust's experience it is exactly the way in which the museum kills any original intention of the object that makes it so interesting. In this sense, the museum is all about the afterlife of works:

> For [Proust] it is only the death of the work of art which brings it to life. When severed from the living order in which it functioned, according to him, its true spontaneity is released – its uniqueness, its "name", that which makes works of culture more than culture. (Adorno [1967] 1983: 182)

Proust, hence, suggests that it is exactly by its connection to death that the museum object provides the viewer with a perspective that transcends the everyday, lived experience. Death, in this perspective, is a potential rather than a loss.

In this chapter we want to take Proust's lead and explore the museum's apparently inert relation to death as a token of its capacity to cause effect. We argue that the most basic attraction of the museum object is that it offers us the 'spark of life' (Deleuze 2001; Dickens [1864–65] 1989); it exposes an anonymous life force that transcends the object itself – that is, it transcends the object's individualised character. Thus, the museum is not a site for preserving past identities in order to pass them on to the present and the future (as Valery would have it) but, rather, a site for passing objects into another state, which is at one and the same time a transformation of the object and of the human spectator.

This leads us, eventually, to the apparently paradoxical observation that, while staking its legitimacy in its capacity to preserve the past, the museum is, in fact, best perceived as a place where history is dissolved and new imaginaries emerge.

But before we reach thus far, we will briefly consider some of the many ways in which museums have been likened to death. We will do so with a focus on museums of cultural history.

Death and the Museum

It is no wonder that museums are often related to death. Physically, museums are filled with dead matter – bones, skulls, fossils, shrunken heads. But more than that, by preserving their objects museums are intrinsically related to the past, to people living before us, famous or mundane, named or part of the masses. As long as museums deal with their collections, they are bound to deal with the dead. In this way the museum 'promises an environment in which temporality is suspended, whether in death or in eternal life, that runs counter to our own experience of life's flux and constant change' (Giebelhausen 2006: 234).

Stability of Matter

The most basic defining character of the museum as an institution is probably the dependence on object collections. The museum stands out as a contrast to the circulation of the market. As soon as an object enters a museum collection it is kept and promised – as far as possible – eternal life (see Otto and Willerslev 2013).

A precondition for creating museum collections is therefore the need to preserve. At a material level the preservation of objects aims, ultimately, at bringing molecular transformation to a standstill (Feller 1973). Museums are places for stabilising material bodies, and particularly with the development in conservation technology in recent decades, this is not simply a matter of keeping objects out of reach of potential threats, but a question of maintaining particular climates and treating objects in particular ways in order for them not to decompose – or, more realistically, for these objects not to decompose with the speed of 'natural' organic decay.

However, while preservation allows for a certain stability of matter, it is clear that this can only come about by isolating objects from the ordinary spheres of social life. The technologies with which museum objects are treated, kept in closed-off collections, handled only by selected experts and kept in carefully monitored climates, stresses how these objects have entered another order.

This obligation to conserve tends to turn museum objects into 'undead' (Žižek 2006: 121) things, things that somehow resist dying even if they should (cf. Willerslev, Refslund and Meinert 2013). While kept out of the flow of life and secluded from any functional relation to the living, they are capable of attaining new roles again and again as they are taken out of the storages and put on display. Thus, they become strangely animated objects that keep reappearing in the world of the living, even if their functional and symbolic relevance has terminated. As Susan Stewart observes:

> Although the given qualities of animated objects allow them to endure beyond
> flux and history, this very transcendence and permanence also links them to the
> world of the dead, to the end of organic growth and the onset of inaccessibility
> to the living. (Stewart 1994: 204)

Thus, there is something *untimely* (Grosz 2004: 113–134) about the museum object which makes its presence to us challenging.

The Melancholic Museum

The preservation of objects apparently turns the museum into an institution for passing on lost worlds. In the museum we can experience the past that is somehow ingrained, but unattainable in our present, and we can preserve life worlds that once existed but have now disappeared (as was the rationale for what has been called 'salvaging collecting'; see Cole 1995; Petch 1998; van der Beek and Vellinga 2005). Likewise, individuals can attain immortal status by making museum collections or donating objects to the museum.

In this way the museum conjures up a negation to the constant flux of life by preserving entities of the past, which we reject giving up on. It clutches onto the dead and allows the dead to demand services from the living rather than letting them go to engage in the ongoing flow of life. This reluctance to let go of the dead links the museum to processes of mourning and the state of melancholia (Boon 1991; Freud [1917] 1957; Willerslev 2013). The museum creates a space where the past hinges upon the present, and where the presence of the past may seem almost unbearable (Boon 1991; Rifbjerg 1998).

Therefore, it is no surprise that it has been suggested that museums should cut this reliance on the past and deal, instead, with current political and social orders and disorders; the current situation of source communities; engagements with local communities and audiences for developing new exhibitions and so on (Ames 1992; Sandahl n.d.).

While these suggestions may all be valuable they also pose a central problem; namely, what is the museum if it is *not* about the past and the dead. If, as we suggested, collections are indeed the defining aspect of a museum, and dealing with collections is, basically, a matter of dealing with the dead, the question we need to ask is not how to put life into the museum but, rather, whether the relation to the dead may be considered not simply pathological and melancholic, but also productive?

The Museum and Non-Empirical Time

In order to explore this question, we would like to go back a bit in museological history, and address two points in the history of the museum that are pertinent to our discussion. The first point concerns the early modern anthropological museum of the late nineteenth century. The development of the early modern anthropological/ archaeological museum was closely linked to prevalent theoretical currents of cultural evolution and diffusionism.

While a central critique of cultural evolution has addressed its neglect of the specificities of cultural context, we may argue that this view from afar was exactly what generated the productive aspects of the theory. With its strong focus on object collections, early modern museum practice created what we may consider a truly museological perspective on the world. By comparing the material evidence assembled in the museum a perspective was created that could never be arrived at through ethnographic inquiry in a concrete locality. In the museum's version of evolutionism and diffusionism what the museum anthropologist looked for were patterns that would link objects in ways that transgressed historical and geographical boundaries (Petch 1998: 78–80). How could pottery, tools and weapons from different time periods and different parts of the world be linked? The aim of this endeavour was not to document or debate the conditions relevant to the present, but rather to seriously deal with the kind of insights that could be extrapolated from the remnants of the past. Thus, by organising museum objects it was possible to trace perspectives to human life that could never be obtained through an ordinary 'historical' perspective.

The second point we would like to dwell upon emerges from André Malraux's work on *Le Musée Imaginaire* (*Museum without Walls*) from 1947. In this original work Malraux argues that the development of photographic reproduction allows for a whole new understanding of art. Whereas before the development of photography our access to art works was based on our experience of these works *in situ*, photographic reproduction allows us to look for relations in art beyond collections, geographies and time.

Through richly illustrated books and catalogues, Malraux argues, we will be able to compare works that have never been placed within the same realm before. And more than that, through the mechanical eye of the camera, we will be able, not simply to compare works, but also to, literally, zoom in on details such as patterns, and compare beyond scales (see Suhr and Willerslev 2012; Willerslev and Suhr 2013). To quote Malraux at some length:

> Thus the angle from which a work of sculpture is photographed, the focusing and, above all, skilfully adjusted lighting may strongly accentuate something the

sculptor merely hinted at. Then, again, photography imparts a family likeness to objects that have actually but slight affinity. With the result that such different objects as a miniature, a piece of tapestry, a statue and a medieval stained-glass window, when reproduced on the same page, may seem members of the same family. They have lost their colors, texture and relative dimensions (the statue has also lost some of its volume); each, in short, has practically lost what was specific to it – but their common style is by so much the gainer. (Malraux 1954: 21)

In this way, it is really the collection and the museum that allow us to locate a category like 'art', by disconnecting the object from any functional or symbolic order it was intended for (ibid.: 14–15). And by 'falsifying' (ibid.: 24) or 'mutilating' (ibid.: 26) objects through photographic rescaling and fragmentation, the museum without walls allow us to establish a perspective that does not only transgress historical or regional 'styles', but also suggests ideas that were not even consciously part of the intentions of the maker of the work (see also Gell 1996 and 1998: 51–65). In other words, the museum makes it possible to extract a creative impetus from these works that does not belong to any creative subject in itself.

The Afterlife of the Object

Without linking Malraux and cultural evolution in any ideological sense, we may say that both of these approaches to the museum look for streams of time and agency that operate beyond the temporality of 'history' and beyond the range of human intentionality. These two perspectives on the museum leads us back to the point which Proust – in Adorno's reading – made clear; that the object in the museum becomes animated exactly by severing the tie to its own origin. In this sense Proust was right in pointing to the relation to death, not metaphorically, but as another order made available by the museum, as the main attraction of the museum object.

But, one may ask, what is the life that emerges that is caused by death? Proust talked about the *afterlife* of the object (Adorno [1967] 1983: 180–181). This afterlife must be considered as one that does not rely on the relevance and identity of the objects in a concrete, historical, actualised setting. Disconnecting the ties to this actualised existence, the museum opens the way for discovering potentials in the object that were not imagined in its original life. If preservation is the technology that allows us to keep the object beyond its normal decay, the afterlives of the object are thus connected to ways of re-assembling these objects in research and display – the ways in which the object may become expressive of aspects that were never part of its original life.

The strange task of the museum, to preserve objects with no really good, contemporarily relevant reason, turns the museum object into something transcendental – but not transcendental *of* a particular event or intention, simply transcendental in the sense that by being severed from the sphere of social relevance it thrusts itself forward as a presence through time. Logically, this implies not *the afterlife* but potentially an endless number of afterlives, as the work may be presented over and over again in different ways and together with different objects. This is not unlike what Rane Willerslev (2013) has described in relation to Arctic rebirth beliefs, according to which the living are considered to be returned deceased ancestors who have already passed through several lifetimes. As he writes,

> People are, so to say, always already in the past. The past then, is not something that comes after the present has ceased to be; rather, the past is always impregnated in the present, even as the present becomes the past. The difficult thing, to understand, however ... is that this repetitious time does not consist in the return of the same, but of the different, a kind of "return of difference". (Willerslev 2013)

So too with the museum objects, the afterlives of which, in a strange kind of way, are all about how the object may be related to life, severed from the actualised existence it once enjoyed outside the secluded space of the museum.

Based in these observations, we will claim that the attraction of the museum object is that it offers us the 'spark of life' (Deleuze 2001; Dickens [1864–65] 1989: 443); it exposes an anonymous life force that transcends the object itself – a kind of anonymous 'soul' of the object that transcends its actualisation, its meaningful location in any specific functional or symbolic order. At the same time it also transcends any particular current political relevance. That is, what is important is not how the museum object may represent this or that grouping but its presence here as an entity from outside any actualised time.

The Spark of Life

Gilles Deleuze's very last essay 'Immanence: A Life ...' (Deleuze 2001) has become one of the most debated pieces of his work (Agamben 2003; Hallward 2006: 24–26). As the title suggests, this short and highly condensed essay develops the idea of immanence as a transcendental life force. Immanence, Deleuze suggests, is a non-individualised life force, 'it is not in something, *to* something; it does not depend on an object or subject' (Deleuze 2001: 26, emphasis in original). This counter-intuitive idea of life as something that does not belong to some*one* or some*thing* is exemplified with reference to a passage in Charles Dickens's novel, *Our Mutual Friend* (Dickens [1864–65] 1989).

In the novel, the despised character Riderhood almost drowns in the Thames. No one has had any concern for him, but as he struggles for his life people suddenly get all concerned with keeping him alive.

> No one has the least regard for the man: with them all, he has been an object of avoidance, suspicion and aversion; but the spark of life within him is curiously

separable from himself now, and they have a deep interest in it, probably because it IS life, and they are living and must die ... . Neither Riderhood in this world, nor Riderhood in the other, could draw tears from them; but a striving human soul between the two can do it easily. (Dickens [1864–65] 1989, cited in Agamben 2003: 159)

So, while Riderhood as a person would not claim any pity or concern from the bystanders, the state between life and death evokes a response. Not for Riderhood, but for the spark of life, which in this particular situation becomes separable from Riderhood as an individuated person. Therefore, what these people are obsessed with is not Riderhood himself but *life as such*, of which Riderhood is simply the carrier, as he struggles for his life. And, as Riderhood slowly recovers as the person known to the people around him, the bystanders lose interest again.

To Deleuze, this struggle in between life and death reveals the non-actualised being, which he terms not 'life' but 'a life ...' (see Agamben 2003, for a semiotic analysis of the title of this essay):

Between his life and his death, there is a moment that is only that of *a* life playing with death. The life of the individual gives way to an impersonal and yet singular life that releases a pure event freed from the accidents of internal and external life, that is, from the subjectivity and objectivity of what happens ... (Deleuze 2001: 28, emphasis in original)

The spark of life, in other words, is neither individuated, as Riderhood's life, nor universal, as God given life. It is a singularised manifestation of the constant transformation of the world (Hallward 2006: 8, 16–17, 27–36). Through Riderhood's struggle for life it becomes possible to see this body as a mere actualisation, a momentary container, of the spark of life. In this sense, the bystanders are not watching Riderhood passing away. Rather, they witness the life force passing through him, which becomes perceptible as he loses subjectivity. This experience is pure immanence, pure *life*, a state that is lost as soon as subjectivity emerges again.

Assembling

In the following we will argue that the museum object is exactly a carrier of life's spark – that is, of life as pure immanence, beyond history and the actual creator. In order to reach such a point, however, we need to destroy the object's identity; that is, we have to go beyond context.

One may speculate whether a single object has the capacity to elicit this spark of life as a singular entity. A classic example could perhaps be the most ancient artworks created by human hands, namely the so-called Venus figurines, like the famous Venus from Willendorf, dated 28–25,000 BC. This figurine, like her other numerous counterparts found throughout Paleolithic Europe and Asia, is believed by some archaeologists to be associated with fertility and reproduction; a kind of 'Earth Mother Goddess' (Cunningham, Reich and Fichner-Rathus 2013: 6). If so, the figurine does not signify an individual or personal deity but a grotesquely overloaded female persona: her face is anonymous and cannot be seen behind the dreadlocks that cover her face, and her abnormally skinny arms are folded, like tiny branches, over an equally abnormally voluptuous chest. The female figurine bursts with life to the extent of being on the brink of collapsing under her own bountiful corpus. In fact, she has no feet and cannot stand on her own. There is a real sense that she holds a life that she cannot really contain and which may be exposed only through her body's destruction. Perhaps it comes as no surprise, therefore, that most of the Venus figures at the Palaeolithic sites were shattered and that too, to such a degree that they could not be reassembled. This points to the idea that these figures may in fact have been designed for destruction, and not, in our view, to support a historical shift of 'vagina to phallus' cult (Campbell 1991: 235), but as a celebration of the excess of life *as such*, the indestructible life force

Figure 11.1   Venus from Willendorf
Source: © Jorge Royan, http://www.royan.com.ar / CC-BY-SA-3.0.

that persists beyond the biological cycle of life and death; that is, the insistence of the spark of life to supersede anything actually living.

However, we will argue the spark of life is not something that belongs to particular exquisite works only. Quite the contrary, all objects possess the spark of life. But in order to extract this spark, we need to present the object in ways that defy the spectator's wish to define it by particular functional or symbolic orders. Therefore, the extraction of the spark of life relies on assembling objects in particular ways, ways that 'kill off' the context, the factual information about the objects that museum labels often refer to (Bjerregaard 2015).

In the following we will offer two exhibition cases that, we suggest, play on the spark of life exactly through particular kinds of assemblages. We will do so through what we may term two archetypes of exhibitions of cultural history that play on the two museological strategies presented above; the evolutionary *series*, and the assemblage of apparently disconnected objects on the same experiential plane, suggested by Malraux.

Pitt Rivers Museum

The first exhibition we would like to dwell on is the court at the Pitt Rivers Museum. Pitt Rivers Museum stands out as one of the most famous ethnographic museums in the world. This fame does not derive from the museum holding particularly unique objects (which it does), as for instance the Mochtezuma headgear of the Weltmuseum in Vienna or the Benin objects of British Museum. At the Pitt Rivers Museum it is the display in itself – which has only been slightly modified since the opening to the public in 1896 – which stands out as the treasured object.

The museum is based on a collection of approximately 16,000 objects donated by General Augustus Henry Lane Fox Pitt Rivers to the University of Oxford (Petch 1998: 82). This collection consisted of a variety of what would be termed archaeological and ethnographic objects. Starting from his personal interest in the evolution of fire arms, Pitt Rivers developed an acquisition strategy based on the ideas of cultural evolution. Thus, collections should be based on typologies under which 'a *sequence of ideas*' (Balfour, cited in Petch 1998: 78, emphasis in original) could be traced. Through organising objects in such sequences, the museum could be turned into a laboratory for exploring the evolution of ideas through material evidence, and the same sequences would work as an educational tool for the public.

However, as one enters the museum, these kinds of orders are not at all apparent. On the contrary, the impression is one of an overwhelming and unordered material attack.

Entering the museum the guest is confronted with an open space with a number of show cases distributed evenly in the space. The show cases are basically placed in one, big open hall, but placed in such a way that they cover each other. Hence, the museum guest has no narrative overview of whether the cases are related in some linear order, and no clear signs of divisions into object categories or regions

Figure 11.2   The court at the Pitt Rivers Museum
Source: Photo © Pitt Rivers Museum, University of Oxford.

are given either. So, visitors are challenged to explore this 'terra incognita' (Dudley 2014: 299) through their own intuition.

As you progress and come close to the show cases you will recognise some kind of order for each show case. One show case will show musical instruments from all over the world, another show case will even go into such detail as to only show musical instruments using membranes, and a third will show equipment for tobacco consumption. And so, every showcase turns out to host one typology of objects, assembling samples from all over the world and from different times.

Contemplating each show case, you will notice that the bases of most of the show cases are filled with drawers. As you open these drawers you will find, under a glass cover, even more objects, some ordered, some less ordered, some in plastic bags, some in small plastic containers. These objects are clearly not organised for display. In this sense, they 'give the strong impression of giving glimpses into the vast, hidden world of what the museum has in storage' (ibid.: 298) – without this material being organised into any particular narrative. All objects in the drawers have a sort of typological relation to the objects on display in the showcase above, but it is up to the visitor to imagine these connections.

The visitor is only given very sparse and basically non-interpreted information on the objects. In a few places you will find a short introductory text on, for instance, smoking, and most of the objects are equipped with brief (apparently original), handwritten labels of this kind: 'Bullock's heart pierced with large nails & thorns, found in chimney, SHUTES HILL FARM, CHIPSTABLE, SOMERSET 1892; placed there to cause harm to someone by "witchcraft". E.B. Tylor coll. Dd. Lady Tylor, 1917'.

What is interesting about the Pitt Rivers Museum is the fact that the museum has maintained its attraction, despite the fact that it has only been slightly modified (in the court area) for more than 100 years. While this attraction has been analysed in terms of the exhibition's capacity to spark surprise and the way in which proprioception is integral to the experience of the museum (Dudley 2014), we would like to focus on the role of objects.

As mentioned, in the Pitt Rivers Museum objects are never placed within a narrative frame, nor within a contextual semiotic. Still, the organisation of objects is not completely random either. While the show cases are indeed ordered typologically, these orders are only vaguely suggested and sometimes almost impossible to recognise.

Thus, it seems as if the display at the Pitt Rivers Museum turns these objects back into a state of potentiality. Rather than placing the object within a defined history, in which each object occupies its own specific and meaningful place, the apparent randomness opens the collection up for potentials that are conventionally lost in the regular narratively or functionally ordered museum display. Indeed, one might think of this as the objects returning to a kind of Lacanian 'imaginary', where all objects are still full of potential, with no designated space in the symbolic order (cf. Pedersen and Willerslev 2012). They float around outside functional relevance or meaningful order.

So, while seemingly dead and forgotten in the show cases no one has touched for a century or more, these objects may trigger associations in audiences that have never been imagined by the museum staff, by Pitt Rivers or, indeed, by the original producers and users of the objects. From their secluded life in the vitrines they almost beg the visitor to make something out of them.

Figure 11.3 Showcase assembling objects related to 'Magic and Trial by Ordeal', Pitt Rivers Museum

Source: Photo © Pitt Rivers Museum, University of Oxford.

In this sense, we argue, the display assembles the spark of life. It extracts a life force from these objects that is not reducible to any singular object's historical origin, its original use, or its symbolic meaning. Returning to Adorno's initial observation on Proust it seems as if it is exactly the seclusion from any kind of meaningful context that allows the objects to attain this kind of attraction. One may imagine the sort of coincidences and practical problems that eventually made the displays at the museum in Oxford a disappointment to the General, who found that the displays did not represent his views (Petch 1998: 82). However, the result is a display that seems to resist being framed within regional or historical contexts, and thereby succeeds in evoking a sense of creational power that is not related to some historical point, but to a structure underlying history.

Hence, the apparent random assembling of objects as we see, for instance, in Figure 11.3 stresses how the spark of life does not belong only to particularly exquisite works as some critics would have it (see Crimp 1980 or Danto 1988). The spark of life becomes present when the objects of the world lose identity, and become carriers of a life force that lies underneath any kind of creation, what Deleuze might term 'creating' in itself; the process through which the world continuously comes about (Hallward 2006: 8, 16–17, 27–30).

The Singular in the Series

The second exhibition we will look into is actually more a *type* of exhibition than a specific exhibition. If there ever was an epitome of the archaeological exhibition it must be the display of series of stone tools. Developed as both an archaeological research method as well as a display technique, the construction of *series* crossed the natural sciences, numismatics and archaeology in the mid-1800s as a way of connecting what might, at a first glance, seem unconnected and contingent empirical findings (Schlanger 2010).

The series worked, thus, to trace currents of development that would not be evident in a synchronic perspective, but only through such a deep kind of diachrony.

Figure 11.4 shows the Stone Age display at the Historical Museum in Oslo as it was to see when the museum opened in 1904. To the untrained eye this may simply look like repetitions of the same. Basically, what this display presents us with is row upon row of deadly weapons: arrow heads of stone, stone axes, guns or even the technological evolution of deadly weaponry. One may imagine how the table-vitrines placed in the middle of the space may have consisted of the same kind of organisation of stone arrow heads. Indeed, one might imagine how this kind of display actually realises what Pitt Rivers had imagined for the collections he donated to University of Oxford, ordering types of objects within sequences of development.

If the series as a methodological tool is intimately linked to evolutionary thinking, its effect in display cannot simply be related to this theoretical background. Indeed, notable recent displays, such as the entomological displays at the Naturhistorisches Museum in Vienna or the 'Wall of Guns' at the National

Figure 11.4   View of the Stone Age display at the Historical Museum, Oslo, 1904

Source: © Kulturhistorisk Museum, Universitetet i Oslo, Cf425.

Museum of the American Indian in Washington DC both play on the series as an effect. So why, one may ask, does this conventional display technique affect us?

We suggest that the series of stone axes exposes an uncanny *excess* of life; an indestructible insistence of pure life, so to speak, which undercuts any cultural order of life. They are akin to the monstrous creature in Ridley Scott's film, *Alien*, which, as Slavoj Žižek (quoting Stephen Mulhall) writes, 'is … a nightmare embodiment of the natural realm understood as utterly subordinate to, utterly exhausted by, the twinned Darwinian drives to survive and reproduce' (Žižek 2006: 118).

While finding its order in the logic of the series, this kind of display evokes a layer of life which goes against that order. It points to a kind of *in*-human part of existence, the point where we lose humanity and are turned into the carriers of *life as such*, an 'impersonal willing' (Žižek 2004). In this sense, this arrangement of weapons turns our attention towards what Freud, according to Žižek, pointed to in his idea of the 'death drive' (Žižek 2006: 66). In Žižek's reading of Freud, the death instinct is, paradoxically, a drive towards the very opposite of death, understood as stasis, namely a drive towards the intensity of *life* or rather what Deleuze calls the 'spark of life', which works in the service of death as well as life (much like the Venus von Willendorf does).[1] In this sense, the series as a display technique exposes instead a life force that becomes present through the elimination of the individual object into the series.

What is interesting for both these cases is the fact that what we may read from them is probably in contradiction to how they were intended to be understood. Both the typology of the Pitt Rivers Museum and the construction of series in the archaeological display were intended as show cases for the capacity of science to order the world. However, in such kinds of displays, which make use of such large quantities of objects materials (true to the collections upon which they are based), it seems impossible to maintain the idea of ordering, and the result is a display that somehow is turned against itself.

Conclusion: Exhibitions and the Death of the Object

We have seen how the museum allows us to experience 'the spark of life' – a non-subjective life force that may be conceived as 'pure life', *life* as a creative force not attached to a particular body. Furthermore we have suggested that this spark of life becomes present to the senses when objects are assembled in ways that kill off our capacity to contextually identify the object – as in the case of the typological arrangement of objects at the Pitt Rivers museum or in the arrangement of stone axes in series. As such, life's spark is paradoxically related to the death of the object as an entity connected to a specific history.

So, in conclusion, we will argue that having objects on the verge of extinction, drags out a spark of life that allow us to see them in new constellations, providing us with new glimpses of the past that have been erased, forgotten, by the production of history (Andersson 2014; Benjamin [1950] 1992). It is this return to a state of potentiality that allows us to stage the museum not as a site for remembering the past, but one of imagining potential futures. While preservation allows us to pass objects through time, letting them last beyond their natural decay, the exhibition opens up another life force which does not belong to the object, but of which the object is the carrier. In this way the museums intimate relation to death is one that, paradoxically, opens up the most essential of life forces, exactly because it does not belong to the world of the living.

---

1   See Willerslev's 'Rebirth and the Death drive: Rethinking Freud's 'Mourning and Melancholia' through a Siberian Time Perspective' (2013) for a detailed discussion of the link between Freud's concept of the 'death drive' and Deleuze's theory of 'infinite becoming'.

References

Adorno, T.W. [1967] 1983. Valery Proust Museum. In: *Prisms*. Cambridge, MA: The MIT Press, pp. 173–186.

Agamben, G., 2003. Absolute Immanence. In: J. Khalfa, ed., *Introduction to the Philosophy of Gilles Deleuze*. London and New York: Continuum, pp. 151–169.

Ames, M., 1992. Introduction: The Critical Theory and Practice of Museums. In: *Cannibal Tours and Glass Boxes*. Vancouver: UBC Press, pp. 3–14.

Andersson, D.T., 2014. Salvaging images. *The Scandinavian Psychoanalytic Review*, 37(1): 61–68.

Benjamin, W. [1950] 1992. Theses on the Philosophy of History. In: *Illuminations*. London: Fontana Press, pp 245–255.

Bjerregaard, P., 2015. Dissolving objects: Museums, atmosphere and the creation of presence. *Emotion, Space and Society* 15: 74–81.

Boon, J., 1991. Why Museums Make Me Sad. In: I. Karp and S. Lavine, eds, *Exhibiting Cultures: The Poetics and Politics of Museum Display*. Washington and London: The Smithsonian Institution Press, pp. 255–278.

Campbell, J., 1991. *Primitive Mythology (The Masks of God)*. London: Penguin Books.

Cole, D., 1995. *Captured Heritage: The Scramble for Northwest Coast Artefacts*. Norman: University of Oklahoma Press.

Cunningham, L., Reich, J. and Fichner-Rathus, L., 2013. *Culture and Values: A Survey of the Humanities*. Boston: Wadsworth Publishing Company.

Crimp, D., 1980. On the Museum's Ruins. *October* 13 (Summer): 41–57.

Danto, A., 1988. Artifact and Art. In: Susan Vogel, ed., *ART/Artifact: African Art in Anthropological Collections*. Exhibition catalogue. New York: Center for African Art.

Deleuze, G., 2001. *Pure Immanence: Essays on A Life*. New York: Zone Books.

Dickens, C. [1864–65] 1989. *Our Mutual Friend*. Oxford: Oxford University Press.

Dudley. S., 2014. What's in the Drawer? Surprise and Proprioceptivity in the Pitt Rivers Museum. *The Senses and Society*, 9(3): 296–309.

Duncan, C., 1995. *Civilizing Rituals: Inside Public Art Museums*. London: Routledge.

Feller, R. L., 1973. Thermochemically Activated Oxidation: Mother Nature's Book Burning. *Pennsylvania Library Association Bulletins*, 28: 232–42.

Freud, S. [1917] 1957. Mourning and Melancholia. In: *The Standard Edition of the Complete Psychological Works of Sigmund Freud, Volume XIV*. London: The Hogarth Press and the Institute of Psychoanalysis, pp. 243–258.

Gell. A., 1996. Vogel's Net: Traps as Artworks and Artworks as Traps. *Journal of Material Culture*, 1, 15–38.

Gell, A., 1998. *Art and Agency: An Anthropological Theory*. Oxford: Oxford University Press.

Giebelhausen, M., 2006. In the museum's ruins: Staging the passage of time. In: S. Macleod, L. Hourston Hanks and J. Hale, eds, *Museum Making: Narratives, Architectures, Exhibitions*. London and New York: Routledge, pp. 234–246.

Grosz, E., 2004. *The Nick of Time: Politics, Evolution and the Untimely*. Durham and London: Duke University Press.

Hallward, P., 2006. *Deleuze and the Philosophy of Creation*. London and New York: Verso.

Malraux, A., 1954. Museum without Walls. Part I of *The Voices of Silence*. London: Martin Secker and Warburg Ltd.

Otto, T. and Willeslev, R., 2013. Introduction. Value *as* theory. Comparison, cultural critique and guerilla ethnographic theory. *Hau, Journal of Ethnographic Theory*, 3(1): 1–20.

Petch, A., 1998. 'Man as he was and Man as he is': General Pitt Rivers' collections. *Journal of the History of Collections*, 10(1): 75–85.

Pedersen, M.A. and Willerslev, R., 2012. The Soul of the Soul is the Body: Rethinking the Concept of Soul through North Asian Ethnography. *Common Knowledge*, Themed issue: Fuzzy Studies, Part 3, 18(3): 464–686.

Rifbjerg, Klaus. 1998. Er det til at holde ud at gå på museum? *Dansk Tidsskrift for Museumsformidling* 18.

Sandahl, Jette, n.d. Waiting for the public to change? [online]. Available at: http://www.kulturstyrelsen.dk/fileadmin/user_upload/dokumenter/KS/institutioner/museer/Indsatsomraader/Brugerundersoegelse/Artikler/Jette_Sandahl_Waiting_for_the_public_to_change.pdf.

Schlanger, N., 2010. Series in progress: Antiquities of Nature, Numismatics and Stone Implements in the emergence of prehistoric archaeology. *History of Science*, 48(161): 343–369.

Stewart, S., 1994. Death and Life, in that Order, in the Works of Charles Willson Peale. In: J. Elsner and R. Cardinal, eds, *The Cultures of Collecting*. London: Reaktion Books, pp. 204–223.

Suhr, C. and Willerslev, R., 2012. Can Film Show the Invisible? The Work of Montage in Ethnographic Filmmaking. *Current Anthropology*, 53(3): 282–301.

Van der Beek, Z. and Vellinga, M., 2005. Man the collector: Salvaging Andamanese and Nicobarese culture through objects. *Journal of the History of Collections*, 17(2): 135–153.

Willerslev, R., 2013. Rebirth and the Death Drive: Rethinking Freud's 'Mourning and Melancholia' Through a Siberian Time Perspective. In: D. Refslund and R. Willerslev, eds, *Taming Time, Timing Death: Social Technologies and Ritual*. Studies in death, materiality and time, vol. 1. Farnham: Ashgate, pp. 79–98.

Willerslev, R., Refslund, D. and Meinert, L., 2013. Introduction: Taming Time, Timing Death. In: D. Refslund and R. Willlerslev, R., eds, *Taming Time, Timing Death: Social Technologies and Ritual*. Studies in death, materiality and time, vol. 1. Farnham: Ashgate, pp. 1–16.

Willerslev, R., Suhr, C., 2013. Introduction. Montage as an Amplifier of Invisibility. In: C. Suhr and R. Willerslev, eds, *Transcultural Montage*. New York and London: Berghahn Books, pp. 1–15.

Witcomb, A., 2003. *Re-Imagining the Museum: Beyond the Mausoleum*. London and New York: Routledge.

Žižek, S., 2004. From desire to drive: Why Lacan is not Lacaniano [online]. Available at: http://zizek.livejournal.com/2266.html.

Žižek, S., 2006. *The Parallax View*. Cambridge, MA and London: The MIT Press.

Chapter 12

Anterior Origins: Merleau-Ponty and the Archaeology of the Body

Dylan Trigg

> *His close escape had left him feeling curiously calm and emotionless, and he looked back on his possible death with fatalistic detachment, identifying it with the total ebb and flow of life in the Amazon forests, with its myriad unremembered deaths, and with the endless vistas of dead trees leaning across the jungle paths radiating from the campong.*

J. G. Ballard, 'A Question of Re-entry'

Introduction

We tend to think of our bodies as not only existing in the here and now, but also being irreducibly alive. How are we alive? One way is to think of ourselves as belonging to the living present. All around us, time converges on our bodies, and through our experience of the world, we regard the body as both a spatial and temporal centre. We are the centre of things, full of the plenitude of time. At the other end of the living spectrum, we know that our bodies will die, and that the materiality of our existence will therefore cease to be. If we know this in advance, we nevertheless are only able to have a relationship with death from the perspective of the living present. However much we look at death, therefore, it still comes from a future that is legitimised in the present, as an event in the unmapped future.

Think here of how this treatment of death impacts our understanding of materiality itself. Our relationship to the built environment, for example, is mediated by our relationship to time, and specifically to combating the incursion of decay and ruination (cf. Trigg 2006). But where does the past fit into this relationship between death and the body? Is the past simply that which is left behind once the death of the body occurs? Or is it perhaps that the past is already implicated in both the structure and experience of death? And for that matter, what is the relation between the living and the dead? Is it, for example, that the dead belong to a time without presence, or can we not think of death as a having a continuation in the present – be it as a latent memory of a spectre?

In this chapter, I would like to suggest an alternative reading of materiality and death. My reading is informed by phenomenology, but moves away from a traditional idea of phenomenology. The conventional idea of phenomenology is that it is a methodology concerned with how we experience things. Thus, to speak of phenomenology as having a particular content is misguided. Phenomenology is a methodology that aims to describe phenomena, be it a haunted tree nestled in a forest or a table with three legs. In each case, phenomenology is the branch of philosophy that aims to restore the world to a state of plenitude. How does the method do this? It asks that we bracket what we presume about the world and return to things with a certain naïveté. In this movement of freeing ourselves of prejudice, we put aside our theoretical baggage and seek to initiate a radical type of inquiry no longer tied with a tradition characterised by historic investigations.

But this rejuvenation of the phenomenal world is not limited to things themselves, but is instead aimed at returning to the life of the human subject. Phenomenology, in its focus on the experience of things, folds back upon the phenomenological subject him- or herself, restoring in them a deeper connection to the surrounding world and a richer sense of what it means to be in the world. This idea of phenomenology, especially as it is articulated in the early thinking of Merleau-Ponty, hinges on the notion that we are at all times involved in a bodily relationship with the world. The implication of this is that in order to understand our place in the world, we need to understand the role of the body as mediating that relation.

Central to understanding our place in the world is considering the fact of our own death. Here, too, phenomenology has a great strength in shedding light on the role death plays, not simply as an event that is located in the future, but as something that structures our experience in the present. This line of thought is especially clear in Heidegger, where death becomes an opportunity for the subject to actualise their authentic existence. This veneration of death provides us with a rich understanding not only of mortality, but also of the role of anxiety in our lives (cf. Trigg 2016).

Yet despite phenomenology's attention to death, what has been overlooked is the role of the past. This may sound odd, given that we tend to think of death in futural terms, as that which impends upon us. Our lives, as we know, are finite, and framed by the ultimate horizon of our own passing. But if we are to frame our bodily existence within the limit of an ultimate horizon, then we also need to attend to the origin of this horizon and not just its endpoint. This relation between death and the past is the topic of the current chapter. More specifically, our question concerns what role an origin anterior to experience plays in shaping our relation to death. This is a complex thought and will require that we step outside the margins of a phenomenology limited to the descriptive content of one's experience. In this movement, we shall retain the centrality of the body, thus also retaining a link with classical phenomenology. However, the body in question is no longer bound by conscious experience, but instead must be approached in terms of the structures that constitute experience in the first place. To approach this thought, three stages are mapped out.

First, I consider the phenomenology of the body in its temporal structure. Here, the critical question is: when is the body located? In the present, in the past, in the future, or in between each of these poles? In fact, I suggest that the body occupies two timescales concurrently: one in the immediacy of the present, the other anchored in the irretrievable depth of the past.

The second thought, then, is, how are these timescales connected? In response, I explore the notion of the body as a 'trace'. And it is this usage of 'trace' that allows us to shift the focus from the body as a centre of experience to the body as a site of archaeological inquiry – a burial ground, as it were.

Finally, we turn to death itself. Just as death as a future event lies outside of the realm of experience, so the temporal origin of the body assumes a parallel relation. Only now, it is experienced not as the annihilation of subjectivity, but as that which has *already occurred* and which the subject is now living through. To begin, then, let us return to the immediacy of experience and consider the body as it finds itself in the present.

Time of the Body

What does it mean to frame the past as belonging to the realm of death? In the first instance, it means recognising that our subjectivity is constituted by a structure that is fundamentally anterior to experience. Indeed, it is precisely this formula that we can use to describe death in a traditional sense: that is, an event that constitutes our sense of self, but at the same time remains anterior to the self. After all, as Epicurus recognised, where we are, death is not. This is not simply a claim to attaining a 'peace of mind' with respect to the fact of death; it is also a structural relation we have with death. If it is a shadow, then it is one that leads us only indirectly to death.

At the same time, however, the shadow of death does not belong to a mythical realm, but instead imparts an affective influence upon our existence. To live in the shadow of death is not simply to occupy an abstract relation to an event. Rather, death is the event that structures our basic experience of time, space, meaning, freedom, and so forth (cf. Heidegger 1996). In this way, death obtains a reality in our existence, even if we can never apprehend death directly. Once more, death evades us, but at the same time resides within us.

We shall return to the term 'shadow', as it marks an importance for our understanding of time. In Merleau-Ponty, too, the term 'shadow' assumes an equal important. The history of shadows within philosophy is a rich one, which finds its most famous incarnation in the Platonic myth of the cave, where the shadow designates a counterfeit appearance. For Merleau-Ponty, this tradition of the shadow as an error in perception is wrong. For him, it is precisely in the shadows where we catch sight of a world prior to appearances as being a correlate between the subject and the world. In the shadows, Merleau-Ponty locates something to be discovered in the zone in between other places. This limit (or liminal) phenomenology departs from an analysis of what appears for a subject, and instead finds its resources in the margins of what is not said (cf. Merleau-Ponty 1964).

It is within this marginal phenomenology that we find death, not simply as a cessation of living tissue in the present, but as the persistence of matter that belongs to another order of time enduring into the present. A living death, so to speak. In this way, death becomes the ghostly survival of an origin rather than an extinction marking the end of that origin, and a survival that relies upon the living body for its articulation.

Here, we can again formulate our critical claim: in order to understand the relation between materiality and death, we need to turn as much to an origin outside of experience as we do a future encroaching upon experience. To begin to understand this complex idea, let us turn now to the body itself to see how this temporal framework is played out.

We begin with a simple question: What is the body? The question has been asked by phenomenologists time and again, and despite the best efforts of Merleau-Ponty, one may be forgiven for thinking that phenomenology venerates the body as a sort of atemporal entity employed to homogenise the world into a uniform state. In fact, it is precisely with Merleau-Ponty that the body gains a dimension beyond its immediate experience of the present. It is worth plotting the development of this movement from lived temporality to a deeper temporality to get a sense of the body's increasing alienage and anonymity.

Merleau-Ponty is known as the philosopher of the body *par excellence*. More often than not, this usage of Merleau-Ponty as a philosopher of the body is employed to refer to lived body or 'one's own body' (*le corps propre*) (Merleau-Ponty 2012). By this, Merleau-Ponty advances our understanding of the body from that of a mechanical or physical set of responses to the world to something that has its own intelligible perception of the world. This intelligibility structures our experience of the world long before we have abstracted the world as something to be understood in conceptual terms. This intelligible structure is also informed by the body as a centre of expression, especially in how we encounter others. Indeed, it is thanks to the expressive structure of the body that intersubjective relations are possible in the first instance.

However, I want to pursue another body in Merleau-Ponty. Alongside the body that is lived in its everyday experience, Merleau-Ponty refers to a body that is older than thought, anonymous, or a trace, and more precisely a prepersonal or prehistorical body that renders experience possible in the first place. At times, he seems to move more from phenomenology to archaeology and the language of psychoanalysis to capture this other body (Merleau-Ponty 1994). It is a body that assumes the role of a corporeal unconsciousness, working behind the scenes, silently and without ever fully coming to the light of reason. Moreover, at no point, so he argues, is this body fully integrated or possessed by us. Instead, it points to an 'original past', in a well-known formulation, 'a past that has never been present' (Merleau-Ponty 2012: 252).

Already in Merleau-Ponty's *Phenomenology of Perception*, the temporality of the body reveals a duplicity that prevents us from regarding it as being present in a wholly unambiguous way. In the first instance, Merleau-Ponty's account of the relation between embodiment and time comes via the idea of the 'intentional arc' (ibid.: 137). The idea comes in the midst of a chapter discussing the relation between embodiment and space. True to his phenomenological roots, Merleau-Ponty regards the body, not as a mechanical unit or simply as a biological entity, but as an organ of expression and value. The body is not simply that which gets us from one point to another, but instead is the means by which we have a meaningful relation with the world, and thus with others, in the first place. This meaningful relation we have with the world is not something that we self-consciously formulate in abstraction. Nor is it a relation we anticipate in advance. Rather, the relation takes place on a pre-reflective level.

Structuring this pre-reflective relation to the world is what Merleau-Ponty calls the 'intentional arc', which he defines as that which 'projects around us our past, our future, our human milieu, our physical situation, our ideological situation, and our moral situation, or rather, that ensures that we are situated within all these relationships' (ibid.: 137). In other words, what we are presented with in this concept is a kind of unconscious arrangement of time, which not only organises time on an intrapsychic level, but also coordinates our relation to the world as a whole. But this configuration of time is not the same as that of calendar time. Rather, what Merleau-Ponty has in mind is the synthesis of time that allows us to have a sense of subjectivity in the first place. Indeed, it is precisely when this arc 'goes limp' that disorders emerge (ibid.: 137).

Elsewhere in *Phenomenology of Perception*, Merleau-Ponty is even more explicit about the role of the body in cohering time. Alongside the intentional arc that grounds our existence in a temporal synthesis, perception itself is the act of synthesising time (ibid.: 249). To understand this, it is helpful to think of the relation between time and space. To perceive space is precisely to arrange this in a temporal fashion – as coming before or after, for example. Likewise, to think of time, we need to think of space, as when we would conceive of the past as being 'behind' us. Such spatial and temporal metaphors are not contingent products of the imagination, but the very manner in which both space and time are conceptualised. This is possible thanks to the centrality of our bodies.

Accordingly, of the nature of perception, Merleau-Ponty writes as follows: 'In every movement of focusing, my body ties a present, a past, and a future together. It secretes time ... My body takes possession of time and makes a past and a future exist for a present; it is not a thing, rather than suffering time, my body creates it' (ibid.).

This mastery over time hinges upon the interplay of the sensing body and the sensible world, with each bound in a co-constitutive dialogue. Time, for Merleau-Ponty, is not the idealised product of the body, but something that is mediated by the body. Time is restored through the creative expression of the body's relation with the world. When entering a room or scanning a landscape, time comes into its own, and is thereby revealed as a site of strange potency for the subject (cf. Trigg 2012).

Yet for all this, there is another dimension to the body's relation to time, which is perhaps more at home in the shadows than in the light. In what follows, I would like to begin to turn the tide on the lived experience of time, and focus more explicitly on an element of time that resists integration into experience. Once we have surveyed this resistant temporality, we shall then be in a position to understand the role it plays in structuring the relation between materiality and death.

Another Time

At the same time that Merleau-Ponty was writing on the unity of the body, he also recognised a hither side to the body that renders this unity possible in the first place. Once more, in the *Phenomenology of Perception*, the relation between time and the body is taken up in the question of perception. The issue here concerns the identity of the subject of perception. Who is perceiving? Ordinarily, of course, we would say that 'I' am perceiving. But who is this 'I', and how does it perceive? Put another way, is it that 'I' perceive or is that some other aspect of my corporeal existence perceives on my behalf?

As strange as this may sound, Merleau-Ponty in fact leans toward this latter idea, characterising perception as much with an appeal to personal existence as he does an immemorial or anonymous structure, as he writes: 'Every perception takes place within an atmosphere of generality and is presented to us as anonymous ... [I]f I wanted to express perceptual experience with precision, I would have to say that *one* perceives in me, and not that I perceive (Merleau-Ponty 2012: 223). This move from the particular to the general carries with it a different account of temporality that is inscribed into the body. At stake in this move is a rupture of lived time and an encroachment of a time outside of conscious experience.

Perception, as Merleau-Ponty has it, in fact distances me from the materiality of my subjectivity. It confronts me with an aspect of myself that is both constitutive of the subject while also being beyond subjectivity, as he has it: 'He who sees and touches is not exactly myself ... the self who sees or the self who hears is, in some sense, a specialised self, familiar with a single sector of being' (ibid.: 224). This description of the subject as both in-itself and beyond-itself establishes a duplicitous structure to time. At all times, the phenomenal subject is carried along in the world by a sedimented and impersonal history, manifest in perception yet irreducible to perception. The result, in Merleau-Ponty's words, is, 'I never have an absolute possession of myself by myself' (ibid.: 250). Beyond the sphere of personal existence, another subject intervenes in the act of perception, there 'confirm[ing] and renew[ing] in us a "pre-history"' (ibid.; cf. Trigg 2014a).

It is precisely at this juncture of personal and impersonal existence that the issue of death emerges. For as Merleau-Ponty understands, in structural terms, the time of perception assumes a parallel role to the 'pre-personal horizon' of birth and death (Merleau-Ponty 2012: 223). As with birth and death, perception arises from 'beneath myself', and it will continue without me 'just as my birth or my death belongs to an anonymous conception of mortality' (ibid.: 224). My existence, such as it finds itself in the present, is masked by 'another self that has already sided with the world' long before 'I' the personal subject arrive onto the scene (ibid.). Already Merleau-Ponty is presenting us with an alternative reading of death. Now, death finds its counterpart in the time before birth, each forming an ultimate horizon that, far from consigned to nothingness, is instead a constituent of subjectivity itself.

We shall return to anonymous or impossible death toward the conclusion of the chapter. But I highlight the topic now as it is an indication of another side to the body that is not obvious to our immediate experience, but which is developed throughout Merleau-Ponty's philosophy. This philosophy allows us to think of terms such as 'passing' and 'materiality' in greater depth than would otherwise be available with a descriptive phenomenology alone. We are able to achieve this through connecting experience with a strata of time that is beyond experience, and can be phrased in terms of an archaeology. It is to this issue we now turn.

Traces and Virtuality

Let us pause to summarise our findings. We have a sense of the body as the bearer of two orders of time. One marks the coherence of time as lived and unified by the subject. The other signals the alterity of an originary past, which is both constitutive of the present without ever being present. In each case, it is the body that becomes the artefact, through which the depth of time can be understood. The plan now is to give some attention to this relation between the materiality of the body in the present and the immemorial notion of an original past.

The key, I think, to approaching this relation between the particularity of the body and the anonymity of an original past is with the notion of the *trace*. It is with the idea of the trace that we come to see the relation between materiality and death as involving the depth of an unlived and unliveable time that is nevertheless preserved in the present rather than being discarded through time. The idea of the trace figures throughout Merleau-Ponty's thinking on time and materiality, and plays its clearest role in the structure of the body, as he writes in *Phenomenology of Perception*:

> When I turn toward my perception itself and when I pass from direct perception to the thought about this perception, I re-enact it, I uncover a thought older than I am at work in my perceptual organs and of which these organs are merely the trace. (Merleau-Ponty 2012: 367)

How to understand this? Merleau-Ponty is describing the moment of reflection, whereupon the thinking organ of the present reveals itself as a prehistoric organ of the past. With this transformation, the organs of the personal subject – my own organs – become the voice of another agency, 'at work' within myself and yet seemingly indifferent to the host entity that it employs as a lifesource.

This sense of the body as being structured by an agency working behind the scenes, in a corporeal unconsciousness, and thus sedimented in deep time, resurfaces in his late writings on nature. In a passage that is typical of the enigmatic style of his later thought, he presents us with the following puzzle:

> The body-object is only a trace – Trace in the mechanical sense: present substitute of a past that no longer is – the trace for us is more than the present effect of the past. It is a survival of the past ... The trace and the fossil ... The living thing is no longer there but it is almost there; we have the negative of it. (Merleau-Ponty 2003: 276)

If the usage of 'trace' in the earlier Merleau-Ponty referred to the structure of perception, then in the latter usage of the term, a move is made from localised phenomenon to the ontology of the body itself. Here, it is not just that perception reveals a prehistory to the subject, which is re-enacted in and through perception, but that the very materiality of the body is being defined in effect by a fundamental absence.

At stake here is not an empirical evolution to be understood in Darwinian terms. Thus, Merleau-Ponty's account of the trace of a fossilised past is not an appeal to a gradual unfolding of history as told through the human body. To be sure, any such account of a material history as a linear process of becoming is nowhere to be found in Merleau-Ponty, much less a process with a particular teleological direction. Rather, the concept of trace finds a closer alliance in the Deleuzian idea of virtuality.

What unites Deleuze's idea of the virtual with Merleau-Ponty's notion of the trace is their commitment to a structure of reality working beneath and behind the scenes of perception. Thus for Deleuze, virtuality comes to signify not a possibility that is then realised, but an already-existing structure of reality, writing of it as thus 'not some confused determination, but a completely determined structure formed by its genetic differential elements, its "virtual" or "embryonic" elements' (Deleuze 1994: 209). This sense of a structural depth in appearances seeks at all times to locate the obscure element from where meaning comes into existence but is never realised. Rather, the 'embryonic' remains just that, an incipient movement, nevertheless different from and never reducible to appearances. Merleau-Ponty's concept of the trace, as it figures in his late writing, dovetails with Deleuze's concept of the virtual, in that both concepts avoid conflating the virtual with the actual. What we perceive in the phenomenal world – not least the human body – expresses itself, to once again cite Merleau-Ponty, as a 'negative' (Merleau-Ponty 2003: 276).

This transformation of the body from a site of personal perception to an immemorial negative to be understood in terms of its relation to a fossilised past means two things. First, the body cannot be understood in solely experiential terms. Instead, we need to understand the pre-theoretical or primitive layers that are constitutive of corporeal perception – and for this reason, render experience possible – yet at the same time remain irreducible to experience. In order to conceptualise the body in this non-experiential way, we are required to think of its materiality in terms of an archaeology, as Merleau-Ponty has it: 'It is to give this depth to the human body, this archaeology, this natal past … ' (ibid.: 273).

Merleau-Ponty's language of archaeology is significant and needs to be explained. With this term, Merleau-Ponty comes to designate a particular type of inquiry. It is an inquiry that takes form in the *'the reflections, shadows, levels* and *horizons between things'* (Merleau-Ponty 1964: 160). This quote comes from a late essay by Merleau-Ponty on the role of Husserl and his 'shadow'. Indeed, this pairing of 'archaeology' and 'shadow' is not incidental. Both terms mark that which is resistant to a direct phenomenology of appearances, but instead must now be approached from beneath appearances (cf. Trigg 2014b). Thus in the aforementioned essay, 'The Philosopher and His Shadow', Merleau-Ponty proceeds to question the very scope of a phenomenological analysis, finding in the tradition a series of limitations that prevent the method from moving beyond a classical idea of intentionality. It is at this point that Merleau-Ponty's critical question emerges: 'Does the descent into the realm of our "archaeology" leave our tools intact?' (Merleau-Ponty 1964: 165). The question indicates the need for another type of inquiry, one that must now be directed to a 'latent intentionality … more ancient than the intentionality of human *acts*' (ibid.).

Merleau-Ponty's usage of archaeology, then, differs from the Freudian image of archaeology as that which is repressed into the Earth. For Merleau-Ponty, the archaeological structure of materiality is implicated in perception itself, and thus evident not least in the human body. Once more, this account of the past adhering and dwelling in the body in no way means a Darwinian process of evolution. There is no radical break from the past, through which 'humanity' suddenly reappears, as Merleau-Ponty writes reflecting on the thought of Teilhard de Chardin, 'That the human entered silently also means: no rupture' (Merleau-Ponty 2003: 267). Without rupture, the past is not 'overcome' but instead assumes a symbiotic relationship to the present. The past perdures. More than this, the undefined presence of a never-lived history figures itself as evident in the body of the present, and is thereby preserved as, in the words of Gaston Bachelard, 'fossilised duration' (Bachelard 1994: 8). If the term 'passing', as the editors to this volume indicate, involves a relation to time, then this movement is not only toward the future but also from the past. The movement carries with it a resurfacing of matter from an immemorial time, yet a time that refuses to be consigned to the inertia of nonexistence.

The transformation of the body from a site of personal perception to an immemorial negative means something else. We see now that the temporal structure of the body cannot simply be captured with the idea of the body as a 'living body'. This distinction between the living and the non-living is undercut by a non-experiential origin that structures the animate quality of life without ever being fully identifiable with life, as Merleau-Ponty has it in his writings on nature:

'Life and nonlife are different only as chemistry of mass and individual chemistry: Are viruses living or nonliving beings?' (Merleau-Ponty 2003: 269).

The question is in direct contradistinction to a phenomenology purportedly concerned with human experience, and that alone. From the perspective of a human subject, a virus or a disease enters the body and is experienced as a form of anti-life. It is experienced as something reduces life to a paralysed state, draining the body at all times of the resources it depends on in order to advance itself in the world. Yet from the perspective of the virus, the body is simply the means by which its persistence is actualised. The implication of this is that what we regard as nonliving or dead is, far from an issue of biology alone, often a cultural value assigned to particular things in the world – be it bodies or viruses. To move beyond this human-centric account of living and nonliving, we need to reconfigure our ideas of death and passing as belonging to the future alone, and instead consider how death can also be formulated as, to some extent, having *already occurred*.

The Pastness of Death

In order to speak of a death that has already occurred, we need to turn back to our engagement with Merleau-Ponty and the role of birth and death in perception. We've already seen that Merleau-Ponty provides us with two timescales. The first is that of lived time. The second is an order of time that enables experience to be possible but resists being reducible to experience. This other body precedes my own existence in the world, marking a pre-history of which 'I' am implicated but never fully possess. With this, we have a dis-possessed subject. At no point do 'I' really claim ownership over my experience, as Merleau-Ponty has it: 'If I wanted to render precisely the perceptual experience, I ought to say that *one* perceives in me, and not that I perceive' (Merleau-Ponty 2012: 250). For this reason, the one who perceives in me perceives *through* me. Through me, and from a time *before* me. A long quote from Merleau-Ponty captures this sense of the origin as being anterior to oneself:

> I am no more aware of being the true subject of my sensation than of my birth or my death. Neither my birth nor my death can appear to me as experiences of my own, since, if I thought of them thus, I should be assuming myself to be pre-existent to, or outliving, myself, in order to be able to experience them, and I should therefore not be genuinely thinking of my birth or my death. I can, then, apprehend myself only as "already born" and "still alive" – I can apprehend my birth and my death only as prepersonal horizons: I know that people are born and die, but I cannot know my own birth and death. Each sensation, being strictly speaking, the first, last and only one of its kind, is a birth and a death. The subject who experiences it begins and ends with it, and as he can neither precede nor survive himself, sensation necessarily appears to itself in a setting of generality,

its origin is anterior to myself, it arises from *sensibility* which has preceded it and which will outlive it, just as my birth and death belong to a natality and a mortality which are anonymous. ... Each time I experience a sensation, I feel that it concerns not my own being, the one for which I am responsible and for which I make decisions, but another self which has already sided with the world, which is already open to certain of its aspects and synchronized with them. Between my sensation and myself there stands always the thickness of some *primal acquisition* which prevents my experience from being clear of itself. (Merleau-Ponty 2012: 223–4)

The passage provides us with a condensed study in the paradox of death. Just as death intervenes upon the material body that will remain long after the subject him- or herself has departed from this world, so it precedes that same body, masking perceptual life with a structure of anonymous existence that can never be fully integrated into the subject, and evoking herein Ballard's allusion to 'unremembered deaths' (Ballard 2006: 453). But this pre-subjective death is not equivalent to birth – that is, as simply the opposite pole of a time. Instead, death as an origin is that which exceeds birth, just as death as a futural event exceeds life – exceeds birth and life, but also bears its presence upon these domains, implicating 'me' the personal subject in its shadow.

As Merleau-Ponty says, to understand our origins – and thus to understand death – we would be required to outlive ourselves, to overcome a phenomenology of lived experience in order to trace and re-trace that archaeology of the body as it comes into existence. As it stands, death masks me from ever knowing myself. Instead, it positions itself in the corner of my eye, present until it's glanced at directly, at which point it retreats back into obscurity. Merleau-Ponty: 'I cannot know my own birth and death'. But this is not simply a question of a failure to empirically grasp a certain detail from one's existence. To reduce death to either finality of matter or the void prior to birth is to risk translating the non-living into the living by dint of prioritising the latter.

This absence of knowledge forges a void or a blind spot in my experience, which itself bears the mark of an anteriority that is equivalent to death. Here, death registers itself not simply as something opposed to life, but instead as another life that runs parallel to our own. If it is a life that has already 'sided with the world' long before I myself have set foot in the world, then it nevertheless lingers in the form of a trace in and through my body. Indeed, I re-enact death each time I perceive a thing in this world. Throughout, my presence is doubled with an alien presence, a presence that cannot be understood in descriptive terms, but instead as a stratum of existence that simultaneously grounds and ungrounds my own existence. To speak accurately of the relation between the body and death, we must speak in paradoxical terms of death as that which has already occurred, is occurring, and will also occur in the future. To speak in such a way means also recognising a limit for phenomenological inquiry, and thus an endpoint for our own investigation.

References

Bachelard, G., 1994. *The Poetics of Space*, translated by Maria Jolas. Boston: Beacon Press.

Ballard, J. G., 2006. *The Complete Short Stories*, vol. 2. New York: Harper Perennial.

Deleuze, G., 1994. *Difference and Repetition*, translated by Paul Patton. London: Athlone Press.

Heidegger, M., 1996. *Being and Time*, translated by Joan Stambaugh. New York: SUNY Press.

Merleau-Ponty, M., 1964. *Signs*, translated by Richard McCleary. Evanston: Northwestern University Press.

Merleau-Ponty, M., 1993. Preface to Hesnard's *L'Oeuvre de Freud*. In: *Merleau-Ponty and Psychology*, translated by Alden L. Fisher. Atlantic Highlands: Humanities Press.

Merleau-Ponty, M., 2003. *Nature: Course Notes from the College de France*, translated by Robert Vallier. Evanston: Northwestern University Press.

Merleau-Ponty, M., 2012. *The Phenomenology of Perception*, translated by Donald Landes. London: Routledge.

Trigg, D., 2006. *The Aesthetics of Decay: Nothingness, Nostalgia, and the Absence of Reason*. New York: Peter Lang.

Trigg, D., 2012. *The Memory of Place: A Phenomenology of the Uncanny*. Athens: Ohio University Press.

Trigg, D., 2014a. *The Thing: A Phenomenology of Horror*. Winchester: Zero Books.

Trigg, D., 2014b. The Role of the Earth in Merleau-Ponty's Archaeological Phenomenology. *Chiasmi International*, 16, 255–73.

Trigg, D., 2016. *Topophobia: A Phenomenology of Anxiety*. London: Bloomsbury.

Index